Mommy Wars

Mommy Wars

Stay-at-Home and Career Moms
Face Off on Their Choices,
Their Lives, Their Families

 Edited by Leslie Morgan Steiner

Random House   New York

Published in the United States by Random House,
an imprint of The Random House Publishing Group,
a division of Random House, Inc., New York.

RANDOM HOUSE and colophon are registered
trademarks of Random House, Inc.

For individual essay copyright information, please see pages 335–36.

Grateful acknowledgment is made to the following for permission to reprint
previously published material:

The New York Times: "Out of Step and Having a Baby" by Molly Jong-Fast
(October 5, 2003), copyright © 2003 by The New York Times Co. Reprinted
by permission of *The New York Times.*

The Washington Post: "The Donna Reed Syndrome" by Lonnae O'Neal
Parker (May 12, 2002), copyright © 2002 by The Washington Post.
Reprinted by permission of *The Washington Post.*

The Washington Post Writer's Group: "Peace and Carrots" by Carolyn Hax
(July 4, 1999), copyright © 1999 by The Washington Post Writers Group.
Reprinted by permission of The Washington Post Writers Group.

LIBRARY OF CONGRESS CATALOGING-IN-PUBLICATION DATA
Mommy wars: stay-at-home and career moms face off on their choices, their
lives, their families / edited by Leslie Morgan Steiner.
p.   cm.
ISBN 1-4000-6415-5
1. Working mothers. 2. Mothers. 3. Housewives.
I. Steiner, Leslie Morgan.
HQ759.48.M66 2006
306.874'3'0973—dc22   2005052066

Printed in the United States of America on acid-free paper

www.atrandom.com

2 3 4 5 6 7 8 9

Book design by Dana Leigh Blanchette

To Perry

Contents

Introduction

Our Inner Catfight

A few months ago, I celebrated a friend's fortieth birthday at the Sulgrave Club, an elegant old mansion in downtown Washington, D.C. Dressed in a vintage black cocktail dress from my mother-in-law's party-girl days, I stood chatting with a neighbor, a mom like me who works part-time in newspaper and magazine publishing. I told her about my idea for a book exploring the tension and confusion between working and stay-at-home moms today.

Another neighbor, a stay-at-home mom whose kids go to school with mine, joined us. This woman is the head of the parent-teacher association at our public elementary school, as constant and welcoming a presence on the playground as a greeter at Wal-Mart. My friend, a former *Washington Post* reporter who makes her living posing provocative questions, asked our neighbor what she thought of my book idea. Specifically, what she thought of moms who work. Without breathing, the stay-at-home mom answered, "Oh, I feel *so* sorry for them."

My cheeks flushed like a child with fever. Fortunately, the guest of honor turned on the microphone and started thanking her husband for the party, so I didn't have to disguise my response. This woman felt sorry for me? For all the moms at our school who work to support their families, to show their kids that women can work, who work to change the world, who work to keep their sanity?

My reporter friend was watching me closely. "She doesn't feel sorry for *me or you*," she leaned over and whispered in my ear. "She feels sorry *in theory* for women who work. It's why she doesn't work. Because she imagines that if you work, you don't have time for your children, your husband, life. She doesn't know what it's really like to work. Just like you and I don't know what it's really like to stay home full-time. That's why you're writing this book—so we can end this catfight."

She's right, that *is* why I created this book. Motherhood in America is fraught with defensiveness, infighting, ignorance, and judgment about what's best for kids, family, and women—a true catfight among women who'd be far better off if we accepted and supported all good, if disparate, mothering choices. For years I struggled to end my own personal catfight over career and family balance—and I tussled mightily to stop myself from disparaging other women's different solutions. I still struggle. Along the way, I've perplexedly watched working women transmogrify into happy (and not so happy) stay-at-home moms, and seen others continue doggedly working, some happily and others with deepening resentment and anger over the drudgery and missed opportunities both at home and at work.

Nearly every week someone tells me how lucky I am—that I have the best of working and stay-at-home motherhood. Until two-thirty every day, I'm a working mom in the advertising department of *The Washington Post*. Then I tear down the office stairs (late, always late), speed-walk home, rip off my business suit and pantyhose, and pull on yoga pants and my Merrell Jungle Slides just in time to grab our two-year-old and pick up the older kids from school. But the truth is I feel like a hybrid—neither working mom nor true stay-at-home mom.

I don't understand moms who find happiness staying home all the time, without work and their own incomes (however large or small). I can't fathom why some working moms stay stuck in too-demanding jobs or careers that they openly resent because of the quality (and quantity) time they miss with their kids. But what I know for certain, because I see it almost every day from each side of the battlefield, is that the two groups misunderstand and envy each other in the corrosive, fake-smiling way we women have perfected over the eons.

● ● ●

Before I tackle how this book came to be, let me explain my own choices. Three observations during childhood convinced me early on to combine work and motherhood:

- I loved children madly and knew I wanted several of my own one day.
- My father, a lawyer, was immeasurably rewarded for his work (he got to buy nice ties, choose whether or not our family went to Florida for spring break, decide when to divorce my mother, et cetera).
- My mom, a Radcliffe graduate and one of the smartest women I know, sipped rum and Coke from a little glass starting at 5 P.M. every day, threw shoes at us from across the living room, and at times became unhinged by the frustrations of staying home raising four children.

During my early childhood, I wore my mother's unhappiness like an invisible cloak. I brought her handpicked daisies on May Day, tried to bring her breakfast in bed on Mother's Day (she refused to stay put long enough), bought a trio of garish painted parrots for her birthday, cooked dinners and made my bed every day, brought home report cards filled with A's, and took care of my youngest sister to lighten Mom's child-care load. As I grew up, I abandoned my campaign to make her happy; I grew dismissive of her flaws and determined to never, ever, repeat the sacrifices that seemed to lead to her inescapable unhappiness as our mother.

Nothing was going to stop me, an optimistic Harvard student in the 1980s, from cherry-picking the best of my mom and dad's worlds. My senior year, Judsen Culbreth, mother of two and editor in chief of *Working Mother* magazine, spoke on campus about the benefits of working motherhood. "The most important factor in a child's life is a happy mom," she said. Her advice flashed like a traffic light turning green; work would be my Route 66 to happiness, freedom, and good motherhood. I could and would have it all.

After graduating, I got a job in New York City at *Seventeen* magazine. My salary, though significantly less than a year's college tuition, covered the rent on a shabby-chic basement apartment in Chelsea, the subway uptown to *Seventeen*'s offices, and five-dollar dinners at the Indian and Israeli restaurants lining St. Marks Place. I was deliriously happy. School was out for good. I was finally working—and at a ridiculously fun, engaging job writing and editing a publication every woman in America has read at least once in her life.

After two years love intervened. I fell (hard) for a brilliant young man I met on the New York subway, a man from a welfare family who dreamed of blue-chip business success. I knew exactly where he could get it. In college I'd organized alumni reunions for Harvard Business School and met dozens of graduates at all stages of their careers. All of them seemed more in control of their lives than any other adults I knew. I secretly wanted to get an M.B.A. too, despite feeling like a traitor to my literary ambitions. My lover figured this out and convinced me to leave the job and city I adored to run off to business school with him.

Despite my Ivy League background, in my world the feminine Holy Grail, no matter a woman's IQ or accomplishments, was attracting men. As a child, I'd watched my mom in the space of one afternoon transform herself from a tear-stained, dirty-apron-clad wretch into a ravishing cocktail-party hostess in full makeup, gleaming black hair, and gorgeous halter dress greeting partners from my father's law firm at our front door. Presenting a perfect front to the outside world of men clearly mattered tremendously. My primary quest had always been getting men to notice my legs, staying skinny, looking pretty at parties, in class, and on subway trains.

But I also craved economic independence. I simply did not want to be my mother. So I traded my glamorous, underpaid pink-collar publishing world for b-school.

Those first months I found myself dumbfounded by the academic material. I nearly broke down in accounting listening to professors discuss credits, debits, and accruals. The droves of former Wall Street analysts intimidated me to the point of muteness. What had I gotten myself into?

Toward Christmas, I went to New York with a study group to interview the founders of Wasserstein Perella, a renowned Wall Street investment bank I'd never heard of. On the train back to campus, three men in suits sat next to me. One tried to start a conversation. The two others joined in the mindless pastime of "Who can pick her up first?," a game

I'd played with decreasing enthusiasm for over a decade. I was no more real to the men than a *Playboy* centerfold.

The closest one asked where I was heading. "Business school," I said.

I will never forget what happened next. The men sat up in unison, like marionettes. They leaned forward. One actually kicked me by accident. At once they dive-bombed me with questions. What did I think of the economy? Was a recession looming? Should they pull out of the stock market? Was it a good time to change jobs?

I held forth on the filthy commuter train, rattling off macroeconomic explanations that would have been gibberish to me three months earlier but sounded good now. When we arrived, the men hovered around me, wished me good luck. No one asked for my number. As I watched them go, a new cloak of equality settled over me. I'd become real. To my surprise, it felt good.

Would anyone understand my excitement? My mother? My Harvard classmates? My colleagues from *Seventeen*? I realized I already knew the women who understood—my female b-school classmates. I headed back to campus to find them. At that moment, like clay being hardened in a kiln, I joined the working-woman tribe.

A year later, I realized what I got in return. Before coming to business school, I'd married my subway lover. To my complete astonishment, this man who had worshipped me poured coffee grounds on my head one morning when I woke him too early. In a deserted corridor on campus he slapped me after I joined an all-male study group. Inside our Volkswagen he yanked the car keys out of the ignition as I drove sixty miles an hour down an interstate highway.

One December night during our second year he became so enraged following a discussion of where we were spending Christmas that he barricaded me in our bedroom. He punched me, kicked me, shattered a wedding photo over my head, and strangled me until I blacked out. When I came to, I saw in his reddened eyes that my own husband was on the brink of killing me. A terrified neighbor pounded on our front door until his fists started splintering the wood. My husband fled just before the police showed up. Rather calmly, they told me they might find me dead the next time.

I loved my husband, even then. But I left him. I hired a divorce lawyer, borrowed money from my mom, changed the apartment locks, and started sleeping with a dresser blocking the bedroom door. My husband began stalking me on campus and at job interviews. At night he paced the street outside my apartment. I thought I might have to leave business school just a few months before earning my M.B.A.

Then my female classmates began calling, asking how I was. My marketing professor took me aside after class to tell me she'd survived an abusive relationship as a young woman. Groups of women paid for my lunches, surrounded me at parties, gave me rides to recruiting interviews, never let me walk home alone. Soon I had five great job offers, three of which were hundreds of miles from my ex. My women friends, along with my mom's support and the wallop of an Ivy League M.B.A. degree, formed an underground railroad to safety and financial independence, far out of reach of my ex-husband's anger.

At twenty-seven, in possession of both an M.B.A. diploma and a divorce decree, I tried to focus on work and rebuilding my personal life. The career part came pretty easily. Outside of work, I felt like a debt-ridden fallen woman. I never blamed myself for being beaten, but there was no denying that of the millions of single men in New York, I'd selected one of the sickest to be my supposed soul mate. Dating again felt like tiptoeing on cut glass, trying to put my foot on the shards that would hurt the least.

I still trusted men as a species. The problem was that in my determination not to make the same mistake twice, I aimed a hot police searchlight on every potential Romeo. Three years following my divorce, after many brief romantic fiascos, I started dating an investment banker whose blue eyes and happy-go-lucky ways made my heart pitch to my toenails. He never balanced his checkbook, wore a Malaysian sarong on the weekends, and shook off my first-marriage confessions with gentle curiosity.

After a year, he proposed in Prague at midnight on the steps of the Jan Hus monument in Old Town Square. He got down on one knee. Tears streamed down his face as he explained that I was the most wonderful woman he'd ever met.

My reaction? Panic. Followed shortly by fury.

Didn't he know that our marriage would probably end in divorce? In my mind, the best I could hope for was that he would cheat on me, surreptitiously cancel our joint credit card and checking account, and prance around in that sarong in front of someone ten years younger. How could he believe in happy endings when I never would again?

I fought my terrors. I humored his romantic dreams. He got his wish for a big white wedding and a long honeymoon. We cried together in our tiny Manhattan bathroom when the pregnancy-test strip shimmered with two blue lines. My husband's faith in the goodness of life thawed me out enough to have a child. But I simply couldn't climb aboard the "married happily ever after" Pollyanna train.

The earth moved for me when our baby was born. During the first weeks of motherhood, I realized I trusted my husband—and life— enough to toy with leaving the working-woman tribe and depending solely on Perry for financial support. By then, I was a marketing executive with Johnson & Johnson, the health-care giant. I'd launched a new product successfully throughout South America, the Middle East, and Australia. I had a shiny United Airlines premier card and change from twelve different countries in my desk drawer next to my dog-eared passport. Chairman Ralph Larsen knew my name.

Still, rocking our newborn son felt like mainlining Valium. I thought I might stay home. My ob-gyn, a mom with three kids, tried to stop me. "You don't want to make such an important decision during maternity leave," she said as I lay on the examining table for my six-week postpartum checkup. "You've got hormones and exhaustion clouding your judgment. Life is long. You can always quit after six months, a year."

I went back to my job the Tuesday after Memorial Day. Max's three-month birthday. I was amazed to be paying another woman to do what I craved most in the world, to stay home with my little bird. While I drove out the driveway, dressed in a black coatdress and full makeup for the first time in weeks, my heart lay beating on the changing table.

I got through the day with a single vow: not to cry.

Soon enough, my boy came to work with me, spending his days at the plush, 22,000-square-foot Johnson & Johnson employee day-care center. I could see his nursery window from the boardroom window. I breast-fed him during lunch. My boss said yes when I asked to work at home two days a week, granting me a gift more priceless than a briefcase of stock options: time with my child.

Due to his time at day care, my son learned to sleep amid chaos, to talk before he turned a year, to trust other people. Ralph Larsen still knew my name. Over the next five years, I worked a variety of part-time and full-time jobs, my career progressed, and I had two more children. I have no doubt that my life, as well as my family's, is immeasurably richer due to my decision to combine work and motherhood.

Of course, it's rarely easy. I don't often have ironed clothes and blow-dried hair on the same day. I could store my three kids' winter clothes in the bags under my eyes. It's not likely that I'm going to be president of any company before I turn forty next year.

I once left my daughter Morgan crying in her high chair during a conference call, shutting the kitchen door with my foot so my colleagues wouldn't hear her wails. More times than I can count, colleagues have wrapped up jobs so I could get to the day-care center before my kids were turned over to foster care. I have not slept for more than four hours uninterrupted in at least six years. I've taken phone calls locked in my bathroom with the fan on to muffle the kid noise in the next room. I just stopped writing to fish my youngest child out of her booster seat, clean spaghetti off her face, hands, arms, shirt, and belly button, wash her dishes, and get her settled playing with her older brother's electronic math gizmo, all so I could scribble a few more lines.

The problem with straddling caring for three small kids and working at a wonderful job is that at times work seduces me into giving more than I should. I rush along deliriously busy, in love with some project. Until *bam*—I miss my children so much it's as though a large block of ice has suddenly replaced my stomach. At times like this I bury my head in my baby's curly hair, smelling her sweet sweat, reminding myself these days are short. I hold my five-year-old's hand all night long when she crawls into bed with me. I let my six-year-old stay up late to keep me company while I take a bubble bath. I pull back from work, reorient myself, and start all over trying to find the right balance.

I don't think staying home full-time would be any easier.

● ● ●

When I was thirty-two, three years into my blessedly peaceful second marriage, sixteen months into the motherhood gig, five months pregnant with our second child, I sat on the floor of our New York apartment in stunned silence. My husband had just come home from work. He stood in the middle of the living room explaining that he'd been offered the presidency of a hot Internet start-up. For context, this was amid the late-1990s dot-com frenzy—twenty-year-old Internet millionaires, triple-digit stock-price increases, companies with funny names like Google and iVillage and paymybills.com springing up like mushrooms. One *teeny* problem: The company offering Perry the job was in Minneapolis. Since we'd been married he'd changed jobs frequently. In less than four years I'd moved four times for him.

Soon I was *lying* on the parquet floor of our two-bedroom, rent-controlled Manhattan apartment, trying not to weep. Within a ten-minute walk lay my son's favorite playground, my sister's apartment, my in-laws' condo, Gymboree, a pediatrician as kindly as Big Bird, five or six Starbucks, the Reebok gym, and at least a dozen museums. I pounded the floor with my fists, arguing that we couldn't possibly move *again,* even for his dream job.

My husband calmly explained that we were very lucky and really had to go. Millions of dollars in stock options, he said. Besides the money, I heard in his voice that he wanted this job more than he'd ever wanted anything—except perhaps me. *This job will make my career,* he said. It was going to cost us, big-time, in terms of my career and quality of life for our kids. But I knew we had to go.

Johnson & Johnson, bless them, let me work long-distance, part-time, from our Minneapolis apartment overlooking Lake Calhoun, which seemed frozen ten months of the year. My salary barely covered the kids' day care. I worked and tried to build a temporary life for us while my husband stayed at his office until the darkness of the midwestern winter threatened to swallow me whole.

I'd promised to go to the arctic tundra for two years. Day after day of working at home, alone, bundling two toddlers into and out of snowsuits four times a day, calling frantically in from business trips to remind

Perry not to miss the 6 P.M. day-care pickup, convincing the kids that Omi, Pop-Pop, Aunt Perri, and Grams were *human people,* not just voices on the telephone. After a year and a half, I resigned from J&J— long-distance, part-time work with no benefits and a minuscule hourly salary wasn't worth it any longer. For the next six months, I was kind of okay. I volunteered at the kids' school. I started writing a book about my first marriage. I brought up moving back East.

"Oh no," said the man with whom I'd borne two children, given up my job and the Upper West Side, abandoned my kids' world-class day-care center, walked away from a big salary and stock options of my own. "I earn more money than you, and I think we should stay a few more years," he told me.

More money than me? A few more *years?* Every single day in Minnesota had felt like exile, a sacrifice for his happiness. I thought of the mornings I'd cried in the shower so that the kids wouldn't hear me. The evenings I'd begged my husband to come home in time to read the kids a bedtime story and he'd replied he couldn't because of a meeting with "someone really important" (as if we weren't). The time, just a few weeks before, with our daughter in the backseat, I had been in a terrifying head-on collision; when I called to tell my husband we were okay, he asked if he could finish up some paperwork before he came to get us. It was suddenly, horribly clear that he was oblivious to the reality of my life and what I'd given up for him. And I'd helped create this monster, by moving for him, by keeping quiet when he worked late month after month, by playing the role of supportive wife just like . . . my mother.

I was so furious that for the first time in our marriage I was speechless. I didn't sleep that night. I lay stiff as a board next to him, listening to the wind howl off Lake Calhoun.

The next morning, my friend Jodi met me for breakfast during our kids' swim lesson. A few years older and with an M.B.A. from the University of Chicago, Jodi started out when women M.B.A.s wore floppy white ties and bulky suits like armor. Happily married for several years, Jodi was an institutional saleswoman at a large Minneapolis investment bank. She'd paid for her mother's breast cancer treatments, bought her a mink coat when she recovered, and taught her three daughters to water-ski barefoot on a Wisconsin lake where she'd bought a cabin—all with money she'd earned herself.

"This is what you do," she began with a Mona Lisa smile, cradling a mug of steaming coffee.

I knew something dreadful was coming. Something along the lines of what I imagined wives told one another in moments of marital stress: *Time to accept the worldly art of feminine subservience. Visit a therapist. Start going to church once a week. Charge a piece of jewelry to his credit card.* I wasn't sure I could stomach this kind of retro advice, especially from her.

"Move back," Jodi told me instead. "Tell him—nicely—that you understand he may need to stay longer. Tell him you and the kids will welcome him back East whenever he's ready."

Later that day I checked my Johnson & Johnson stock fund. If I sold all the shares I'd earned over eight years, I'd have enough to move East, rent an apartment large enough for the kids, pay for day care. Barely enough. What if I hadn't saved that money?

I sent my résumé to the paper I grew up with in Washington, D.C. Three weeks later, the publisher called to tell me of an opening at the Sunday magazine. *My* dream job this time, a chance to combine what I'd learned at business school and J&J with my passion for publishing.

I didn't break all our china or stage a three-hour fight. I told my husband it was his turn to move for me. And then I shut up.

I think few things frighten a man as much as an opinionated wife who suddenly falls quiet. One morning at breakfast Perry cleared his throat and said, "I've been thinking about what you said about moving back home. I guess you're right. I'll start looking in D.C. right away."

We left Minnesota in February.

Washington welcomed us with pink and yellow springtime fireworks—sunshine that made us lift our faces skyward, daffodils and cherry blossoms lining the streets like our own ticker-tape parade. Perry and I bought a house less than two miles from my childhood home, settled into our new jobs, decided to have a third baby, and got pregnant on the first try. He had moved for me. I carried that fact around like a kid with a new puppy at the end of a leash. Perry also promised we'd never have to move again. I tried to believe him.

A happy ending.

But those white-knuckled weeks of fury in Minnesota had hacked a new pathway in my working-mom psyche. The job at the *Post* required full-time work, at least at first. The hours away from my kids were worth the leverage my job would bring. Not just worth it to me, but worth it for the kids. Repeated moves for a parent's career do not make an idyllic childhood. Max had never had two consecutive birthdays in the same state. In four years he and Morgan had been in five different nursery schools, had been terrified by shots and exams by four different pediatricians, had gotten attached to and detached from countless babysitters. The trade-off I faced as a mother was crystal clear: work, earn money, have a voice in where and how my family lived, or depend on Perry 100 percent financially and give up our right to protest his career choices despite the short- and long-term emotional costs. Going back to full-time work was the road I had to take.

But along the way to renewing this commitment to working motherhood, ironically I also learned to swim in an ocean of sympathy for stay-at-home moms who feel they can't object when told they have to move to (or stay in) places they or their children hate. However, I still didn't understand these moms and their lives. We all started out kind of the same. School. Work. Marriage. Babies. (Not always in that order.) How—and why—do some moms know to stay home? How do others decide not to?

I've struggled to find my own balance. One crisp October morning my car key wouldn't turn in the ignition. My reaction was to sob for four hours, which made it difficult to go to the office. Once I stopped crying, I thought hard about my life. I'd been working full-time running *The Washington Post Magazine* for nearly two years, clocking long (and admittedly thrilling) hours and sleeping even less than usual. I'd moved into an old house that we were renovating, cared for our two toddlers, and gotten pregnant. I was moving so fast I could hardly slow down to snuggle my children in bed.

No wonder I couldn't stop crying. That day I resolved to cut back at work, and a few months later I reduced my hours (and my salary) by 50 percent, although I'm happy to say I kept the parts of my job that continue to thrill me.

But finding your own balance between work and family can be a torturous task. The easy divining rod—financial need—explains only a portion of working-mom choices. On my block there's a family who cannot afford for the mom to stay home. But they rent a small apartment, go without a car, and send their children to a mediocre public high school so she can. Two houses up the hill lives one of D.C.'s most successful Realtors, a mom with two small kids, a cell phone permanently attached to her ear, and a rich husband who could easily support a stay-at-home wife. Both women (and their kids) seem happy to me. The fundamental question remains: Why are some moms still ardently working and some so happily not?

The far more troubling query: Why is there this catfight between working mothers and stay-at-home ones? Despite the snarling most of us witness at times (and engage in ourselves), aren't we moms ultimately united in our quest to stay sane, raise good kids, provide one another with succor and support, and protect humankind from the overly aggressive, overly logical male half of the species?

The evidence, unfortunately, does not support a united sisterhood among women. Just a week or so ago, dressed for the office at 8 A.M., I (somewhat) frantically dropped my kids off at their schools while my husband sat on a plane to Atlanta (I think—could have been Chicago or Vegas or anywhere *not here*). In the space of twenty minutes on the playground, three different stay-at-home moms lobbed greetings that felt like sly, wholly unwarranted commentary on my life:

Mom number one: Oooh, pantyhose! I've forgotten what those feel like!
What I heard: I haven't had to work in so long. Aren't you jealous?

Mom number two: Oh, don't bother slowing down! You are always rushing somewhere!
What I felt like retorting: Yes I'm in a rush! My husband is out of town—again. I've been up since 5 A.M. feeding, dressing, and cajoling three savage small people. I didn't even have time to brush my hair. Now I've got to go to the office when I already feel I've worked a whole day! And you expect me to chat?!

Mom number three: I don't know how you do it. (Accompanied by patronizing smile.)
What she meant: I don't know *why* you do it. You must be in really

desperate need of money or self-esteem if you are willing to neglect your children in order to work. Not me—I love my children more and am clearly the superior mother.

But at least the stay-at-home moms talked to me.

Later that day I was dressed in sweats, sitting on the floor at the kids' weekly computer-enrichment class, trying desperately to (a) stay awake, and (b) amuse our toddler for an entire hour with props from my purse. A slew of working moms rushed in to pick up their kids, clad in child-unfriendly leather skirts and high-heeled boots (quite similar to the ones I had recently peeled off), impatient for their children to finish up. They glanced at me on the floor as if I were an oversized rodent. In lieu of a greeting to their children, each spit out a version of "Hurry up—we've got to be—" One just rapped on the glass door to get her kid's attention. Maybe she didn't remember her kid's name. (Strike that: way too bitchy.) In one day, I rocketed from damning the holier-than-thou stay-at-home moms (*no one loves their children more than I love mine!*) to damning those snotty working moms (*What makes them think their contributions to the world are more valuable than mine?*).

There is no good reason for working moms to treat stay-at-home mothers like dirt (invisible dirt, but dirt nonetheless). Working moms might conceivably be grateful to moms who stay home and run our schools, our communities, a good chunk of our kids' worlds. And stay-at-homes might arguably appreciate the working moms staying late to get the big promotions, fighting to increase women's presence on company boards and the front page of *The Wall Street Journal*, campaigning to win elections. Without the money, the power, and the loudspeaker successful careers bring, women will never have the collective bargaining power to make the world better for ourselves, our children, and all the women who can't leave abusive husbands, the ones who wear veils, the moms who earn less than minimum wage cleaning houses and don't have choices about birth control or prenatal care or any other kind of care.

That same morning on the playground, right after the stay-at-home moms had had their verbal way with me on the blacktop and I was scurrying out of the school yard, my daughter's pre-K teacher beckoned me with one finger.

"Shit," I thought. "I don't have time to talk to her." But my inner-mom voice prevailed—she must have something important to say about my daughter. So I went to her.

She had on one of her thirty-three-year-old son's old Redskins T-shirts, pulled down over a faded purple Indian batik skirt. Her long white hair hung to her elbows. Her red lipstick was on crooked. If you'd put a crown and shimmery dress on her, she'd have looked just like an aged Good Witch Glinda headed for the Wizard of Oz nursing home. The other parents and I call her the Goddess of Pre-K. In a city renowned for its expensive, elite private preschool programs, this public school teacher, who's been in the same classroom for twenty-six years, rules with an imaginary golden wand, turning a crop of tearful, terrified four-year-olds into calm, well-behaved, curious five-year-olds who love going to school each day.

She gently but firmly grabbed my elbow, exactly as I'd seen her do to my daughter on Morgan's bossiest days. She'd overheard those stay-at-home-mom comments. Wisdom radiated from her green eyes, almost buried in their wrinkled pockets. "Did anyone ever tell you how beautiful you are?" Mrs. Rahim whispered so that the swirling crowd of stay-at-home moms, lingering by the school door, couldn't hear. "You are a happy mom. Your face glows with it. That's what matters most to your kids. I think you should have ten more children. Now go to work." I could tell she wanted to pat my Liz Claiborne–clad tush as I walked away, smiling as if she'd tied a pink balloon to my wrist.

Today, right before lunch (i.e., a quick hop to the cafeteria to get ice for my Slim-Fast), I ran into another working mom in the hallway and spent ten precious minutes commiserating by the water fountain.

"How are you?"

"Well, I was up at 3 A.M., nursing the baby and writing a PowerPoint presentation for the VP group that I have to give in fifteen minutes. How are you?"

"Oh, yeah, no sleep here either. Last night Morgan kicked me all night, Max peed on me, and when I woke up at 5 A.M. Perry wanted to have sex."

Conversations like this sustain me for days. They provide psychic nourishment when life feels like a bizarre twenty-first-century game show with me as the lone contestant. Throw her a child who vomits on the way to school the day of a big presentation! Chuck an irate client across her path! Have the cat swallow a phone cord at 10 P.M.! Make her go to New York with only twenty-four hours' notice! Break her cell phone, the dryer, and the microwave *on the same day* and see how she reacts! Working moms understand me in ways stay-at-home moms—even my own mom and close friends—never will.

I have to work. I wouldn't be myself if I didn't. My job (most days) makes me feel energized, important, successful—a happy mom to my kids. I have combined the best of my mother's and my father's worlds, largely through years of education and careful career choices that have afforded a handsome prize: rewarding, lucrative part-time work that leaves time for my family. Financial independence factors mightily in my decision to continue working. As I hope I've made clear, I could never leave something as crucial as my family's income solely to someone else, even if that someone else is my husband.

Even so, say that life and luck conspired against me and I had to choose between a demanding fifty-plus-hour-per-week job that left no time for my children or no work at all. I'd choose my kids every time (assuming I could find a way, financially). Because as much as I prize economic independence as a crucial element of providing for and protecting my children, their psychological well-being and the joy I get from being the emotional linchpin of their lives mean more to me. Much more.

The time I do have with my kids is a scarce resource, precious as black pearls. During the week I don't go to girls' night out, to client dinners, or anything else. You're never going to find me on a moms' retreat away from her children. My kids know I can never get enough of them. The biggest punishment Morgan can muster is to put her hands on her hips, stomp her feet, and command imperiously, "Mommy, you go back to work!"

Working motherhood offers a surprising and invaluable benefit: It forces my husband to be a more involved father and a better husband. Because I work, my husband orders our groceries online, makes the kids breakfast every day, periodically takes them to doctors' appointments, and occasionally even makes our bed. Last week was typical: He took Max to school every morning, came home one day at four forty-five to coach the kids' basketball team, and squeezed what he assured me should have been a three-day business trip to California into one day.

He wouldn't have done any of this if I stayed home all the time. Sure, he'd want to. He'd have the best intentions. But the immediacy of his work pressures as the only breadwinner, coupled with my availability as a last-minute substitute, would make it too easy for him to put work first. *Honey, can't you take Max to school today? Babe, all the other guys are staying for the whole trade show. But we have to move to Arkansas—I won't get this opportunity again.* And so on. Like many families with stay-at-home moms, we'd become artificially divided— Mom doing the June Cleaver thing, Dad whistling away at work. My husband probably wouldn't realize what all of us had lost until he became a grandfather.

What puzzles me is that despite the fact that I've crafted a pretty ideal work/family situation, I'm still jealous of the trust stay-at-home moms seem to have in their husbands and in life, a breezy Carol Brady belief that everything will always turn out fiiiine. Some days I dismiss their confidence as sheltered naïveté. Other days I'd kill for even a small dose of faith that neither my husband nor life will leave me stranded destitute on a highway someone else chose. That I'll never need to foot my kids' tuition bills with my own money. That a car accident or sagging economic times will never rob my family of financial stability. That the nagging ache in Max's knee is definitely growing pains, not bone cancer, so I'll never need my more generous health insurance to hire cancer specialists to save his life. That the man I depend upon for food and shelter won't betray my trust.

Whether it's luxurious blindness or a kind of faith I lost long ago, I don't know. Whatever it is that separates me from true stay-at-home mothers makes me sometimes hate them. For a minute.

Then I regain my equilibrium and remind myself that it's *my* life I should judge, not anyone else's. I know that twenty years of work, coupled with surviving a disastrous first marriage, means I make profoundly wiser choices today. I've learned that some scars never heal, but the wounds don't kill you, either. Being responsible for my life, my children, my choices, sustains me in even the darkest hours. The gift of facing life headfirst is knowing that self-reliance, not just the paycheck that makes it possible, is the true key to happiness (or something close to it).

So I'm back where I started. How can some moms stay home? Why is it that others, like me, so clearly cannot? Do we all fight our own private battle about whether to work or stay at home? Does that explain why we're so bitchy to women who've made different choices?

My confusion and curiosity about other moms' lives is what led me to create this book. I *needed* to hear from happy stay-at-home mothers and hard-driving career moms about what life is truly like for them. To bridge the gap between working-mom fantasies and fears about stay-at-home lives (and vice versa), twenty-six writers have laid out, step by step, how they've made their choices and why the decisions are right (or not so right) for them, their children, their husbands, the world. I found it provocative, in the best sense of the word, to juxtapose the stay-at-home mom elucidations with the working-mom ones, and to mix in a few hybrid part-timers like myself. In order to end this catfight and emerge united, we need to explain ourselves to one another.

Most of the debate in the United States about the benefits of working versus stay-at-home motherhood has been taken over by experts: researchers, academics, politicians, journalists. Many of them aren't women. Some aren't even parents. The most authoritative (and fascinating) answers come from moms themselves.

So let's hear from them.

Mommy Wars

Neither Here nor There

Sandy Hingston

People often ask how I found this book's contributors. In truth I could have stood outside my house and flagged down the first twenty-six minivans driving by; every mom has a unique story about why and how she combines work and family. But I found our first contributor via one of womankind's most tried-and-true methods of connecting with other women—an old boyfriend. I asked one about his favorite female writers, and he recommended Sandy Hingston.

Sandy lives in Pennsylvania with her husband and two teenage children. She is a senior editor at *Philadelphia* magazine and the author of nineteen historical romance novels, including *The Suitor* and *The Affair.* In 2004 and 2005, her parenting column, "Loco Parentis," was recognized with the Gold Award from the City and Regional Magazine Association; it has also won the Clarion Award from the Association of Women in Communications.

Some of us working moms find ourselves caught in a gray zone between work and home. We are working but have scaled back our ambitions. Our employers, our colleagues, even our husbands, may not comprehend what we've given up in order to have more time and energy to devote to our children. But we know. Sandy's essay brings to life the pros, the cons, and the frustrations of having it all and ending up in the middle of nowhere.

Eight years ago, when my son had just turned three, I went for the first job interview I'd had since quitting work the week before he was born. The woman who conducted the interview was funny and charming. I felt an instant bond. I aced the copyediting test she gave me. We spoke about the magazine I'd be working for if I got the job, and she pumped me up. We went to lunch in the company cafeteria and discovered that we both loved egg salad and were Lithuanian American (which doesn't happen often). Things were moving right along.

Then, over cups of herbal tea, the woman said, "You say your son is three. What makes you sure you're ready to go back to work now?"

I was prepared for the question. I'd practiced my answer. I held my hand up and ticked off my fingers: "Jake's in prenursery school two mornings a week now, and doing fine there. The same school has full-time day care, so that transition should be smooth. His sister just started kindergarten, and he's jealous of her 'big-kid school' anyway. He's very verbal, so he'll be able to express himself if something at day care is making him unhappy. And—well, this job just seems perfect for me. It's time to go back."

That was all five fingers.

But the woman wasn't looking at my hand. She was staring at my face. Because right from the word *prenursery*, I'd been crying, silently crying, great fat slobbery tears rolling down my cheeks and throat and onto my neatly pressed blouse.

She handed me a tissue. I dried my eyes.

We both knew it was the end of the interview.

Two years later, different interview, different magazine, different job offer—one I could say yes to without sobbing. For one thing, my male predecessor had structured the position to accommodate his novel-writing aspirations: He was in the office the first two weeks of every month, when the magazine was in the throes of production; the last two weeks, when things were slower, he worked from home, via computer—a setup that sounded heavenly compared with conventional full-time. And no one could say I'd asked for special consideration because I was a mother; I was simply inheriting the status quo.

For another thing, Jake had finally begun kindergarten. My husband's work as a musician could be arranged so he'd be there for the kids after school. I would have it all: a real job, a great job, decent money, terrific people to work with, plus those two weeks a month when I would be a full-time mom. I sat Jake and his sister, Marcy, down and explained how wonderful life was going to be from now on.

And it *was* a wonderful life. While I was at the office, I never thought much about what the kids were doing. When I was home, the office seemed very far away. I had more patience for playing Legos or leading the Brownie troop when I knew that in only two weeks I'd be dealing with adults who respected my talents again. True, the commute was a bear—an hour and a half each way. In the weeks I was working, I dropped Marcy and Jake at school in the morning and didn't get back until it was time to tuck them in. But—though it took me a long while to admit this to anyone, even myself—I loved my time alone in the car, alone in the silence, or in noise, if there was noise, of my own choice and making, in contrast to the unending tumult that was Marcy and Jake.

And oh, how I loved the homecomings, turning the key in the front door in the violet glow of evening and being greeted like the Allies liberating Paris, by the kids, yes, who threw themselves at me in delirious adulation, but also by my husband, Doug, passing the child-care baton with weary gratitude. Then it was upstairs—"Up the blue waterfall!"—to the pleasures of the tub, and into jammies that I had washed and folded on the weekends, and bouncing into Mom and Dad's big bed for half an hour of *The Boxcar Children* or *Little House on the Prairie* or *Winnie-the-Pooh*.

Part-time parenting was pleasurable, and I was good at it, as good as I was at fixing dangling participles and sorting out faulty parallelism and conjugating *lie* and *lay*. I was the Selkie Girl, sleek as a seal in my dual roles, better than anyone else because there were two of me.

It took some time for the fragility of the construct Doug and I had created to manifest itself. There were foreshadowings, ghostly intimations that all was not well in Toyland. That first year in kindergarten, Jake pushed a fellow student hard enough that we got to meet the principal. In the autumn of first grade, he hurled his lunch across the room and then hit a girl named Enjoli with a chair. The spring after Columbine, he took a nail clipper to school and damn near got expelled. ("It's not a *weapon*," he said scornfully when we attempted to explain how the world had changed. "It's a *nail clipper*.") The following year, when a teacher suggested that Jake hadn't done his best at a task, he locked himself into a bathroom stall and refused to come out, announcing his intention to "just kill myself." This tripped a school-district alert process that landed him in anger-management therapy. All this time, Doug and I presented the perfect concerned-parent front, siding with the school in every instance, promising disciplinary action on our end, doing our best to impress everyone involved with how dedicated we were to putting things right.

What was needed, the therapist and Jake's teachers and the principal and Doug and I agreed, was consistency and follow-through: consequences laid out in advance, punishments doled out as threatened. It sounded great in theory. But what it ran up against was my deep conviction that Jake's problems were at heart *my* problems—that if I was a real mom, there for him every day at pickup and not just half the time, he wouldn't be hostile and impatient and sarcastic and rude. I felt this way even though I loved my job—maybe *because* I loved my job. Instead of coming down harder on Jake, I came down harder on myself, and doubled up the perfection: perfect Christmases, birthdays, summer vacations. The Halloween costumes I sewed were museum-worthy. Cupcakes for class parties were Martha Stewart fantasies of fondant and flowers.

And I justified the hours I was away with the money I was making. New Nikes? You got 'em. Another Barbie? You betcha. A $120 collectible *Star Wars* helmet? Little man, nothing's too good for you.

Somehow, it wasn't helping. Jake just got angrier. I felt so lucky to have Marcy, solid and sensitive Marcy, with her straight A's and goody-two-shoes ways. She was her brother's perfect foil. I'd fallen into writing a parenting column for the magazine, producing gritty, drawn-from-life portrayals of child rearing as it really is. Only—they weren't, really. I skated on the side streets of Jake's problems, riffed drolly on Marcy's entrée into the teen years, each column neatly tying up the issue of the month—racism, Britney wannabes, attention deficit disorder. I heard from lots of parents who said they loved my stuff. My mistake was taking praise for the columns as praise for *me:* What a good, wise mother! And all the time we as a family were devolving, heading into a tailspin, catalog-shopping for the emperor's new clothes.

My daughter, in the summer before she began high school, took all the willpower she had hitherto directed at earning good grades, excelling at trombone, and making varsity in three sports and turned it to one purpose: getting very thin. It is proof of just how far my head was stuck in sand that Marcy dropped nearly forty pounds before I noticed how odd her eating habits had become.

I knew she was dieting, but I'd dieted when I was her age. I had just never done it so obsessively—or successfully. Holding herself to less than a thousand calories a day, sobbing when circumstances forced her to consume foods with uncertain nutritional values, working out feverishly at the gym, my daughter reduced herself to a wisp, convinced that in radically altering herself, she would change her world.

Shylock never paid more dearly. For her meticulous troubles, for her painstaking efforts, Marcy began her freshman year at high school and discovered . . . that nothing had changed. That the boys she idolized still preferred girls she considered idiots. That though she was rail-thin, she was still agonizingly self-conscious and shy. Instead of coming to what seemed to Doug and me the logical conclusion—might as well start eating again!—she curled up on our sofa and fell into what Jake's therapist (we were all seeing her now) diagnosed as depression.

My perfect family had become a perfect mess.

Like Alice down the rabbit hole, I was plunged into a new world, one with its own vocabulary and rules of order. Therapy was as foreign to me, the child of parents who'd never admitted there were problems, let alone discussed them, as the Cyrillic alphabet. It took all my concentration, in the face of our therapist's gentle questioning, to keep my good-mother persona intact. Now and then I flubbed it big-time; on one memorable visit, in my daughter's presence, I referred to her as a "whack job." The therapist stared in shock, then asked me to repeat what I'd said: "I'm sure I must have misheard you."

"No, she called me a whack job," Marcy confirmed. "But it really didn't bother me. She says things like that all the time."

In the therapist's narrowed eyes, I read something no one had ever, ever, accused me of before: I was a bad mom.

We didn't dive into quarry-deep psychological waters in our family therapy; we only dabbled our toes. But it was a strange and different way of thinking about our relationships to one another, brought into focus by a woman who knew only what we showed her about ourselves. What I learned from it was that the more I showed her, the more I felt we were getting somewhere.

As a mom, I came to see, I was pretty bad. Failure was new to me, and I found it liberating. The key to what had gone awry at home—what fed my daughter's unfeeding, and my son's fits of temper—was precisely what made me so good at my job. Each month, it was my responsibility to see that the magazine was perfect: no typos, no grammatical mistakes, no errors of logic or omission. When you spend your days aggressively seeking out imperfection, you begin to see it everywhere: in the bedspread that's askew, in the lawn that's mowed haphazardly, in the A-minus that could have been an A.

Before we could heal, I would have to learn to turn off my relentless drive for finding flaws. I would have to understand the truth in those weary platitudes: "It's not the end of the world." "Everyone makes mistakes." I strove to loosen up. Occasionally, we did something on the spur of the moment—and it turned out okay. I became braver in dealing with situations that had once made me panic: asking directions, making reservations, packing for vacations, all those control-freak moments that filled our daily lives with high anxiety. I had a responsibility to my children to try to become, in my late forties, a grown-up at last. And part of growing up was figuring out how I felt about the decisions I'd made when it came to my job.

Conventional mother wisdom tells me I'm right to work because my family won't be happy unless I'm happy. What does it mean, then, if my work makes me unhappy—but maybe less unhappy than staying home would? Conventional mother wisdom says that the best, the finest, gift I can give my children is to be interesting and involved, and that I can't have that without a career. Maybe not. I'll never know what our lives would be like if I'd stayed home full-time, been there for all the concerts and parent-teacher conferences and hockey games. Maybe Jake wouldn't be so angry. Maybe Marcy wouldn't be so thin. Or maybe they would.

What I do know is this. We women, we're supposed to be the ones making the choices these days, calling the shots, controlling our destinies. And despite my desperate efforts to keep it all together, I'm really not in control of anything—not my family, not my career, not my relationship with my husband, not who becomes president of the United States. I'm not even in control of me. When I'm at work, I wish I were home. Tending to my children. When I'm home, I think longingly of work—where I have space, can breathe. The only time I feel as if I know who I am anymore is in the car, when I ride bareheaded between my two hats, neither here nor there.

This realization, the recognition that having it all is the same as having nothing, has had the effect of making me softer, more tolerant. Childless women, the ones who've made or been forced into that choice—I've stopped seeing them as doppelgängers, my thinner, richer, infinitely more leisured lost self, what I would be if my womb had never come through. And where once I pursed my mouth when prospective mothers announced their intention to return to work full-time in six weeks, now I tell them how much I admire them, how sure I am they'll cope, thrive, be fine. When I wheel my grocery cart into the checkout line behind a woman whose toddler is screaming for candy, I smile at her, thinking, "Bad day" instead of "Bad mother."

We are all good mothers, the best we know how to be.

The Mother Load

Terri Minsky

Terri Minsky is the creator of several television shows, including *Lizzie McGuire, Less Than Perfect,* and *The Geena Davis Show.* She is the executive producer of *The Lizzie McGuire Movie,* and has written for *Sex and the City, Flying Blind,* and *Central Park West.* She lives in New York City with her husband and two children and frequently can be found three thousand miles away in Los Angeles. Stay-at-home mom, part-time working mom, eighty-plus-hours-per-week working mom—she's done it all and lived to write about it.

Here's one of my mother's favorite stories of my childhood:

At the age of nine, I come home from school weeping: I have no friends; no one plays with me during recess. My mother, in what becomes her lifelong trait of taking my misery as her own, comes to school the next day and hides behind some shrubbery, where she watches me on the playground racing around and jumping rope and clearly not lacking for company.

My mother repeats this story every time I tell her I'm feeling insecure. I think the moral is "You're not insecure, you're just delusional." But now that I have a nine-year-old daughter of my own, and an eleven-year-old son, I realize what the real lesson is: I can't be a stay-at-home mom because I would spend every waking hour behind shrubbery.

My mother's story suggests I'm hardwired for hovering. Add to that three years I spent on the fertility roller coaster, riding the hopeful highs and the crushing lows, feeling as if I were the only woman in New York not pregnant or pushing a stroller. I went out of my way to avoid the many playgrounds on the Upper West Side. I was a sullen baby-shower guest. I completely stopped speaking to a friend who told me she planned her pregnancy to ensure that her child had a spring birthday.

The moment I learned I was pregnant in early 1993, life became all about the kid for me. I took the oath of our generation that I would not, would never, give my child any reason to mention my name in therapy. I wanted my children to feel they'd hit the mommy mother lode.

Year one, I was a stay-at-home mom. My days consisted primarily of photographing Sam, often while he was sleeping (in fact, entire rolls of that), then running down to the one-hour developing shop and ordering double prints, which I picked up exactly sixty minutes later. I made albums and scrapbooks and journals and carefully labeled and stored all the negatives and extra prints. My idea of an "event" was a sale at Monkeys and Bears, the tony children's wear store in the neighborhood. I arrived a half hour before the store opened the first day of the sale. My own wardrobe was black and entirely elastic.

I shunned all store-bought birthday-party invitations and made my own. One year I sewed them. Every playdate was an arts-and-crafts extravaganza. Finger paints and Play-Doh didn't cut it for me. When a child came to our house, I produced googly eyes, Sculpey clay, Shrinky Dinks, Mod Podge, special scissors that cut fancy deckled edges, bags of cloth swatches, boxes of beads, fabric paint, glitter glue, stamps and ink pads, the Eric Carle set of designed tissue paper, decorate-your-own T-shirts, picture frames, treasure chests, puppets. I wanted to be the gold standard by which all kids judged their parents.

Just to be clear: I'm not bragging about this.

I wanted only what every parent wants—for my children to be happy. But first I had to define happiness for them, and I went with excess, constant surprise, wish fulfillment before the wishes were made, before my kids even knew what wishes were. As a two-year-old, Sam formed his first material attachment, to a four-dollar *Lion King* figurine. Inevitably, it slipped from his hand during some stroller nap, and rather than wait a day—okay, an hour—to see if he could love another toy, I rushed to the store and bought four more, all they had in stock. He was never without it again, until he discovered T. Rex . . . well, I think you see where I'm going with this. I'm actually too embarrassed to describe the riches that befell my children as rewards during the potty-training process. Let's just say it was Christmas with a toilet instead of a tree.

I was constitutionally unable to see them suffer. Discipline, time-outs, denying my own flesh and blood a sixth bottle of juice just because it would, quote unquote, "rot her teeth"—all of that fell to David, my husband. As did the dreaded Ferberizing—following Dr. Ferber's method of teaching your child to fall asleep by letting him cry for increasingly longer intervals until he figures out you've discontinued the blissful experience of rocking him to sleep. I don't know who suffered more, Sam or me, but I do know David had to Ferberize us both at the same time.

Annie was born when Sam was seventeen months old. Two months later, I went back to work as a writer on the television series *Central Park West*. If nothing else, I had to support this insatiable shopping habit I'd developed on behalf of my children. But it really was too good a job to pass up—a TV show shooting in New York, the brainchild of zeitgeist master Darren Star, who already had *Melrose Place* and *Beverly Hills 90210* on the air.

As it turned out, this wasn't the hard-core office job that kept me away from my kids. I could get to work late, I could leave early, I could write at home, so neither my children nor I had to deal with major separation issues. It had been more than two years since I'd spent any significant time in all-adult company, let alone as the only one with children. I was about as clueless as a German tourist trying to decipher a New York City subway map. I couldn't remember the last book I'd read that didn't rhyme. I had no good industry gossip, and nobody here wanted to gab about breast-pumping machines and babyproofing your apartment. The job itself lasted only a matter of months until the show was canceled. For the next five years, I was a work-at-home mom, which I kept telling myself was the best of both worlds, but when I look back on it, I see now it was also the worst.

Work was a distraction from Sam and Annie; Sam and Annie were a distraction from work. It turns out I'm not all that good at compartmentalizing or managing my time, but until this point I had never really had to be. I had always gotten things done before. Now I was turning in scripts late and sometimes not at all. I would sit bolt upright in bed at 3 A.M., freaking out about how I was going to do my share to support this family, vowing to myself that today I would get all the work done that I hadn't managed to do yesterday and the day before that and the day before that and the day before that. I would shut the doors to my living room, determined to concentrate, and then look up to see a little face staring mournfully at me through the glass. Was I really going to ignore that just so I could stare at a blank screen? Of course not. The mommy part of me was never going to take a backseat to the writer part of me.

Unless I had forty-five minutes left to go in my workday and had produced barely half a page of stuff I didn't loathe. I'm one of those writers who needs hours of staring at the computer to write anything worthwhile, and now I had to weave those hours around parent-teacher conferences and ear infections and making cookies for a bake sale and jumping up to see what that horrible crashing sound was. I would set very reasonable, not overly ambitious goals for myself: Write five pages today. We're talking sitcom script pages with wide margins and double-spaced dialogue—I wasn't giving Proust a run for his money.

As my available work time ticked away, I would become increasingly tense. Mommy wasn't opening the doors for a hug; it was the Writer, and she was snapping, "You have to leave me alone! I have to get this done!" Which was then followed by Guilty Mommy, who wouldn't let Frustrated Writer do anything until she apologized. You know, it's scary when you see the last scene of *Psycho,* where Norman Bates is in a padded cell and his two personalities have finally merged and you're thinking, "Wow, he looks relaxed."

So, I had the Holy Grail of "it all"—marriage, family, career—and, for the first time in my life, antidepressants. Yet everything I did felt half-assed. I hadn't written more than a script or two a year for five years. I spent entire days in my bathrobe, and it wasn't a particularly attractive bathrobe. I had an all-purpose sleep/work/gym wardrobe of leggings and oversized T-shirts, and had been known to go forty-eight hours straight in the same clothes. My main mode of transportation was bicycle, which I could ride with four grocery bags suspended from the handlebars. It took me a really long time to figure out I couldn't handle "it all," even longer to stop feeling horribly incompetent about that.

In the mid-1990s, having children was considered a serious liability for female television writers. One executive, a woman who knew of my fertility problems, greeted the news of my second pregnancy with this sentence: "You're as useful to me now as if you had a brain tumor." I thought, Oh my God, she's going to realize she said this grotesque thing and call me back any minute, begging my forgiveness. But she never did; actually, she thought her sentiment so apt she repeated it to my agent. I take tremendous satisfaction in the fact that a script I wrote for her, which died at ABC, was picked up in 2000 by the Disney Channel and became the series *Lizzie McGuire.*

This same year, I wrote a pilot about a fabulous single girl who marries a widower with children and becomes Instant Mom. It wasn't my idea, and I had no higher expectation for this script than anything else I'd written. But this one was picked up, and Geena Davis agreed to star in it.

This is like you just passed your driver's test and somebody hands you the keys to a Jaguar. You have to drive it. Even if you feel like you'd be happy with a beat-up Toyota. And everyone keeps saying, "Boy, you're so lucky, what a fantastic car, better not let it get dented or stolen or scratched." Which is what you know for certain is going to happen if you so much as get behind the wheel.

Sitcom writing is not the job for people who want to spend time with their kids. For nine months of the year, you just don't get to. Eighty-hour weeks are typical. An "easy" job is one where you sometimes get home before midnight and have some weekends off. You eat most of your meals out of Styrofoam delivery boxes. And you spend nearly all this time in a conference room from hell, sitting at a table covered with cold French fries and empty soda cans and used napkins and open soy sauce packages and the trade papers, which everybody's reading while they're supposed to be working from the hundred various drafts of that week's script, also scattered around. Usually at least one person is quizzing the room from some dictionary of vile sex terms printed off the Internet.

But for me the main drawback of the job was its location on the other side of the country, which meant moving my family to Los Angeles. Any satisfaction I may have allowed myself in my accomplishment was subsumed by guilt. I never for a moment considered going without them, and likewise never intended it would be a permanent move. It was for one year, an extended family vacation, with the promise of many trips to Disneyland. So I wasn't adequately prepared for what happened when I finally went to work.

I loved it.

I loved being in the company of adults. I loved being able to swear freely and not worry that I might be corrupting anyone. I loved having my own office, and this one had a button on the desk that would make the door swing shut. It had been so long since I had gossiped about anything besides other people's nannies. I made new friends. I bought new clothes. I had my hair streaked for the first time and bought three hundred dollars' worth of makeup, which I actually wore for a while. The night we shot the second episode of the show, I was so overwhelmed with the pure joy of being in this place with these people that I wept and hugged everyone, including the network executives. People asked me if I was drunk.

I felt like Hollywood had for some reason conspired to throw me a massive surprise party, and everyone who came chipped in on the gift of a giant ego boost. But I can't say I was especially proud of my contribution to my own show, or even that I made much of one. I was one of four executive producers, the one with by far the least experience. I may have stated my opinions, but I didn't insist on them. I sat relatively quietly while we added a hot-for-five-minutes dimwit to attract male viewers. I said little as we broke a story in which Geena "accidentally" bakes a cake in the shape of a penis. And I wasn't altogether surprised when the show was canceled.

But the record shows we all enjoyed that year in Los Angeles. We rented a house, the first we had ever lived in, with this incredible yard that had hammocks and a fish pond and little waterfalls and a tree house and grapefruit, orange, and avocado trees—quite a different piece of real estate from our New York City apartment. We took trips to Newport Beach and San Diego and cut school one day to go to Disneyland. It actually did feel like an extended family vacation.

We moved back to New York, as scheduled, a year later. I realized with something akin to panic that I had to escape our apartment if I wanted to keep playing with the big people. I just couldn't slide back into my former life; I couldn't return to writing in the living room. I rented myself an office, where I was alone, just me and my blank screen, trying to write myself another job. The following year a pilot I wrote became an ABC sitcom called *Less Than Perfect*.

Uprooting my family again was not an option, so this time I went to Los Angeles by myself, making a deal to run the show for its first thirteen episodes. It's only for four months, we told the kids; I swear I'll be home for Thanksgiving. Then the show was picked up for an entire season, and for three months after I "came home," I spent half of every week in Los Angeles. The kids' good-byes went from tearful to furious at warp speed:

You lied! You said you wouldn't go back! I hate you! I HOPE YOU NEVER COME BACK!

You try getting in a town car and driving away from that.

So why did I? I could say it was because I had to, if I intended to remain a television writer, live in New York City, and send my children to private school. All of that is true. But it was mostly because I wanted to.

That year, I missed a lot of things in my children's lives. Big things that I loved: the first day of school, parent-teacher conferences, the annual apple- and pumpkin-picking excursion, choosing their clothes for

Picture Day. Little things that I loved even more: laughing over Shel Silverstein poems at bedtime, the way my kids look right after a haircut, the wrinkled notes from school they pull out of their backpacks that they were supposed to give you last week.

But this was something in my life I didn't want to miss. Getting a show on network television is a thousand-to-one shot, and I had hit it. It's not the kind of opportunity you can tell yourself you'll take the next time it comes around. Obviously it sucked that it was an opportunity three time zones away from my family, but that's where it was, so that's where I had to be.

Every time I spoke to Sam or Annie during those months, they would ask, "Mommy, do you love your television show more than us?" And I would tell them no, of course I didn't. Their next question always was, "Mommy, then why are you with the show and not with us?"

First I tried "This is hard for me, too." They would point out I could solve that if I would just come home. When I said, "But I have to be here," they would say other people could run a TV show, but I was the only mommy they had. (The perfect age for a prosecuting attorney: eight years old. Eight-year-olds are merciless.)

I could never come right out and say to my children: I want to do this. I need to do this. This is who I am, and it's taken a lot of therapy not to apologize for that. At my children's school, there are mothers who hold meetings with administrators to discuss the juice policy. I would put a fork in my eye if that were my life. But I'm grateful to the parents who immerse themselves in our school, and I would like to think that somehow, I'm returning the favor. No, not by writing a television show for their children to watch. But maybe by letting their children know they can someday turn the trauma of their teenage years into an interesting career. As I agonized, friends told me I was setting an example for Sam and Annie to pursue their dreams, and that as adults they would appreciate that. The problem was, I needed something to comfort them at that moment, and I didn't have anything.

The best I could do was minimize the torment. After the first year, I turned *Less Than Perfect* over to another show runner, also a mother who had faced her own struggles having a family in this business. The fact is, there are a lot more of us now, and we do have workplace conversations about how much homework our kids have and why sleepover birthday parties often turn out badly. We can be late to work to attend school field trips and doctor visits. I've had women thank me, and tell me I helped make that possible. Had I known anyone would ever say that, I would have had an answer to those horribly difficult conversations with my children.

But we haven't had any of those lately. I still go to Los Angeles several times a year. My kids don't love it, but they accept it. The trips are shorter and the good-byes are manageable.

Before my most recent trip, Sam and I were walking up Broadway together. I asked him, if it had been up to him, would he have wanted me to work, or be at home?

We happened to be walking down a block where I had pushed him in a stroller, where I had stood with him as he counted buses going by, where he collected bottle caps from the sidewalk despite my begging him not to. Now here he was, dressed in his baseball uniform and carrying his bat bag; I could see his whole history on this stretch of concrete. And I was talking to him like the adult he nearly is.

The next day, I told this story to a roomful of network executives in Los Angeles. I was pitching a pilot about a woman who goes back to work after several years of being a stay-at-home mother. I may have gotten out of my living room, but as a writer, I rarely venture five feet from my own life.

I repeated Sam's answer to me: "I would have wanted you to do what made you happy."

As soon as I said it, I started to cry.

And so did the other moms in the room.

Sharks and Jets

Page Evans

One of my goals when I started out was to find stay-at-home mothers interested in telling their stories. Although they are supremely important and powerful in the lives of their families, and often involved in their schools and communities, their voices are rarely heard on a national stage during the years they devote themselves to their children's daily lives. Although their buying power is formidable, as any Procter & Gamble brand manager knows, their influence is anonymous and silent. Every few years a politician might commandeer a cute soccer mom for a photo op, but rarely are stay-at-home moms asked to open their mouths or pick up their pens to tout their opinions.

It was important that stay-at-home moms have a voice in this book, but I worried about how to find them. How do you contact women who've never published anything? Then one by one I found them, mostly through word of mouth. Page Evans is a neighbor, a local freelance writer, and stay-at-home mom. Her work has been published in the anthology *2Do Before I Die: The Do-It-Yourself Guide to the Rest of Your Life, The Washington Post,* and *Washingtonian* magazine. She lives in Washington, D.C., with her family.

Jenny's six-week-old boy and my three-week-old girl slept blissfully as our matching all-terrain strollers bumped along the redbrick Georgetown sidewalk. Our babies' noses were barely visible under hats, snowsuits, and blankets of fleece. Marching our way up Wisconsin Avenue, whirling past Fresh Fields and Guy Mason Park, Jenny and I chatted breathlessly about the ups and downs of motherhood, about breast-feeding and sleep patterns. It was a sunny but cold January morning. A dusting of snow had fallen the night before, covering chunks of gray frozen slush, remnants from a storm days earlier.

Jenny and I had known each other for years and had become even closer during our parallel first pregnancies. We'd laughed as our belly buttons popped out the same week like the white plastic pieces on roasting chickens. We'd been through prenatal classes together and shared the same ob-gyn; a snapshot on my fridge shows us bumping bellies at my baby shower. And while Jenny is a gourmet cook, turning out puréed parsnips on a school night, I'm the queen of takeout. I do have one specialty: pumpkin pie. Baking several a week, I'd put on more than forty pounds in nine months. "Page's pumpkin pie" became the running joke during my pregnancy. So when Jenny went into labor three weeks before I did, I brought her a pumpkin pie with homemade bourbon whipped cream to dollop on top.

After I delivered an eight-pound, two-ounce baby girl, she brought me what I never imagined needing: an inflatable donut to sit on. It was the most useful—and needed—gift I received.

But on this sunny day, a chill crept between us, old friends, new mothers. It started when I asked about her plans to go back to work. I figured she might be available for a few more weeks to power walk and talk with me about the puzzling and at times terrifying behavior of our infants.

"I'm going back next week," she told me. "There's a big deal in the works, and I have to be there."

Trotting alongside the stroller, my ninety-pound yellow Lab lurched toward a squirrel scurrying up a bare tree. "Emma," I scolded, tugging her leash. "My God, that's so soon," I said to Jenny. "Aren't you going to feel terrible leaving him?"

I wanted to take back my words as soon as they hit the crisp air. But it was too late. I had launched the first salvo. "Sorry, Jenny, I don't mean to put a guilt trip on you," I said hastily.

She looked straight ahead and gave the air a quick shrug, as if a snowflake had landed on her cheek. She went on to tell me about buying a bionic breast pump so she could continue nursing at her investment-banking job. I half expected to hear grand plans of FedExing milk back to D.C. from different business-trip locations. There was a tinge of pride in her voice. At least, that was my perception. I got the impression that she was feeling pretty good about (a) fitting into a size 4 dress just weeks after giving birth, and (b) doing it all.

Yep. She was doing it all, all right. Jenny had regained her mind and her body, and soon would regain her job. I had none of these. Hell, I could barely get my daughter into her car seat without feeling like I needed a Ph.D. The click-in strap would never click. Everything was a struggle.

My baby didn't sleep. I, in turn, didn't sleep. I breast-fed on demand, with fresh milk coming in every forty-five minutes, soaking through countless Playtex nursing pads, leaving rings of yellowish residue on all my oversized nursing shirts. I'm sure I smelled. The well-heeled customers at the Georgetown Safeway often seemed to sniff as they walked by in the dairy aisle, me hoping they'd assume the stench was coming from dried-up sour milk on the shelf and not my body. I was tired. I was resentful and self-righteous. Perhaps even a little paranoid.

And then Jenny launched a salvo of her own. "I don't know, you know." She turned to me. "I think I'd just be so *bored* if I had to stay home all day with a baby," she said, still pushing her pram.

Bored. The way she said it, it was like she was spitting on me.

And there we were: a stay-at-home mom and a working mom, strolling along in icy silence.

Looking back, I see that the dissonance in our friendship had the makings of a Broadway musical. Sort of a *West Side Story,* fighting it out behind each other's backs instead of in back alleys. The Sharks and the Jets.

Stay-at-home moms versus working moms. Bored. Guilty. Bored. Guilty. Bored. Guilty. I hear fingers snapping and tongues hissing.

"You must feel guilty," the stay-at-home mom sneers, pulling out her switchblade, taking another jab.

"You must be so bored," the working mom says, spitting in disgust.

Spit. Jab. Spit. Jab. Spit. Jab.

I imagine Jerome Robbins choreography. The stay-at-home moms in their park attire of rubber clogs, khakis, and T-shirts. The working moms in their pencil skirts, pressed blouses, and Ferragamos. The T-shirts haughtily push their strollers in single file, their noses inching higher as they pass the Blouses marching single file in the opposite direction holding briefcases, their noses down—to the grindstone.

They pretend not to notice each other. Then, slowly, longingly, they look back. Because we all do, no matter what our choices. We question our decisions, our roles, our lives. Are we doing the right thing? Are we happy? Are our children happy?

Happy children. Isn't this what we want, whether we're working or not? For me, having children who know they're loved and are happy and kind is all I want. Sure, it would be great if they turn out to be smart, athletic, and funny, but happy and kind, there's no gray area there.

There is a gray area, however, in how we judge one another and how we landed these roles we've come to play.

I stepped into the role of stay-at-home mom without auditioning for the part. I had worked on the Bush '88 campaign (I've since switched parties) after college and then went to work as a TV reporter on Maryland's Eastern Shore. The market was a small one, but for me it felt like a stepping-stone toward my dream of becoming Oprah. When I was growing up, my family referred to me as Bawbwa because I was so nosy. (I prefer curious.)

After a couple of years, the dream lost its stardust. In a business too pressed for time to see anything but the next story, I'd interview the victim of some heinous crime, only to tear up while holding the microphone. The interviewee would end up comforting me. Clearly, my skin wasn't thick enough for the job. My long hair always got caught in my mouth during live shots, and my raspy voice caused concern with viewers. I think they assumed I had a chronic case of strep throat. No wonder my one and only fan letter came from a prisoner at the Eastern Correctional Institute. Figuring prison was no place to host a talk show, I threw in the microphone, left the Eastern Shore, and headed to graduate school in Washington, which also happened to be where the boyfriend who would later become my husband lived.

After moving to D.C. and marrying, I got a master's, had a brief stint producing an independent film, and did some freelance writing before having my first baby, Peyton, at thirty and the second, Katherine, at thirty-three. Since there was no "real" job waiting for me on the horizon, I more or less coasted into the role of a stay-at-home mom. It's not even something Bobby and I discussed. Taking care of my own children just made sense to me.

I knew I wanted to be there for my two girls in a way my mother wasn't there for me. Mom was—and is—an artist. Not an oh-isn't-that-a-nice-hobby artist, but a professional one. She shows at galleries and her work hangs in two museums. Now, of course, I couldn't be more proud of her and her accomplishments, not just as an artist but as a person, mother, and grandmother. We often joke that she's a better grandmother than mother. My girls love having an artist as a grandmother. And as an adult, I love it too. Growing up, though, I was often embarrassed by my "working" mom. She'd pick me up from school—usually running late—in a paint-splattered Chevrolet Impala station wagon. Often wearing bell-bottoms, a tie-dyed T-shirt, and a scarf tied around her head like a pirate, Mom looked every inch the quintessential seventies chick. I'd open the car door, inhaling paint and turpentine fumes, hoping none of my preppy friends would see the multicolored abstract landscape painting through the back window. Or, God forbid, a nude!

And the lunches she made. Well, let's just say I was not the envy of every kid in the cafeteria. A hastily made peanut butter and jelly on wheat (for some reason, I always seemed to get a heel) was the main course, followed by an orange or apple thrown on top. No chips. No dessert. I remember salivating over classmates' lunches, begging for one of their homemade Toll House cookies. One girl's mother used to make an extra batch for me, probably aware that my mom wasn't the cookie-baking type.

When she wasn't painting, playing classical piano, doing yoga, or taking French, my mother was teaching art at the women's prison, volunteering at an inner-city day-care center, and helping cultural causes around town. On top of all that, while raising three children, she was married to a man with a political career. Dad was the U.S. congressman from Delaware from 1977 to 1983. Before that, he co-chaired the Republican National Committee. Both jobs kept him in Washington during parts of the week, leaving Mom at home, juggling. Preparing the perfect lunch, making sure my hair looked nice, and helping her kids with their homework weren't at the top of her priority list (or weren't always feasible). I get that now. I didn't as a child.

So it was with this baggage that I entered motherhood, determined to be, as they say in the Army, all that I could be. I wanted to be interesting like my mother but also available for my two little girls. I wanted them to know that they were my priority.

What I've found, though, is that motherhood is hard. And staying at home is not as easy or fun as I originally envisioned. I didn't slip into the role as naturally as I thought I would. Yes, there are moments of sheer bliss. But there are also moments of utter exasperation and, dare I say, boredom. Sometimes pushing that baby swing in the park can feel cathartic. You get lulled into the syncopated rhythm of it. But other times that same rhythm can feel like Chinese water torture—especially when your child wants to go "higher, Mommy, higher" and your right shoulder is about to pop out of the socket from pushing.

Or I'm in the car, listening to an interview on NPR with the author of the book I'm aching to read and both girls demand to hear Abba's greatest hits for the umpteenth time. And then Katherine needs to know—a sense of urgency growing with each question—where God lives, who made up words, what happens if you sit on a cloud, how waves are made, where thunder comes from, and why lightning blinks. Then I get home, physically and mentally spent, wondering how some mothers make it look so easy. The phone rings. It's another mom from the girls' school, whom I've never been able to say no to. "Oh, Page, you are such a sweetheart. Do you have a minute? We need your help . . ."

Shit.

Part of the problem, until recently, has been my inability to say no. No one tells you when you decide to stay home that you're rarely actually at

home. Between carting the kids to and from school and various activities
and playdates, you get sucked into the vortex of volunteerism. Once you
become a yes-mom, it seems, everyone—schools, churches, neighborhood parks, theaters, children's hospitals—wants a piece of you.

I remember the first few weeks after Peyton started pre-K there were
sign-up sheets to volunteer for the various causes: the annual auction to
raise money for scholarship funds, the book fair, chaperoning field trips,
reading to the students, helping make sandwiches for the homeless.

I felt pressured to do everything I could to make life better for my
children and their school. I imagined daggers being shot in my back if I
didn't do my fair share. I'd overhear comments like "Well, we'd call so-
and-so to do it, but she's working." Or I'd see a mother with four children volunteering, doing it all, and figure, "Well, I only have two kids, so
I should be able to do it too."

For stay-at-home moms without so-called "real" jobs, volunteering
becomes a social payback of sorts. I feel obligated to volunteer, to say
yes, to prove my worth. But who am I proving it to? *What* am I trying to
prove? Do I feel pressure from other parents when I see them volunteering? Do I want to show my children I care enough about them to chaperone a field trip to a local wetland, make papier-mâché masks for a play,
help sew stockings in the classroom at Christmastime, chop vegetables to
add to soup for the homeless, be on the auction committee? Do I feel like
I'll be struck by lightning if an older woman from our church asks me to
help with an art project for inner-city adolescents and I can't make it?

YES! Yes. Yes. YES! Yes. And yes.

The problem with saying yes so often is that I've found myself doing
more volunteering than parenting. One day I woke up and thought:
"The whole reason I'm not working is to raise my children, but now I'm
paying a babysitter to take them to the park so I can volunteer and not
get paid."

And it's not just the pressure to volunteer that weighs on mothers,
working or not. There's also pressure to enlist our children in endless activities. I know one working mother whose first-grader takes karate, vi-
olin, and a dance class all in the same day—a school day. Where is the
downtime? Where is the time for just doing nothing, for playing, for letting children use their imaginations?

It has taken me a while—nearly seven years—to find a balance that works for me as a mother. Scratch that. I'm still searching for that balance, hitting bumps along the way.

"So, what do you do, do you work?" a fifty-something gray-haired man in a black turtleneck and tweed jacket asks. We're standing in a claret-colored living room at a book party in Cleveland Park, and the bartender has just handed him a glass brimming with bourbon over ice.

"I'm basically a stay-at-home mom," I say.

"Oh, well, that's such an important job. Kids grow up so fast, don't they?"

"Yeah, they do," I say.

And that's the end of it. Turn and pivot.

But wait. Wait! Don't you want to know what I think about what's going on in the world? I want to scream out. I've spent the past seven years trying to improve my mind, to prove that I'm more than "just a mom." I see more plays, read more op-eds, take classes, visit museums. I'm in a book club. I write essays. I read *Us Weekly* in the checkout line. (Whoops. Might not mention this fascination with pop culture—too revealing of latent lowbrow tendencies. Okay, better not admit to liking *People,* either.) Driving car pool and discussing favorite food groups is not all I'm about. Yes, I'll gladly discuss those things, but I don't want to be defined by them.

But then I think, "What's wrong with being just a mom?" I know plenty of mothers who mother completely and mother well. They don't work or volunteer. They're mothers through and through. And they're happy with that role. It's almost as if they have a calling to do it.

There's a serenity about them that I admire. I wish I had it, but I don't. There are times—those stolen moments—when being a stay-at-home mom is enough. More than enough. Still, there's an undercurrent of restlessness and insecurity I can't seem to shake.

This insecurity usually reaches a crescendo when I'm out with my "working mother" friends. Whether she's a stockbroker or White House official, I'll try to read everything I can about her job before our dinners. For someone who barely scraped by Economics 101 in college, scouring the business section is not a natural choice. I usually turn straight to Style or Arts.

Sitting at a front table at Mendocino Grill on M Street, I mention having read something about some business issue and its effect on the market that day. My stockbroker friend draws a blank.

"Oh, God, I don't know what was in the paper today," she informs me. "I didn't have time to look at it."

The waiter places our salads on the table, and I recognize the gray-haired man I'd met at the book party walking by with his wife. He doesn't recognize me.

Later in the evening, my high-ranking government-official friend, sipping Chardonnay, tells us about a political argument she had recently with a former official from the Clinton administration. "I mean, I'm sitting there talking to this woman, thinking, What the hell does she know, she's just some fat stay-at-home mom now."

Yikes.

"Oh, Page. You know we don't put you in that category."

I try to make a joke out of it. "Yeah, well, I know I'm not fat at least."

The thing is, I know the conversation could have easily swayed the other way. I know of one working mother who was about to return to a publishing job after a three-month maternity leave. At a dinner party in Georgetown, gathered around an oval mahogany table of twelve, she talked openly about how torn she was over her decision to return to work. Votive candles flickered among silver monogrammed mint-julep cups crammed with white tulips. The general conversation—up until this point—had covered politics, the local real estate market, and *The Da Vinci Code*. Now eleven coiffed heads turned in her direction.

"I don't know," the working mother said, her voice rising. "I know I'm going to be a basket case that first day back. But what am I supposed to do? I love my job and they're being really flexible with my schedule. It's the best thing for right now. Plus, the pay's great. I mean, they've got me in golden handcuffs."

Pushing the scalloped Gruyère potatoes aside and carving into her filet, a stay-at-home mom with a baby the same age interjected from across the table: "You'd have to peel the skin off my body before I left *my* baby."

"Anyone need a little more wine?" the hostess asked.

The jabbing and spitting continues. When are we going to lay down our weapons and start high-kicking in unison? If someone were looking for the weapons of mass destruction concerning motherhood, we need look no further than our own judgmental tongues. Until we as mothers, as women, stop judging one another for the choices we've made, I can't envision a "One Singular Sensation" finale to this musical of motherhood. Maybe if we tried harder to cut the competition and cut short harmful thoughts before they become harmful words. Or maybe it's a matter of not trying so hard to be accepted but trying harder to be accepting.

A few years ago, I found myself sitting in a back pew of a church in Alexandria, Virginia, for the funeral of a friend's mother. We sang "Amazing Grace" in the oppressive August heat. I wept for a woman I had met only once.

"She was the type of mom who would cut the crust off her kids' peanut-butter-and-jelly sandwiches," the minister remarked. He talked about her patience and gratitude. "She didn't care so much about being a good businessman or -woman; she cared about being a good human being."

I didn't know if I was crying for my friend's mother or for the fact that motherhood is infinitely more complicated than cutting the crust off a sandwich. If only it were that simple.

Last fall, when Katherine was three, I enrolled her in a dance class. There she was, bedecked with a bow, pink leotard, and tutu. I felt myself tearing up, imagining we were in some sort of Kodak commercial. I could hear the orchestra and voice-over. "Share a moment. Share a life." Okay, so maybe it's Folgers I'm thinking of. Whatever. Still, I could see images of my little girl—all atwirl, smiling as the sunlight streamed in, enveloping her in a golden haze. I'd be in the corner, coffee or camera in hand, looking on with pride.

But the Kodak moment was not meant to be. As parents, we were under strict orders not to watch.

"You moms talk too much," the dance teacher said. And she was right. It probably was distracting. I mean, three- and four-year-olds need every ounce of concentration when they're dancing around a church basement, pretending to be Ariel while a Little Mermaid cassette crackles from a boom box balanced precariously on a folding metal chair.

So I told Katherine that Mommy had to run some errands (Starbucks) and would pick her up at the end of class.

One latte later, I was back. I peeked into the room to see Effie and Natalie and Rosie and other little girls pretending to swim around the floor like Ariel. But Katherine was not part of this Disney drama. Scanning the room, I felt a slight panic come over me until I spotted her in the corner, crying. The class hadn't ended, but I rushed in to see what the problem was. I could feel the teacher's eyes lock on me, imagining what she was thinking. "Overprotective parents. That's why I didn't want you here in the first place."

I got to Katherine, who could barely look up amid her small sobs. "Oh, Katherine," I said. "Are you okay? Did you not want to dance today?"

"I wanna go home," she squeaked.

That's when I saw it: a puddle spreading out around her like an amoeba on steroids. Her pale pink tights had turned a shade darker, and urine seeped out of her ballet slippers.

I stood there, frozen. The Disney music droned on, and the kids were starting to look our way. *If you even think of teasing her for this, you'll have to deal with me first,* I wanted to tell the smug little ballerinas. My Kodak moment had turned into a Prozac moment. Scooping Katherine up, I raced into the dark hall and located a bathroom. She was drenched, except for her tutu. I peeled off her tights and leotard, wrapping them in paper towels. I threw the soggy slippers into a trash can.

And there she was—stripped down to her tutu. "Look at me, Mama, I don't have any underwear on."

Although the sheer tutu provided slight coverage, I couldn't leave the church with an X-rated toddler. So I took off a black T-shirt I had on under my sweater and put it on her. She looked like some sort of mini motorcycle-riding cross-dresser.

But attire aside, Katherine and I had places to go. I was already running late to pick up Peyton, who was taking a yoga class that afternoon. Yep. Kiddie yoga. A friend had offered to take her to the class, provided I pick her up. Since the studio was across town and pickup would be during rush hour, I didn't know how I'd swing it. So my gut reaction was to say no. I said yes anyway.

After stopping by a friend's house nearby to purloin a pair of underpants for Katherine, we arrived at the hot-yoga studio, out of breath but on time. We sat in the waiting room, Katherine in bare feet, tutu, and black tee, I in my itchy wool sweater. The temperature in the studio had been turned down for the kids, I was told, but it seemed someone forgot to do the same in the waiting room. With beads of sweat slowly inching down my back, I kept wondering why we were there.

Well, I knew why. I had said yes, yet again. Do you want to do this? Sure, we can do that. Sure, I'll pick her up. Sure. No problem. Oh, yeah, I'm sure she'll love it. Sure, sure, sure.

One thing I was now sure of: We all needed to get out of hot yoga. Peyton looked pitiful. I could see her through the glass partition, trying to do a down dog but looking more down-and-out. Meanwhile, the dried urine on Katherine's legs was starting to smell in the heat. I noticed a together-looking mother eyeing Katherine's getup. Crossing her leg and clutching a pale blue leather purse closer to her kelly-green cashmere cable-knit sweater, she sniffed slightly. For a moment I had visions of her reporting us to social services. Katherine complained about being thirsty. I was thirsty too. Parched, actually. And then came the hives. The itching started on my inner arms and spread to my torso. Wool on my skin.

Peyton finally emerged from class.

"Hi, Mama. Do I have to do yoga?"

"We'll talk about it later," I told her, not wanting to offend the friend who had brought her here, or the yoga instructor standing beside us.

"But Mama," she whined. "It wasn't very fun."

"Okay, honey," I said, jaw clenched. At that point, the only thing I really cared about was being polite. God forbid we offend the hot-yoga instructor by complaining.

Maybe I had hoped there would be a payoff for all this hive-inducing craziness. I should have been more sympathetic. But I wasn't. I was mad. Mad at Peyton for being so honest. Mad at Katherine for whining while we waited. Basically, I was mad at myself. Why did I bother doing all this stuff? Was it making them happy? Was it making me happy?

Fuming, but still managing to paste on that oh-this-was-great face, I paid the yoga instructor fifteen dollars for this hour of "fun." My friend—buff, bronzed, Botoxed, and blow-dried—overheard Peyton's assessment of the class and chimed in. "I hope she'll try it again. My girls really love it."

"Oh, I'm sure," I said. Sure.

"I mean, with everything going on in this world, I just want them to find an inner place where they can go, you know."

"Yeah, right," I thought. I wanted to tell her what she could stick in that inner place.

"I know," I told her. "I'll talk to Peyton when we get home. I think she's just a little tired today."

"I'm not tired, Mama," Peyton added helpfully.

"She's *not* tired!" Katherine yelled, stomping her bare feet on the carpet.

The itching was becoming unbearable. I needed to get outside. I needed to take my sweater off, but I had nothing but a bra on underneath. I needed air.

"Are you mad at us, Mama?" Peyton asked on the car ride home. "I'll do yoga if you want me to."

"No, sweetie," I said, clutching the steering wheel. "You don't have to do yoga. I just thought it might be a fun thing to do with your friends."

"Well, I guess it was okay," she said. "I could maybe try it again."

I felt like such a failure. Here was this six-year-old who was just trying to please me, becoming a yes-person just like her mother. I kept wiping the tears away with my sleeve so the girls wouldn't see me crying. I realized that if I didn't pull myself together, this pathetic image of a sweaty, hive-ridden, hysterical mother would forever be embedded in their childhood memories.

"I just want you guys to be happy. That's all I want."

"Then why are you crying?" Peyton asked.

"Mommy's just a little tired today," I choked out.

"I'm not tired," Katherine said proudly, but without the usual tinge of defiance.

Home, washed, hydrated, and in a change of clothes, I told the girls to play outside while I got dinner ready. I microwaved organic macaroni and cheese, boiled a bag of frozen peas, chopped cherry tomatoes, returned phone calls, and popped open a Rolling Rock. Out the window, I saw them marching through the grass, looking for leaves to twirl around like helicopters, digging for the perfect rock to paint, collecting acorns. A yellow oak leaf clung to Peyton's brown curls, and Katherine's pink corduroys were etched with grass stains around the knees. They laughed and squealed and ran around. It was the most fun they'd had all day.

Finally, a Kodak moment.

This was where we should have been all along, if only I had been able to say no to all those self-inflicted pressures and yes to time with my kids.

Resisting the temptation and the peer pressure to overschedule my two girls has given us more room for downtime—and conversation. Saying no is like a 12-step program. I fall off the wagon more frequently than I care to admit. But being aware of my propensity to say yes when I should be saying no is the first step toward a peaceful life. What is it they say? The first step is recognizing you have a problem. My name is Page Evans and I can't say no. But I'm trying. I'm learning to appreciate parenting by being present with my children.

The Kodak moments may be few and far between, but at least when they happen, I take note. I feel joy.

It's been months since our hot-yoga fiasco. Katherine and Peyton's after-school program is decidedly more laid-back. While Katherine naps at home with a sitter I pick Peyton up at three-fifteen and we head over to Marvelous Market on MacArthur Boulevard for lemonade and chocolate croissants. Eventually, she'll discuss what went on in school that day, but not until she's had a good amount of decompression time.

"Caitlin and Melissa started a club and they said I couldn't be in it," Peyton says one afternoon, searching for sympathy.

"Really?" I ask. "What kind of club?"

"I don't know, but they said that me and Mary Anne and Harriet can't join."

"Well, that's not very nice, is it?" I say, trying to disguise what I'm *really* thinking. That those f-ing brats better not mess with my daughter. "Listen, Peyton, you need to remember how not being included makes you feel, right? You never want to make anyone else feel that way. And besides, any club that excludes people is not something you want to be in. That's not nice and it doesn't make people feel nice."

"What's exclude mean?" she asks.

"It means to keep someone out," I tell her.

"Well, Mrs. James said we could start a club as long as it doesn't eggs . . . what's that word again?"

"Exclude."

"Yeah, as long as it doesn't exclude anyone," she says. "So anyone in the whole first grade can join if they want."

We then delve into another topic, something that sends her to the science teacher the next day because, once again, I'm not equipped to answer.

On a breezy day in mid-April, just before Katherine's fourth birthday, I arrive in the nursery school car-pool line shortly before the noon pickup. The children, some fidgeting, sit on blankets listening to a teacher reading *One Fish Two Fish Red Fish Blue Fish*, waiting their turn to be taken to their car. When the teacher opens the car door and buckles her into the car seat, Katherine slumps down in a state of exhaustion, her barrette dangling from a strand of blond hair.

I ask how school was only to get a muffled, unintelligible response. An hour later, after splitting a turkey, cheese, and tomato sandwich for lunch, we head to the park to log time on the swing, slide, and sandbox. My eyes glaze over, and I switch to autopilot. Pushing, pulling, climbing, digging. My brain feels like it's been replaced with brioche, and I want nothing more than to lie down on the teak bench next to the sandbox.

"Mommy, I'm tirsty."

I hand her a juice box, and we plop down on the hill behind the swing set. We pull up a few blades of grass, and I show her how to make whistling sounds by holding the blade between my thumbs, pressing it to my lips. It sounds more like a chipmunk gasping for air than a whistle.

Lying back in the grass, we look at the clouds, turning shapes into animals.

"That looks like an alligator with a balloon," Katherine says.

"Maybe he's on his way to a birthday party," I say.

We lie there for a while longer, watching the clouds drift across the blue sky.

"It's such a bootiful day, Mommy," Katherine says.

"Yes, it is. It is a such beautiful day."

Act 2, scene 2

Peyton and Johnny, my friend Jenny's son, ended up in the same class at nursery school. Several times a week, Jenny and I would sit in circle time, children perched on our laps, singing the "Good Morning to You" song. Afterward, she'd rush downtown to her office; I'd rush to, uh, Starbucks, where a grande latte and *The New York Times* awaited.

We have different schedules, yes. But we have similar parenting styles. Neither of us fits the stereotype of our so-called titles, working mom versus stay-at-home. For her children's birthdays, Jenny bakes cupcakes from scratch. She even uses the "Seven-Minute Icing" recipe from *Joy of Cooking.* My cupcakes come straight from Safeway, their iced tops rivaling Mount Fuji. Happily, we don't take ourselves quite as seriously as we did postpartum. With a little humor and humility, our divergent paths have wound up meeting somewhere in the middle. Her two boys (the second's a couple of months older than Katherine) couldn't be nicer or better adjusted. I saw them a few days ago, playing in Montrose Park near the woods. They were collaborating on a sculpture made from pebbles, sticks, and leaves. Towheaded Johnny, now seven, held up a dark green leaf, inspecting its veins as the sun shone through it. Curious, kind, and happy.

Happy children. That's the bottom line for mothers. At least it seems to me it should be. Working, not working, or somewhere in between, our children will—with any luck—take their cues from us. And that, indeed, would be a grand finale.

Crank up the orchestra, take a bow, and close the curtain on motherhood, the musical. The reviews may not be in yet, but I'm working on giving it my best performance, making adjustments night after night as the show goes on.

Baby Battle

Susan Cheever

Susan Cheever is the author of five novels, four memoirs, and two biographies, including *My Name Is Bill: Bill Wilson—His Life and the Creation of Alcoholics Anonymous*. Her most recent book, *American Bloomsbury,* explores the lives of Emerson, Hawthorne, Thoreau, Margaret Fuller, and Louisa May Alcott in 1850s Concord, Massachusetts. She writes a column for *Newsday* and teaches in the Bennington College Writing Seminars and in the graduate writing program at New York's New School University. Her work has won a Guggenheim Fellowship and a Winship Medal Award and has earned a nomination for a National Book Critics Circle Award. She is on the boards of the Corporation of Yaddo and the National Council on Alcoholism and Drug Dependency, and on the Author's Guild Council. She lives with her family in New York City.

There is a war going on in the streets of New York City.

Platoons of mothers in bicycle shoes and designer sweats wheel divisions of gleaming, clanking strollers down the sidewalks, chattering into their cell phones and blocking the passage of other pedestrians. These are the Stay-at-Home Mothers.

Their adversaries, the Working Mothers and the Women Without Children, straighten their sleek success suits and try to stay out of the way.

"It's not just the strollers," said a Working Mother friend recently as we barely escaped being mowed down by a squadron of juice-cup-wielding Stay-at-Home Mothers. "It's the stroller *entitlement.*"

The Stay-at-Homes hang together as if they are from a different planet than the mothers who chose to go on working, or the mothers who *have* to go on working. They regroup in the playgrounds, brushing the crumbs off their strollers, Björns, and tricycles. If a toddler under a nanny's care has an accident or a tantrum, the Stay-at-Homes cluck and shake their heads knowingly. *That child needs a mother.*

Women without children are whipsawed by hostility from both camps. The Working Moms look down on the Stay-at-Home Moms: *What on earth do they do all day? How can they be so dependent?* The Stay-at-Home Moms feel sorry for the Working Moms: *Do they know what they're missing?*

Why are children such a divisive force between women?

What happened to the good old days when women used to fight with men?

Last week, a mother and her toddler were in my local supermarket in the evening, at a time when few children are there. The toddler was mounted on a tricycle with a metal handle protruding about three feet at a forty-five-degree angle from the seat. The purpose of the handle— parental control—had apparently been forgotten. As the toddler sped down the aisles, the handle brought down a paper-towel display and threatened the eggs. "Gabby! *Gabby!* GAB-RI-ELLE!!" the mother's voice escalated as she looked the other way and manically loaded her cart with an assortment of Lunchables, Dunkaroos, and other junk foods manufactured to temporarily pacify and ultimately enrage our country's children.

As little Gabby approached my shopping cart, she began to slalom, sending the handle zooming from side to side and knocking loaves of freshly baked bread into the aisle. Clouds of choking flour rose around us as I dodged flying baguettes. I was about to grab little Gabby and summon her irresponsible mother.

Flashback.

Only a few years ago, I *was* that mother.

Before that, as a single woman twenty-five years ago, I fiercely protected my single rights. I had a great job and I did what I pleased. I was thrilled not to be encumbered by a family. When the people in the apartment next door bought a piano for their little girl, and her endless practices bothered me, *I hired a lawyer to limit her practice time.* Why should families have more rights than single people? I chose to be single. They chose to have children. Therefore I was as entitled to my silence and freedom as they were entitled to their family.

I looked down on women with children as fools, dupes who had fallen for a myth created for the purpose of their own oppression. Women with children were trapped, dependent on their husbands for money and for whatever else they still had the brains to need. Just the presence of a child seemed to reduce intelligent women to blithering idiots. Once at the gynecologist's office I watched as a group of chic, smart, professional women kicked off their Chanel sling-backs, left their briefcases unattended, and crawled around on the filthy floor making goo-goo faces at someone's sluglike progeny.

"Ohhh, she's so adooorable," cooed a real estate tycoon.

"And look at that face!" squawked a Citibank vice president.

I was appalled. Even if I ever had a child—and for most of my twenties and thirties it was the last thing I imagined doing—I would never, ever, behave like that.

Marriage and pregnancy at the age of thirty-eight didn't change me. I was amazed at the fatuous way people spoke about childbirth in my Lamaze class. "I want to share Cathy's pain," one of the husbands intoned. The leader nodded approvingly while I burst out laughing. Even my husband smiled. We flunked Lamaze. When strangers cooed at me and reached out for my burgeoning stomach, I wanted to bite them.

"Oh, it's such a celebration," gushed one friend with a new baby, a woman who had formerly been a brilliant journalist. She and I had once spent two hours searching for the perfect lip gloss—a pale pink called *Prrr*. She used to be *fun*. Now she appeared to be drooling. As I watched her change her baby, exclaiming over its small green excrement, I took a vow. I would have the baby—there was no way to avoid that now—but I would never lose my mind. I planned for full-time help. I signed a contract for a new book. I rented an office.

Then I had my baby, my Sarah.

The moment I held her in my arms, I became a different person. You could say that I joined the human race. For the first time in my life, my connection with someone else sliced through the web of defenses, fear, and pride that had separated me from the world. I had been married twice, but holding Sarah was my first experience of love. My heart seemed to melt. My mind no longer interested me. This tiny baby became the center of my world. I crossed over.

As soon as I got home from the hospital I went out and bought the biggest, most expensive stroller I could find. I wanted my precious girl to be safe. With her tucked into the stroller, I resented anyone else on the sidewalk. Everything seemed like a threat to the only being I had ever loved. I took Sarah everywhere with me, even in places where she wasn't allowed. To me it seemed criminal that my baby wasn't supposed to be with me at all times. Why should she have to be alone with a strange babysitter instead of at the movies with me? I took her to expensive restaurants and delighted when she threw the foie gras on the floor and smeared her adorable face with *quenelles de brochet*. Other diners frowned at us; I ignored them.

On airplanes, where baby Sarah was particularly fussy, I demanded extra help from the staff and often threw enough of a tantrum to get an extra seat—no one wanted to be close to us anyway, not even my husband. I personally took the time to explain to hapless complainers that my child was a *child,* and that people who were not enchanted by the noise of children were uptight, intolerant puritans who had probably never had an orgasm. *Weren't you ever a child yourself?* I would hiss. If someone suggested that I might think about controlling my daughter, I would lean over them menacingly. *So you think I'm a bad mother?* These confrontations never ended well.

As a mother I felt like the keeper of the flame, a woman who had been entrusted with something infinitely sacred. I had done nothing to earn the gift of this child. Watching her sleep I sometimes felt enveloped in a golden cloud of unconditional grace. I kept on working—I had signed the book contract—but I slowed way down, and my old Armani success suits are still gathering dust in the back of the closet. Suddenly, I looked with pity on people who had never had children. How sad. They had never loved. They didn't know what they were missing.

My baby daughter is twenty-two now, and although she remains at the center of my life she has also developed a life of her own. My beloved son is fourteen. I've had decades of being a mother first and a writer second. I kept on working when my children were born, partly because I didn't have the luxury of having to decide whether to be a stay-at-home or a working mother. I took a professional hit and lost a lot of the sharpness and brashness that were my trademarks. I spent hours on the floor oohing and aahing over tiny hands and feet. I wrote and edited among the blocks and plastic castles in the pediatrician's waiting room and missed deadlines to attend parents' meetings. My lip gloss was whatever I could find at the bottom of a bag filled with lunch passes, old homework papers, and half-empty juice boxes.

Lately though, as my children become adults, I am noticing a change. I have become dependent on getting eight hours of sleep a night. I get regular haircuts and spend more money than I should on clothes. For the first time in a long time I'm annoyed by children like little Gabby and the way their mothers defend them. I'm crossing back over. I can almost feel it. I'm changing sides again.

Why does having children, while bringing out our most loving, effusively maternal selves, simultaneously ignite our fears and turn us against one another? After all, women with children—whether they work or stay at home—might get together to make this world a better place for all women with children.

What's all this anger really about?

For one thing, we're too sleep-deprived to be tolerant or temperate. I remember the caul of exhaustion I lived in as the mother of young children. In those days the most erotic thing a man could say to me was "Why don't you just go back to sleep." My idea of lingerie was earplugs and a sleep mask—neither of which blocked out my children clamoring for my attention.

Women do the lion's share—perhaps it should be called the woman's share—of the child care and household work in this country. A recent National Labor Bureau study shows that women who work still spend twice as much time as men on child care and housework. We live with the results of half a revolution: Women have earned the right to work as hard as men do, but men did not take over half the work at home. Every woman knows her pediatrician's telephone number; I have yet to meet a man who does.

What worsens our predicament is that women lack core representation in our government. Photographs of the Senate still look like "Class of 1970" men's college-reunion photos. One of the great mysteries of modern politics is that women, who comprise more than half the population, still comprise less than 20 percent of the government. More women vote than men, but we don't vote for one another. Certainly gender is not the defining reason to vote for or against anyone, but if more women voted for women, at least we would be governed by those who have walked in our flip-flops and pushed our strollers and hunched over our changing tables at 4 A.M. Have we been so indoctrinated by a patriarchal society that we secretly think men are more fit to govern? Are we so hardwired by advertising and fairy tales that we assume the best child care always comes from a mother even if she's a resentful nervous wreck?

Working and stay-at-home moms today are like the famous psychology experiment in which too many rats are put in a cage with too little food. The rats *have* had enough sleep, nevertheless, they kill one another. The stakes in the baby battle are high—nothing is more precious than our children and being able to provide for them and ourselves. The level of resources is low. There isn't much support for women who work—support like office child care, flexible hours, and reasonable maternity leaves. There isn't much support for women who stay home—like tax breaks, financial protection in case of divorce, subsidized medical care, or even licensed child care. Kennels are more strictly regulated than child-care agencies; veterinarians get paid more than pediatricians; men who can hire better lawyers tend to walk away with more advantageous divorce decrees than their ex-wives who have spent two decades with zeros on their income tax forms.

No wonder every woman who has made a different choice seems like an enemy. What if you are right? What if I am wrong? What if in working we are damaging our children by being absent and preoccupied? What if by staying home we are sacrificing our independence and our ability to financially take care of our children and hurting them in another way?

And so we fight.

Guilty

Dawn Drzal

Dawn Drzal was an editor at Viking Books from 1989 to 1999. She became a stay-at-home mother soon after the birth of her only child. She lives in New York City with her husband and son. Her articles have appeared in *The New York Times, The New York Times Book Review,* and *Food & Wine.*

My life has always been about books. My first real job out of college was as an editor at a New York publishing house, and for fifteen years I couldn't believe they paid me to do it. I loved working with authors—Pulitzer Prize winners such as science writer Deborah Blum and poet Carl Dennis; Dr. Jerome Groopman of *The New Yorker;* inventor Ray Kurzweil; cookbook writer Molly O'Neill. I treasured the peculiar intimacy of the editorial relationship, the understanding I gained of how another person's mind worked by going through her book line by line. I enjoyed the inevitable conflicts, the spirited discussions in which each of us argued our case for a particular deletion or turn of phrase or grammatical point. The editor/author relationship is the best sort of collaboration, in which the sum of two minds immeasurably improves the parts.

I've always known New York was my real home. I have a photograph of myself bundled in a blue plush coat, my hair shorn into a hated pixie cut, trying to feed a squirrel in Central Park during my first trip there when I was six. I certainly never felt I belonged in Trevose, the suburb northeast of Philadelphia where I grew up. Even to my child's eye, everything about the place seemed mediocre and sad, especially the women at the local mall pushing strollers or dragging stumbling children. Those women, who wore stretch pants long before it was fashionable and didn't seem to have the will to brush their hair, looked so trapped and miserable that I swore to myself never to become one of them. Until I could escape for real, I escaped into one book after another.

Neither of my parents went to college. I don't remember hearing higher education discussed once at home, even as my graduation from Nazareth Academy approached. If girls from my school went to college at all, they went down the driveway to Holy Family. Still, even though I had no conception of where I wanted to go, I knew I would die if I had to stay, so I tunneled diligently away at my studies in the blind hope that someone would notice.

It was a sort of miracle that my godfather, my late father's best friend and a judge, decided to stop by our house a few days before Christmas and see me off to my senior prom.

"What colleges have you applied to?" he asked.

"None," I replied.

I still remember the look on his face.

Luckily the admissions office of Williams College was open between Christmas and New Year's. I managed to make the January 15 deadline. My acceptance letter was my ticket out of Trevose.

Editing was my first career. My life changed abruptly when I had a child, my only child. Suddenly, seventy-hour weeks didn't seem tenable anymore. For five years I've stayed home and taken writing workshops, occasionally editing business proposals for my husband's company, while I raised my son. But he'll be starting first grade this year, and already he doesn't need me in the same way he once did. What will I do with the next part of my life?

I can't envision going back full-time to the work I once loved almost as passionately as I love my son. I'm not the same woman. Somewhere along the way I misplaced my persona, the one who brazened it out for all those years. My job, now that she is gone, is to answer the very literal question of what to do without her.

I was secretly terrified of my infant son from the moment the nurse squeaked out of the hospital room and left me alone with him. During my pregnancy, a completely uncharacteristic and enjoyable placidity had descended on me, displacing my usual state of anxiety about work and life in general. An irresistible narcosis would overwhelm me every afternoon, and I would lie down on the floor next to my desk with my feet against the door in case someone tried to open it without knocking. After an hour or two I would surface to the insistent buzzing of the telephone on my desk, a sound that used to strike fear into my heart, as if it were a signal from a distant planet, and try to rouse myself by imagining what call could possibly be important enough to answer. The only things that mattered to me besides sleep were some truly violent food cravings—one week a gallon jar of kimchee, the next three dozen clementines or French fries with hot sauce or a porterhouse steak blanketed with sea salt and malt vinegar. If I had thought about this psychic cushion between me and the world at all, I suppose I would have considered it a result of my new perspective on life, not a chemical gift that would depart with appalling suddenness. Even though my son was born on Midsummer's Day, the most cheerful day of the year, the light in that hospital room seemed as stark and chill as a Bergman movie.

Prior to our son's birth, my husband and I both arranged to take three months' leave to welcome him into the world. We rented a large, airy house on the North Fork of Long Island, where we planned to escape with our newborn from the heat and grime of New York City. The baby nurse who rescued us during the first days home from the hospital had not figured in our idyllic Long Island fantasy. There was no way we could do without Glenda, so she came along too.

Instead of feeling more competent with each passing day of motherhood, I became more and more dependent on Glenda during those three months. I began to be haunted by a feeling of existential dread. While she attended to my son, I spent hours at the kitchen table, chin propped on my hand, staring out at the sparkling bay. On Glenda's day and a half off every week, she took the train back to New York to see her own children. My trepidation turned to outright terror. If my husband happened to be out when the baby woke from a nap, the hair on the back of my arms and neck would stand up, my heart would pound in my ears, and I could hardly pull in a full breath. Was something wrong with him? What if he kept crying after I fed and changed him? The afternoon would stretch before me like a wasteland. Sometimes I would begin to cry myself.

It didn't help that nursing, which I had looked forward to as the ultimate bonding experience, turned out instead to be an ordeal for both my son and me. Nowhere in my obsessive reading of pregnancy books had I come across an "immature sucking reflex" in a full-term baby, which (compounded by a dairy allergy) was finally diagnosed in my son many long months later.

When he fell asleep in the middle of nursing, I would sit absolutely still for hours rather than wake him. Often I would almost dispassionately observe how much physical pain, from a cramp or loss of circulation in my arm, I could endure before I would take the chance of shifting my position. If I remembered to put a book on the arm of the glider before I sat down, I couldn't find the courage to risk turning the pages.

I remember how bemused a houseguest was when she came downstairs one morning to find me desperate for a cup of tea. "Why didn't you make one?" she asked.

I explained that I couldn't put the baby down, and it was too dangerous for him to be near boiling water. When she suggested I put him in his bouncy seat in the middle of the kitchen table, I was as impressed as if she'd discovered the secret of cold fusion.

The night we returned to the Upper West Side of Manhattan from the North Fork, I reluctantly said good-bye to Glenda. I put our son in the middle of the bed and settled down next to him and my husband to watch television. Now that we were back in our own apartment, I was determined to relax and incorporate the baby into our lives, as all the books said we should. But the longer I sat there, the more violently my stomach knotted up. Finally I burst into tears.

"What's wrong?" my husband asked, putting his arms around me.

I tried to stop crying because I didn't want to scare the baby. "I can't remember ever being able to watch TV without this horrible feeling of dread," I sobbed. "Who am I fooling, trying to hang out with him? I'm afraid he's going to suffocate in the comforter. Or fall off the bed."

"He can't roll over yet," my husband said sensibly.

"That's not the point," I said. How could I explain that I was convinced that a terrible tragedy would befall us—as in fairy tales where a witch curses a baby in its cradle or a single pinprick brings on a hundred-year coma—no matter what precautions we took?

I knew I wouldn't sleep at all if I put the bassinet next to the bed. So I rolled it just outside our bedroom door, but the ten feet between me and the baby did nothing to keep me from listening for his breathing now that there was no baby nurse to watch over him all night. That first night in our home was as fitful as the vigil I kept on a cot outside my grandfather's room the night before he died. I was ecstatic to be awakened in the middle of the night by the baby's cries of hunger. I fed him and dozed with my back propped uncomfortably against the headboard, unwilling to put him down until the light came up outside the windows.

It now seems obvious to me why I didn't get more comfortable with my son over time, as most new parents do. I wasn't afraid of dropping him by accident. I was afraid that part of me wanted to drop him on purpose. One of the many good reasons I had waited until the age of thirty-six to get pregnant was to develop iron self-control, so that I could be sure I would never hit and scream uncontrollably the way my mother did at twenty-two.

One tiny flare did go off about a week after we got home. I had been awakened by my son's hunger cries every night since the departure of the baby nurse and was suffering from the sleep deprivation I had always feared when I contemplated motherhood—having always been inordinately fond of sleep. When I stumbled to the baby's bassinet, I saw that before I could nurse him I would have to change an exceptionally sticky, smelly diaper. A hot wave of nausea and irritation coursed through me as I picked him up. Uh-oh, I thought, here it comes. I was pierced by a memory of clambering under the dining room table, my mother's fingernails raking my ankle as I pulled away from her grasp. "Come out of there, you little bitch, or I'll kill you!" she screamed. But I knew she'd kill me if I did come out, so I just cowered farther into the corner and prayed she wouldn't rip the table away from the wall. Her fury obliterated the world and me with it.

Then I caught a whiff of the ineffably sweet smell of my son's head. I pressed him against my pounding heart and rubbed my cheek on the warm fuzz of his scalp. I don't know how long I stood there like that, breathing him in, before I realized that all the anger had drained out of my body. From that moment it was banished. All the fevers and nightmares and tantrums in supermarkets and on street corners in the years to come would fail to produce more than a flicker of impatience in me.

My husband and I soon realized, without the baby nurse to walk our son around twelve hours a day, that his gas pains were unusually severe. We began a series of visits to allergists and lactation specialists, lab tests, and elimination diets that ultimately resulted in a diagnosis and a much happier baby. I was ashamed to discover that the cries that had made my hair stand on end were those of real distress. I had mistaken genuine mother's intuition as neurosis lingering from my childhood fears that I would never make a good mother.

When our baby was four months old, I returned to work. I made a valiant attempt to continue nursing, consuming so much fenugreek tea that my sweat smelled like maple syrup, rushing home at lunchtime to nurse, dutifully lugging my Medela breast pump back with me each afternoon. But nothing could help me to keep pace with a hungry four-month-old. It also didn't help that my boss, the mother of three, got a kick out of pounding on my door whenever it was closed and yelling, "Are you pumping in there?" Within a couple of weeks, my milk dried up completely. With it dried up the psychological protection conferred by breast-feeding hormones, although I didn't discover that until later.

One morning in October, I left my apartment in my favorite suit, a forest-green wool Regina Rubens, artfully tailored to camouflage my remaining thirty pounds of "baby fat." Unfortunately, I realized as soon as I stepped out of the lobby that it was already eighty degrees outside. I was not about to go upstairs to change; I had nothing to change into. I walked across Seventy-seventh Street to Broadway and stopped at New World Coffee for fortification. Coffee and wine were my only compensations for my failure and disappointment at no longer being able to nurse.

Because I was a few minutes early, I sat down on the bench outside to drink my coffee without being jostled by fellow subway commuters. I closed my eyes and tipped my face up to the sun. October had always been my favorite month. It was with a creeping sense of horror that I realized I couldn't sense the warmth of the autumn sun on my face. It was a peculiar numbness, a weatherlessness that I hadn't felt since my father's death when I was fifteen and realized I couldn't smell the burning leaves my boyfriend and I had raked into a pile. It hadn't occurred to me until years later that I had been, understandably, depressed. It unnerved me to recognize a similar symptom now.

Sitting up straight, I breathed in the familiar smell of exhaust from double-parked delivery trucks and tried to get a grip. The spindly ailanthus trees were just starting to turn color. A sky the color of faded denim heralded another scorching day. I tried to banish thoughts of global warming from my mind. As the M104 bus disgorged passengers who scurried off to the Seventy-ninth Street subway station, I realized I was now late. When I tried to get up I found I was unable to move. I sat clutching my tepid coffee, paralyzed by the thought of going to the office.

Well-groomed young women, fresh from the gym, strode by in pumps. Men engrossed in their cell phone conversations looked like a stream of lunatics talking to themselves. A few old people rattled by with their collapsible silver carts, trying to finish their shopping before the heat became unbearable. Some mothers hurried their children along to school; others, wilted as though they'd already gone through half a day, wheeled half-dressed toddlers in expensive strollers.

I had gone back to work expecting to reconnect with my old self—the thin, self-assured young woman who took pride in satisfying the competing demands made by the publishing house, my authors, literary agents, and dozens of others every day. Instead I remained the sluggish, beleaguered self I had dragged out that morning. Pregnancy had—quite literally—transformed me. I was beginning to realize with something like horror that I wasn't going to change back now that the baby was born.

Sidewalk traffic gradually thinned. There were more strollers and joggers and only the occasional harried-looking commuter sprinting toward the subway. Students began to drift out onto the street, moving in slow motion. Buses became sporadic.

I still couldn't make myself move, not even to reach for my cell phone to say I'd be late. I cast about wildly for something, anything, to get me off that bench. Then a brilliant thought popped into my head: I needed a cigarette. I was seized with the conviction that nicotine, my nemesis of twenty years, was the answer to my problems. A pack of Dunhill Reds would restore my mood, tame my appetite, give me back a taste of the bad girl I used to be, before my body was held hostage to an Olympian standard of health by a baby, born or yet to be born.

As I walked the half block to the filthy newsstand where I had fallen off the nicotine wagon the last time, years before, I felt more cheerful than I had since having the baby. On a different bench with a fresh cup of coffee, I struck a match. I inhaled deeply and waited for the hit that had never failed me.

Nothing happened. True panic set in. This unwelcome transformation had clearly extended to my *brain*.

Eventually, I did get off the bench. My best friend, like almost all good New Yorkers, had long been seeing a therapist, who in turn recommended a good psychopharmacologist for me. Sitting with a box of Kleenex in my lap, I was told I was suffering from postpartum depression, which most commonly strikes about four months after delivery. I told him I had never been depressed before, at least not like this. As he wrote out a prescription, he assured me it was not unusual for perfectly healthy women to develop these symptoms. Cigarettes and coffee had been my attempt to self-medicate. The Wellbutrin and Depakote he prescribed patched me up well enough that I could continue working.

I left work six months later. I left the career I loved because, by the time he was nine months old, my son started to cry inconsolably each night after the babysitter left. I had gone back to work after my maternity leave fully expecting to combine motherhood and career as several of my colleagues had done for years. But there had been a merger while I was away. I wasn't allowed to work from home one day a week as new mothers in my department always had, and that and countless other indignities tipped the scales in favor of leaving. If I hadn't had a child, I would have looked for a new job, but the job I returned to was no longer worth the pain of being away from my son.

One evening I heard myself say calmly to my husband, "This isn't why I had a child. I'm giving notice." I was surprised at myself. I had expected to agonize endlessly over my decision. Instead I found I had made it already.

I don't mean to imply that I left a career that had defined my life for fifteen years because my maternal turf was being invaded. I left because I could not live with the bitter knowledge that while I was busy keeping my son at arm's length, his babyhood had all but slipped away. Only my fear of what I was about to lose enabled me to come home and face what was—for me—the real work of becoming a mother.

Despite my misgivings about staying at home, it was hard not to be seduced by my son. Everyone agreed he was an unusually charming baby, with round cheeks, cornflower-blue eyes, and a mouth that made my female friends predict he'd be a lady-killer. There was one problem. He didn't look like me or my husband. After one too many milkman jokes, I took a curl from his first haircut to a salon and said, "I want this." The hairdresser looked dubious. I insisted. After that, people would say, "I see where he gets that beautiful red hair." I would nod and smile, or, if I liked them, I'd tell the truth.

For the first month or so it was all I could do not to cry several times a day. I choked off tears every time I sang him to sleep, cleaned up the tide of toys and food that threatened to cover the floor of the apartment, looked at the clock to find it was only 9:47 A.M. I tried not to feel suicidal about the fact that I—who had recently edited books about consciousness and complexity theory—was reduced daily to helpless weeping by the challenge of what to pack in a diaper bag.

Ironically, it wasn't nursing but the dairy allergy (aggravated by the baby formula we'd resorted to occasionally) that proved to be the bonding experience I had hoped for. Our pediatrician said that our son had a better chance of outgrowing his allergy by age two if we were absolutely scrupulous about keeping his system free of any trace of dairy products. Now that he was old enough to eat more than baby food, being scrupulous was becoming more of a challenge. So, as a former cookbook editor, I made it my mission to eliminate from his diet every trace of dairy, down to lactalbumin and sodium caseinate.

Every day at noon I would pack up the babysitter with tiny cartons of soy milk and cinnamon graham crackers, lest my son accept a forbidden cookie. Then I would go food shopping, setting out for a distant organic market or ethnic enclave to hunt down new prepared foods or a particular exotic ingredient for his meals (which my husband and I enjoyed as well). When the babysitter left at six, she would deposit him in his high chair, freshly bathed, and he would happily watch me sautéeing onions or marinating tofu or cooking his favorite dinner, red lentils with garlic, onions, and ginger. One Sunday morning he surreptitiously consumed the centerpiece of a brunch for his grandparents—two pounds of Barney Greengrass eastern Gaspé smoked salmon. Caught in the act, he popped a lemon crescent into his mouth and grinned. At a year and half he stunned a Danish friend of ours by asking for seconds of pickled herring. He outgrew his dairy allergy and, alas, his adventurousness with food, too. But I had proved that no one on earth could take care of him as well as I could.

Gradually, I felt more energetic and even managed to organize a move out of our beloved fifth-floor walk-up with something like my old efficiency. We settled into the floor above the home of our dreams so we could keep an eye on a yearlong renovation. I began to feel almost happy as the leaves changed in Riverside Park outside our windows . . . until my beautiful red hair started falling out.

One of the medications, while stabilizing my mood, had slowed my thyroid so sufficiently that I couldn't budge the thirty pounds I had carried around like an albatross since my son was born. I had tolerated being chubby for the sake of my sanity and my family's well-being. But the threat of patchy baldness, which I now learned was a not-uncommon side effect, was another story.

Since it was possible that my hair wouldn't grow back, I wasn't willing to lose any more of it. So when my doctor insisted I gradually taper off this drug before switching to another, I not only stopped taking the drug but also stopped seeing him. What followed was a hellish two or three weeks in which my rage—always simmering although never directed at my son—was fueled by withdrawal from one drug and not yet controlled by another. I should have gone off someplace where I wouldn't do any harm. However, part of the problem was that I thought I was fine. It felt good to explode after all those months of being barely alive.

Late one afternoon, my husband and I were in the middle of our daily argument that predictably escalated into a screaming match. Immune to my husband's attempts to placate me, I had forgotten that my eighteen-month-old was in the next room until he ran in and wrapped himself around my leg, sobbing and begging, "No, Mommy, no, stop it, stop it!" I saw in my son's eyes the monster I feared I would become as a mother— the monster who had terrorized my own childhood.

The words that had seemed unstoppable a moment before dried up in my mouth. I picked him up, kissed his wet cheeks, smoothed back his damp hair, and reassured him that Mommy and Daddy were fine, we were sorry, we loved him. After he fell asleep, I knelt by his crib, tears streaming down my face. "I swear to God I will never, ever, lose my temper like that in front of you again," I whispered. As I stood to kiss him good night, my tears dripped onto his cheek, and he swatted at them with the back of a plump little hand.

There is a price to be paid for everything, though. The cost of conquering my rage was a wave of depression far more vicious than the first. Depression is anger turned inward, the therapist I eventually sought out told me. From then on the monster showed her face to no one but me.

We moved into our new home in December, and there were days on end when I couldn't leave the apartment except to drag myself to therapy appointments. Some days my whole being hurt so much that I had to close my eyes each time my foot hit the pavement. After the sessions I bolted home to the safety of my bed.

I believed, because I needed to, that my son thought I was fine. I got up rather cheerfully with him in the mornings, cooked him breakfast, played with him. My own earliest memories were of endless hours watching TV with the sound off while I waited for my sleeping mother, who had threatened to strangle me if I made any noise. I made dinner when the babysitter brought him home at night. For all anyone knew—I told myself—I could have been running a Fortune 500 company during the intervening hours.

When I was awake I would fantasize about being dead, guiltily, the way one would allow oneself to imagine an illicit affair. I never seriously considered suicide because of what it would do to my child. Even in my darkest hours I knew that a bad mother was better than a dead one. That may have set the bar pitifully low, but that's where I needed it. I took solace in depression's greatest refuge: denial.

Of course all of this was terribly hard on my husband, who struggled to preserve a semblance of normalcy in our home and in our dealings with the outside world. He'd married a woman who worked seventy hours a week and rarely went anywhere without four-inch heels. Now he came home to an overweight crybaby wearing mint-green fat shorts around the house.

Matters came to a head when our neighbor across the hall invited us to her New Year's Eve party, children included. It was literally steps away. Our sons were best friends. There was no getting out of it. My poor husband was so starved for social interaction that even I realized it would be unkind not to go. The thought of getting dressed for a party and facing strangers, especially those in the book business, reduced me to a sniffling, sniveling puddle. But I forced myself to go.

Knowing what a challenge it would be, I started dressing at four o'clock. I had to lie down for an hour and a half after taking a shower. Trying to decide what to wear took two hours and two crying jags. Makeup, which I had not put on in six months, took another hour. And for some reason the effort of pulling on my black suede boots was so exhausting that I lay prostrate on the bed until my husband came and found me at about nine. "What are you doing here? Aren't you coming? Helen's editor is making fondue. You love fondue."

"Okay," I said as I took his hand and stood up for what felt like the final walk to the guillotine.

There, stirring cheese over a flame in the center of the living room, was my old self, young, blond, and utterly sure of herself. I bit the bullet.

"Hi," I said to Helen's editor, a little too enthusiastically. "I'm Helen's next-door neighbor. I used to be an editor at Viking."

The blonde hardly lifted her head from the bubbling cheese. She flipped her cloak of hair to tell her boyfriend to turn the flame down. I turned away.

I would have been angry, if I hadn't done exactly the same thing hundreds of times myself. Of course everyone wanted to talk to her. She was an attractive book editor at a major publishing house. And to think I used to believe it was my magnetic personality that made people buttonhole me at every event. Now, as I reintroduced myself to agents and industry people I'd known vaguely, I inevitably ended up a victim of the "greet and turn." It was ignominious, being shouldered out of a conversation after the carefully phrased question "Are you working outside the home these days?" Time after time, my answer was a short, helpless, truthful "No."

To hide my brimming eyes, I retreated to the back bedroom, where the children were playing. My boots made it impossible for me to sit comfortably on the floor, and the boys gave me dirty looks for intruding on their space. My husband came and found me. "What are you doing hiding back here?" he asked.

As if the answer wasn't painfully apparent.

By eleven o'clock I had safely escaped to bed. My husband complained somewhat bitterly the next morning about ringing in the new year alone. I would never be able to convey what a superhuman effort it had taken to get there, and stay there, at all.

One afternoon soon afterward, I was lying in bed thinking about my mother. I had stopped speaking to her just after my wedding, had not talked to her during my pregnancy or even after the birth of my son. "Better mad than sad" had been the motto of generations of women in my family. My mother's personal favorite was "Mad keeps me going." But I had begun to realize I was getting nowhere nursing the same old grievances.

In a sudden burst of industry, I climbed out of bed and went in search of an old shoe box full of photographs from before my mother's divorce and remarriage when I was five. I hadn't remembered there was such a profusion. Few of them included my father, and the ones that did were full of obvious tension. But there were many of my mother, most of them in severely impeccable Jackie O. ensembles out of place on the front walk of our modest twin house. I appeared in a number of these, as carefully dressed as she was, my golden hair in a perfect bun topped with a grosgrain bow, wearing a yellow-and-white dotted swiss dress in one, a pink belted coat with fur collar in another, but always with spotless white tights and a tiny pocketbook. Now that I had a son, I knew there was only one way to get a child of two or three to stand still for such elaborate grooming: fear. I had a vague memory of holding absolutely still as my mother brushed and curled, buttoned and fluffed.

Every day seemed to be Easter in these photographs. We looked like a politician's family. Who were we posing for? Was it my father? I noticed that many retakes of me were necessary in order to perfect this Potemkin village of happiness. In the first photograph, my face would be mulish or glum or tear-stained. In the second it would be twisted into a grimace more or less resembling a smile. But the photos that filled me with an emotion I couldn't name, that made my heart feel as if it were a bar of soap slipping out of my grasp, were the ones in which a baby girl—me—stared round-eyed into the camera, her eyes filled with a dumb, beseeching despair.

I picked up a shadowy Polaroid I hadn't looked at closely before. My mother stared out at me hollow-eyed, cadaverous, her hair teased into an untidy beehive, barefoot in front of a toddler's overflowing toy box. My overflowing toy box. I recognized the look in her eyes from my own mirror. Could it be that my mother's "nervous breakdown" had been postpartum depression? It runs in families, my therapist had told me. This photograph was proof. Suddenly her impatience, her slaps, her screaming fits, her bouts of tears, seemed all too understandable.

What had delivered me from the same fate but the accident of having been born in a different time? Holding that Polaroid, I finally understood that I was a better mother not because I was a better person, but because I was lucky. I had sophisticated medication, a supportive and loving husband, a therapist, and a full-time babysitter. And thank God I did. Who can say what I would have done had I been alone in the house with a baby all day, every day, at twenty-two? After all these years, I pitied us both—and forgave her and myself.

Mother's Day was approaching. Early one morning, on the spur of the moment, I decided to send my mother a message. I had only two happy memories from my early life with her. One was of the inflatable baby pool in our backyard. The other was of picking violets in Pennypack Park in Philadelphia. I must have been only three or four, but I remember how we lay on the grass together, how the warmth seemed to come from the grass itself, and how she laughed and smiled a lot and didn't raise her voice or slap me once all afternoon. On the Internet I found a small pot of African violets, on sale. Deciding it must be a sign, I enclosed a note: "Remember Pennypack Park?" was all it said.

My mother called me two days later, crying. She proceeded to give me something few people get in this life: the apology I had fantasized about and replayed endlessly in my head for forty years. She admitted everything she had denied over the years (so I had *not* been crazy after all) and told me she had been "the Wicked Witch of the North, East, West, and South." She said she had been haunted all these years by the memory of her screaming and how I would slide down the wall and shake and not be able to stop. She said she would give her right arm to be able to undo what she had done to me.

After the conversation with my mother, whole hours began to pass during which I realized I hadn't thought once of killing myself. I began to enjoy the rush of the wind off the river as I came down the hill, and the swish it made in the stately oaks in Riverside Park. I applied to a nonfiction-writing workshop at the 92nd Street Y. I went to Barneys and bought some tight Italian capri pants now that I'd finally dropped those thirty pounds. And I started to feel odd when people referred to me as "the redhead." To my husband's great relief, I returned my hair to its natural dark blond.

My mother accepted our invitation to my son's third birthday party. She and I began a shy, awkward renegotiation of our relationship, which is now solid. I'm happy to have my mother back in my life. I'm happy for my son, too. He has both sets of grandparents, especially important since he is our only child.

The transformations of motherhood, like those of pregnancy, have taken place on a visceral, subterranean level, under my skin and inside my heart. Some have been chemical, some so painful they felt surgical. Some are, no doubt, ongoing. They will surely continue to make me into the mother I need to be for my son, and for myself.

I don't know what I'm going to do with my life after I put my son on the school bus this September. But after I spend some long autumn afternoons alone in the apartment, I expect to find that the decision has already been made.

The Donna Reed Syndrome

Lonnae O'Neal Parker

Feeling like a cartoon character with an angel and a devil whis-
pering in each ear ("Stay home with your children!" "Go to
work to protect your independence!"), don't we all sometimes
long for a few months to immerse ourself in the opposite
lifestyle without any long-term consequences? Lonnae O'Neal
Parker, a staff writer for *The Washington Post* "Style" section,
actually got a trial period to see how she liked being home full-
time. Lonnae is the author of *I'm Every Woman: A Black
Woman Remixes Stories of Marriage, Motherhood, and Work.*
She lives in suburban Maryland with her husband, Ralph, and
three kids, ages ten, six, and two.

can't recall what kept me late that night. It was some event I had to cover as a Style writer for *The Washington Post,* but by that time they had all begun to blur. I don't remember the details. I just remember the drive home.

It was cold, but I kept the window down and the radio blaring. The night air and a heavy bass line filled the roomy cockpit of my car, but they were not enough.

I was falling asleep.

I don't ever remember closing my eyes, but every few minutes I'd be jarred awake by rumble strips on the shoulder of the road, and I would pinch myself, hard.

"Wake up, Lonnae!" I hissed angrily.

But by that time, I was too far gone.

When my second daughter, Savannah, was a month old, my husband began working as a market analyst for a pharmaceutical company outside Philadelphia. For the next two years, he'd go up on Mondays and return to suburban Maryland Fridays.

Though my young cousin lived with us and helped with the house and the girls, I became mother and, largely, father to Savannah and four-year-old Sydney. I spent days hurtling from baths and lunches and field trips and Friday treats to interviews and transcripts and events and deadlines. I made the parenting decisions: how much nap time, how many cookies, Tylenol or Children's Motrin, spankings or time-outs. And I plotted all the logistics: work schedules and pickups and drop-offs and handovers.

By the second year of my husband's commute, I was exhausted. And everything in my life began to suffer. At work, I began to feel flat and stale. I began recycling old images, plagiarizing myself. At home, I often missed dinner. Or sometimes I got there just in time to cook real quick before reading a bedtime story or playing a perfunctory game of concentration and conking out, usually before nine.

Typically, I am obsessive, compulsive, a little freaky when it comes to control—sometimes I think I can bend spoons with my mind. There's just a certain pitch at which I like to write and mother and engage in my world—but now I couldn't keep it together.

I felt like a hag.

That night in the car, each pass over the rumble strips reminded me of how far I had pushed myself. And that night, fatigue pushed back—hard.

You can do it. You're almost home. You're almost home. I willed myself to keep driving.

Finally, I turned onto my block, then into my driveway, and waves of relief washed over me.

My husband, Ralph, was home that night and heard me pull up. He says he wasn't worried the first ten or fifteen minutes when I didn't come into the house; he just figured there was something good on the radio. But fifteen minutes turned into twenty. After twenty-five minutes, he stepped outside. Even standing on the porch, he could see my face. My head was back and my eyes were closed.

The car was still running.

Before that night, I had been unable to face the reality that something had to give. But falling asleep in the driveway helped me realize that while it seemed I had it all, perhaps that was just a little too much.

It was time to cast about for a simpler life—a model of routine and order and organization and competence. I wanted a life where women kept house, raised kids, and kept their eyebrows looking really good.

That's about the time I began fantasizing about Donna Reed.

Ralph and I still live in the first house we ever bought—the second-smallest on the block. A modest three-bedroom split-level situated near the end of a cul-de-sac, in a regular middle-class way-outside-the-Beltway Maryland neighborhood. We dream of bigger, better-appointed, location, location, location. Still, right now, either of us alone can afford what eight years ago it took both of us to buy. Which is why I had always had options. Perhaps not the option of lavish entertaining, or even soaking in a tub without staring at the brightly colored zoo animals on my kids' bathroom wall, but options like six months' maternity leave with each baby and, now, maybe, a little time off. I realize that is a luxury a lot of women, who are a lot more stressed or have many more kids and a lot less house, don't have. But I was thoroughly postmodern. Which meant in addition to having options, I was self-absorbed and felt entitled enough to explore them.

I had never seen an episode of *The Donna Reed Show,* an ABC family sitcom that ran from 1958 to 1966, a year before I was born. Still, Reed was, for me, iconic—a cultural touchstone like June Cleaver and Jane Wyatt (who played Margaret Anderson, wife of the Father who Knew Best). But Reed resonated more because she also seemed to conjure a touch of glamour, a hint of sexuality. Home, hearth, hugs, and high heels—that's what I wanted, to mine the feminine mystique, surrender pliantly to the cult of domesticity. So, even though my husband had just accepted a position that brought him back to the Washington area, I signed up for six months of unpaid leave.

And let the fantasy begin.

For a time, doing simple household chores felt spiritual and cathartic. It connected me to the women who had come before. My mom said Mondays had been her mom's laundry day, so I took it as my own. I pretreated and soaked and spot-removed and scrubbed. I got out what my children got into. And all the career satisfaction I had ever had was rivaled by the sight of my toddler's startlingly white, lemon-fresh tees, pressed crisp for added punctuation. It brought me a serene, uncomplicated joy that crashing a story on deadline never had.

My neighbors teased me about my sudden lifestyle change. "I hate you," one of them told me.

I believe she was joking, but I was aware that my extended leave made me an anomaly—an object of curiosity, maybe a bit of jealousy, and perhaps a little scorn. Donna Reed wasn't a model for the women I knew as a black girl growing up on the South Side of Chicago. I came from a tradition of women who worked. Who went out and hit it every day and imparted to their daughters no options other than college and career. On many levels, my choice separated me not only from my neighbors but from a part of myself as well.

Still, when I finally sat down to watch a few episodes of *The Donna Reed Show*—Dr. and Mrs. Alex Stone and their kids, Mary and Jeff—courtesy of TV Land, I knew immediately what I had been responding to. Reed negotiated her world with an ease and an authority I had only pretended. She was up early, perfectly coiffed, and bacon grease never stained her apron. Her children listened and responded, and she handled them with a skillful and nuanced touch. Like the time Mary accepted two dates to the "big dance" but was left dateless when the boys found out. Reed counseled her daughter that she must wield her girl-power with kindness and wisdom—be an indulgent and just ruler over the white-bread, repressed boys she went to school with. And Mary listened faithfully. For Reed was deep and beautiful.

Reed also kept her dashing husband whipped. Their on-screen kisses were chaste, but he smacked her on the bottom once, hinting at a passion waiting only for the studio audience to disband. It was a passion she leveraged into power. A passion she manipulated and tweaked to maintain her ruling order.

I was surprised at Donna Reed's subterfuge—like the time she dyed her hair platinum and didn't want her husband to know. She covered, stalled, dyed it dark brown and then back to its original color, and the good doctor, probably thinking about smacking her bottom again, was none the wiser. I deeply appreciated that nod to the need for occasional covert household action. Reed was a pragmatist, a temptress, queen of the realm. She brought deep measures of herself to bear in order to secure what she had to have, even if it was just respect for her meat loaf and matching table linens.

My husband got caught up in the Reed spell as well. He was now the sole provider—able to share the minutiae of his day with a newly attentive wife. "It's great having you home, having my dinner ready when I get home," he would say, and I'd just smile.

My eyebrows looked good.

Still, even though Donna Reed was my fantasy girl, I knew going in that I'd be cheating on her regularly. For all my nostalgia and revisionist stirrings, I was under no illusion about the stuff that happened off-camera: that there were times even a wonderful mother wanted to smack her kids and tell her husband to shut up. That keeping a house perfect meant sometimes your hair and nails couldn't be. That Donna Reed must have at least occasionally tired of hospital corners and longed for intellectual stimulation.

So, of course, I added a few new-millennium, New Age touches to make my vintage fantasy world possible. I no longer wrote regularly for the *Post,* but freelancing brought me exposure and a bit of extra cash, as did occasional speaking engagements. I took dance classes sometimes and worked out three or four times a week. And I fed my literature-starved soul with Toni Morrison and Ralph Ellison, Ernest Gaines and Isabel Allende.

Though my focus had shifted, I maintained an ambitiously busy life. I mothered lavishly but on my own terms. I volunteered one morning a week in my daughter's first-grade class, but keeping all my day-care options open for six months meant I could drop my kids off whenever I needed and keep them with me whenever I wanted.

For a time it was the perfect combination of all my worlds. And when the last of my loved ones left in the morning, all I could do was smile, fold my apron, and get ready to run a few miles on the treadmill.

Life was as sweet as a 1950s sitcom.

About six months in, the fantasy showed signs of strain, began collapsing under the weight of its lofty expectations—its disconnect with the salient facts of my life.

I had seen the signs over the holidays. I wanted to take the girls to have their annual Christmas pictures taken, but my husband—saying we didn't have the money and a nice Kodak would do just as well—vetoed it.

He *vetoed* it.

It was a notion that was unfathomable to me, since I had always worked hard. I had a powerful memory of having money—which turned out not to be quite as powerful as actually having a little bit of money—and the strain of being wholly subsidized was beginning to take its toll. It was beginning to alter the power dynamic in my house. I had to plead and bargain and barter for things I used to be able to buy.

There were other signs as well. As much as I loved a clean house, I was limited in my ability to mop floors consistently—constrained by outside interests, lack of domestic expertise, too much time in the workforce, and perhaps too few chores as a child. I had difficulty developing regular routines or remaining focused enough to keep more than a few disparate parts of the house cleaned and organized at any given time. I grew frustrated and overwhelmed by the ease with which the girls razed my clean living room, or by Ralph's failure to tie his socks together.

Donna Reed didn't have these problems. She had a crew of set designers and technicians to make sure her wood floors gleamed. I didn't even have wood floors; I had linoleum.

Still, I was as determined to hang on to the fantasy as I had been in crafting it. In February, when my first six-month leave was up, I requested and received another six months off. I continued to freelance and read and volunteer. And I canceled my older daughter's day-care option—both to save money and to add to our time together.

But the cracks in the fantasy widened further.

That spring, I was trying to line up more regular writing assignments because being broke wasn't cool at all. I had gotten kind of sneaky—having my mother or sister buy things I couldn't afford and back-dooring them into the house so my husband wouldn't find out.

And although I had had a couple of well-paying speaking engagements, that also meant I had to have a new BCBG suit to wear to them, the cost of which offset my honorariums. My expensive tastes and lack of self-control were running afoul of my unemployed status.

One April morning I woke to find my house a wreck. My husband would be home from work early, but I was desperate to work out and hungry for a little library time with my toddler. I was racked by guilt and indecision. Overwhelmed by dust bunnies. Shaking off my helplessness, I grabbed the phone book.

Molly Maid, Maid to Order, ah, Team Clean. Here we go, I thought. The conversation went something like this:

"My house is a wreck. Can you come out this afternoon?"
"Sorry, ma'am. We're booked for the day."
(Pause.)
"Okay, what about if I double your usual fee?"
"We can be there at two."

When my husband got home he marveled at our new sparkles. And I claimed credit—took great pains to point out the tub and windows and extra-special elbow grease I had applied to the stove. (Because even Donna Reed lied to her husband.) And although he eventually noticed the extra couple of hundred dollars missing from the checkbook, I don't believe he made the connection.

I still took pride in a clean house, but it was different from the pride of accomplishment or the satisfaction of drudgery in service of a goal. Alone with myself for a concentrated period, I had faced my limitations and used my husband's money to overcome them.

But even though I couldn't admit it to anyone, I suspected that very soon, once again, something would have to give.

In early summer, I took my older daughter, Sydney, to Guatemala for a month. I had been there two years earlier and was eager to give a boost to my Spanish and expose my daughter to another culture. Though there was no money in the budget for this, I secured a couple of writing assignments to make it happen.

When I got back in July, I knew it was decision time. I was restless, losing touch with the part of me that had built a career as a newspaper reporter. Friends began assuming I had made a permanent lifestyle change and asked about the kids and the house and my tableware plans but no longer asked about my job and when I'd be returning. And I realized how isolated I had let myself become.

As we were driving downtown one afternoon, Savannah asked me where all those dressed-up ladies were going. They are going to work, honey, I told her. And she corrected me. Mommies don't work, she said.

I was tired of having no money. And my husband, once enthralled with his stay-at-home wife, was dropping not-so-subtle hints about all the things we could do if I made a more regular financial contribution. I stayed busy with the hundreds of details of running a house and coordinating family getaways and kids' summertime schedules. But increasingly, my husband found all sorts of please-take-the-car-to-the-shop, the-clothes-to-the-cleaners, the-coupons-to-the-Safeway errands to fill my vast quantities of "free time." "What did you do today?" became a loaded question.

I no longer had the confidence, or, more accurately, the inclination, to argue with him about the value of my home work, tempered as it was by the cleaning-service expenditures I now fessed up to, and by my own lack of restraint. There were too many things I wanted to buy, too many places I wanted to go.

Still, I had a hard time admitting that I had to either drastically scale back my purchases or return to work. A hard time reckoning with the notion that I could never fully give myself over to baseboards. From a distant psychic recess, Donna Reed still beckoned.

One August morning, a year after I left work, I picked up the newspaper and realized how much I missed my job. I missed going to the office, sharing stories with colleagues. And I missed feeling competent and accomplished at what I did. That day, without ever directly articulating my intentions to my family, I asked my boss if I could return. Though I had left on good terms, I was tentative, no longer sure if I was a reporter or a housewife who used to be one. Still, I was rested. I had new images, new connections with my family and my world and myself. And now I was ready to see if I could translate them into creativity.

I returned to work four months ago.

Most days, I'm still optimistic when I walk through the office doors. Glad I left, but glad to be back. Happy once again to hustle and bustle and mix it up with the other nine-to-fivers.

But some mornings the idea of planning the day over cornflakes while the girls watch *Arthur* or *Clifford the Big Red Dog* is incredibly seductive. And sometimes it actually hurts to leave—mornings like today when my three-year-old screamed and cried and begged, "Mommy, please stay!" And I just kept walking.

If I had magic powers, I would ration my children's love. Shave a little off the top of the little one—who sometimes can't bear to allow me to walk from my room to the kitchen without wrapping herself around my neck—and save it for the not-so-distant times when she gets busy with her own life and forgets to call. But I don't have those powers, so I have to enjoy my children now.

And when my seven-year-old is an old woman, I hope she remembers that once a week, for a year, I volunteered mornings in her first-grade class. And I hope she loves me for it.

I'm a working mother, in and out of the house, and I've learned that overarching balance is elusive, mythical, so I just take it one weekday at a time. Still, I'm sustained by memories of my year of living as Donna Reed and my new, post-postmodern realization: I can have it all, just not on the same day.

Mother Superior

Catherine Clifford

Catherine Clifford's decision to be a stay-at-home mom was by default. After spending her twenties and thirties racking up credits in the competitive world of New York magazine publishing, writing and editing on staff for *Self* and *Longevity* and freelancing for twenty other monthly magazines, she moved to the Maryland suburbs and bore three children in three years. Bested by the mundane but immutable demands of finding and keeping good childcare, she leapt into the full-time stay-at-home mom fray herself. Like Alice down the rabbit hole, she was surprised by what she found in Wonderland. She explores the simple yet sticky conundrum at the heart of the tension between working and stay-at-home moms: "Children need their mother."

There's nothing like having five older brothers for turning a girl into a feminist. Throughout my childhood, as a female and the youngest, I was usually derided and dismissed on the scarce occasions that my brothers noticed me at all. In cahoots consciously and not, my mother ranked the needs and wishes of males, specifically her husband and sons, above those of herself, my much older sister, and me, whether it was who got the biggest piece of cake, the car on Saturday night, or the engagement ring that my grandmother had left to *me* (cue *Psycho* music and stabbing motion).

At the same time, my mother was incredulously, openly thrilled that I was a girl—the bonus she got after five sons. And because I was her last, I did receive more of one asset than anyone else: her time.

I was young when no one thought twice about quoting what little girls were made of, and I did lots of girly things with my mother, albums' worth of lovely, corny mental snapshots: the two of us making candy, baking cakes, reading *The Wizard of Oz*, playing games, going shopping. She organized ice-skating outings, train trips, cooking clubs, hikes to find wild-animal tracks. My mother was there, just there, busy but able to find time to talk or listen or have fun or get mad or be a jerk or comfort me—in short, to have a full-fledged relationship with me. She described herself as a housewife but also (and this is just a sampling): wrote a weekly column for the local newspaper and feature articles for national magazines; participated in local, state, and national politics; took a long walk or bike ride or swim almost every day; housed two foster children and three exchange students for a year each; and, already possessing a master's in economics, got her second master's in library science. Her husband and seven kids may have been the most important things in her life, but we were far from the only things.

I adored my mother—at least I have ever since she died six years ago and isn't around to tick me off anymore—not least for her model of motherhood: Convention be damned, construct your life as you want.

● ● ●

That I would have a career was never in doubt. What career I would have did not become clear until it had started. After graduating from college and working at a few unimpressive jobs at impressive places—Harvard, the BBC—I was in New York City casting about for stimulating employment that didn't require much in terms of actual qualifications. I happened to meet the managing editor at the then-fledgling *Self* magazine. I immediately liked her, and *Self*'s informal, intelligent, estrogen-rich atmosphere. Mainly on the basis, I think, of "Harvard" and "the BBC," *Self* offered me a job as a researcher, which sounded good enough to me.

After two vastly fun and instructive years in research, I was promoted to staff writer, a great job, then senior writer—still great, and, naturally, more work. Senior editor was the next step up, a promotion I asked for partly because I wanted new challenges but mainly because it was the only way to get noticeably more money. Encouraging new writers, smoothing awkward syntax, having more say in the magazine's content—all that was very satisfying. The job also meant, though, a lot less working with words and a lot more memos, meetings, and hours. The managing editor advised me one day that if I did some savvy job-hopping, I could be managing editor somewhere within a couple of years. My reaction was to feel flattered, and to recoil. The closer I got to the top, the grimmer the work seemed to get.

Sure enough, soon afterward I was offered the position of managing editor at one of the big fashion magazines. But by then I knew that that kind of success wouldn't make me happy, and I bailed altogether. Luckily, eight years in publishing meant I had as much freelance writing and editing as I could handle. Besides, I had new diversions siphoning off my attention: a husband, a house, and our efforts to have a baby.

I was twenty-nine when an old friend gathered some high school alums for dinner out. One was a friend/crush I hadn't seen since graduation, and by the time the waiter brought my chimichangas, I was halfway gone. A date turned into a weekend turned into the kind of superglue, soul-mate bonding that had Nick mentioning marriage after only six weeks. Among the many major attractions for me was that Nick was so counterculture, a spiritual type who used his Yale degree to become a car mechanic and union organizer. I mean, the guy's last address had been an ashram, for God's sake. He moved in with me in New York, and we were married shortly before I turned thirty-one.

I had long known that I wanted children, so Nick and I quit using contraception a year after our wedding. Nothing. Over the next four years, we collectively endured endless tests, four operations, months of hormone treatments, eight rounds of Pergonal IUIs (daily injections of fertility drugs and monthly intrauterine insemination), two rounds of in vitro fertilization, and, halfway through, a physically and psychically excruciating miscarriage.

I can't say I handled prolonged infertility gracefully; I harbored death wishes for anyone I knew who got pregnant. But as a couple, Nick and I coped relatively well. The seam that began to pull apart was a surprise, to wit, that Mr. Natural had morphed into a Master of the Universe. As I was pulling over into a slower lane, Nick was getting serious about being a Success at his new Wall Street job, working increasingly insane hours—weekends, nights, vacations, thirty-plus hours straight. He was *never* home. Yes, we had more money. What resonated with me, though, was a quote from a shrink I'd interviewed: "The currency of love is time." We still got along great on the rare occasions I saw him, and we weren't talking about how I never saw him. But no amount of discussion made a dent in Nick's commitment to be an unfailingly loving, attentive, devoted companion—to his clients.

It took a long time for me to stop loving Nick; to this day, we're friends. We'd been married almost six years when, cleaning out a closet, I found a packet of letters he had written me in our first months together. The contrast was stunning. Not "Okay, so the honeymoon's over," but "Oh. The marriage is over." The reality hit that he had left emotionally long ago. Leaving Nick, our home, the lifetime together that we had taken for granted, is still the most anguishing decision I've ever made. What made it both harder and easier was something that, even after years of feeling lonely and abandoned, shocked me as much as anyone: I fell in love with someone else.

It wasn't the first time I had fallen in love with Kirk. Barely taller than me, with Golden Boy looks and an aw-shucks demeanor, Kirk was the quintessential great guy with a rusty pickup, always willing to help college friends move. My counterpart from a parallel universe—the only boy among three sisters—Kirk was funny and smart. More strikingly, he appreciated how funny and smart I was, equally impressed that I was pretty (thank you) and that I changed the oil in my VW myself. I fell in love with him at regular intervals from college on, and we remained close friends most of the other times. But he lived in Washington, D.C., and I always had other boyfriends and, it's safe to say, issues to work through. Then, as my marriage crumbled, I fell one last time wildly, madly, crazily in love with him. Seventeen years after I'd first met Kirk, I moved into my own apartment in New York and got a job three days a week editing at a small health magazine called *Longevity* to add predictability to my income, and we began alternating weekend visits to see each other.

Neither of us had any doubt that we were in it for keeps. We wanted children, we were both thirty-six, and I was nothing if not intimate with infertility, so we let nature take its course. Nature had more nasty tricks up her sleeve. After maybe a year and a half and no pregnancy, I reluctantly dug out the doctors' phone numbers. Now we were thirty-eight and the prognosis was bleak: In vitro was our only hope, and an exceedingly slim one at that. We booked a slot at an IVF center with a six-month wait, and debated IVF (could I go through it again?), adoption, or staying childless. When a couple of months later I didn't get my period, I knew I wasn't pregnant, so I thought, "*Now* what?"

"What," to our and the doctors' amazement, was a baby, a one-in-a-million miracle pregnancy that just *happened*. Kirk and I were wild with excitement, and wild with anxiety about everything we had to do. Though Kirk was willing to move to New York, I could freelance from anywhere, and *Longevity* offered to let me do my deputy-editor staff job long-distance. So I lined up an ob-gyn and hospital, packed up my New York life, and when I was six and a half months pregnant, moved into a new house with Kirk. After unpacking, childbirth classes, checkups, acquiring baby equipment, and fixing up a nursery, every frantic thing we had to get done was done. There was just enough time left to check off one last item. At thirty-nine, when I was eight months pregnant, we had a very joyful wedding. Seven and a half years after I'd started trying to have a baby, our daughter Darcy was born.

There's no point in trying to describe my emotions. It would be fatuous to suggest that I was more elated, enraptured, or devoted than any other new mother (although I may be, still, more consciously grateful). I'm not religious at all, but after years of internal demons muttering about how I'd been cheated, I felt whatever the oxymoronically agnostic version is of this: There is a God, and God has been really wonderful to me.

Once I was a new mother, two principles ruled my consciousness:

1. I loved my baby so amazingly, inexpressibly much, I would do anything to keep her happy and healthy.
2. Unfortunately, I didn't have the faintest idea what I was doing.

Did I believe in the family bed? In pacifiers? In letting her cry herself to sleep? Should feeding be on demand or according to a schedule? Books I read explained that you simply needed to choose the approach you agreed with, then apply it consistently (since inconsistency apparently correlates closely with cavities, low GPA, and matricide). My response: "How the hell do I know which approach I agree with? I've never done this before!"

However, when it came to working, staying home, or straddling the two, I did know. It never occurred to me not to work. While I of course respected any choice a woman made, yadda yadda, modern, enlightened women like me, who very much wanted to care for a baby but also had successful careers and strong feminist beliefs, seemed happiest if they could pare their jobs to part-time, which I could. Kirk's and my incomes were almost exactly matching, so we needed my half if we wanted to live in a safe town with good schools less than an hour from Kirk's office. My plan was to work from home and, I blithely told everyone, go up to the New York office for a few days once or twice a month, the preposterousness of which I understood once I had a colicky, nursing newborn with reflux.

I answered a classified ad in our local weekly placed by a nanny available during school hours. Not having any idea how lucky I was, I struck gold. Lulu, a young Filipina, was nothing short of a fairy godmother, coaxing delighted giggles and coos from Darcy that all of our doting hadn't elicited. As you'd imagine, the entire galaxy rotated around

Darcy. Still, I don't remember feeling torn or envious as I handed her off to Lulu each morning. I had work to get done. And anyway, unless I was on a crucial work call (signaled by frenetic air slicing and head shaking), I was always available for nursing, consultation, and to observe extra-cute behavior.

When Darcy was nine months old, I was driving to the National Institutes of Health for research materials and suddenly felt very carsick. What the—? It couldn't be. Yes, it could. Eight months later our son, Liam, was born. It had never occurred to us to use contraception; the first pregnancy was so clearly an astronomical fluke. And anyway, if we could have more kids, you bet we wanted them. So at almost forty-one, I now had two kids under a year and a half.

I had happily surrendered huge portions of my life to having one baby already, but it was during Liam's first night home from the hospital that I had an epiphany. Having just given birth, groggy with painkillers, I was beyond exhausted. Around 4 A.M., Liam woke up and we entered that serene stop-motion world of predawn feedings, where no one exists except you and your baby and the newspaper deliverer. I took my time nursing him and burping him, rubbing my cheek against his fuzzy head and getting high on new-baby smell. Then after checking his diaper and swaddling him tightly, I laid him back in his bedside bassinet and crashed on my pillow. He fussed; I jiggled the bassinet. He started to cry; I patted him halfheartedly, trying to convey, "Look, kid, you had your turn, now I have *got* to get some sleep." He cried harder.

Suddenly, as clearly as if I'd said it out loud, I thought: "None of this is about you or what you need. It is *only* about this little baby and what he needs." I roused myself, held him, and I don't know what else I did except that it was whatever it took to get him happy and back asleep. That's when I really got it: Life with me at the center, or even *sharing* the center, was over. To some, this realization may seem obvious, terrifying, or the beginning of misguided self-denial leading inevitably to seriously low self-esteem and other mental-health problems.

To me it felt like I had finally grown up.

Longevity had recently folded, and although I'd curtailed my writing to keep up with two kids, I was still turning out regular articles and a monthly column. Kirk had switched to a better-paying job, so we were at least close to even, financially. Then after Liam's first birthday, Lulu left to have her own baby. Her replacement was okay, but just okay, and my open office door started to see a marked uptick in traffic from kids who now found the alternative to me a lot less appealing. Darcy started nursery school two days a week, which, with drop-off, pickup, and school activities, nibbled the edges of those work mornings down to a couple of hours. For the first time, I started to feel bad about how my children were spending half their days, but not to worry: Lulu's replacement left after several months because it turned out she had no desire to babysit three—yes, three—kids.

This time I wasn't so dense about why I was suddenly nauseated, but it still blew us away. "How did we go from hopelessly infertile to baby factory in three years?" marveled Kirk. Or as one of my brothers put it, "Boy, Catherine was late out of the gate, but she sure is making up for it in the home stretch." When Kirk and I were forty-two, Darcy just over three, and Liam not yet two, another girl, Marron, was born.

We persuaded Lulu to come back and bring her one-year-old daughter. Working at home with four toddlers underfoot unavoidably multiplied the interruptions and tarnished the professional tone of business calls. My interview tapes started sounding like this: "But aren't there conflicting results—*sure, sweetie, that's fine, shhh*—from later studies?" I started taking shorter (and lower-paying) assignments with longer deadlines. Then Lulu got pregnant again, and this time we had to say good-bye to her for good.

Now we descended into the dark ages of the nanny hunt. Legal part-timers are hard to come by anyway, but as soon as I mentioned the number and ages of the children—one, three, and four—prospects lost interest, such as the one who said "I'll call you back" and hung up as I was pathetically bleating, "But you don't have my number . . ." Nanny agencies wouldn't return my calls. When we did find candidates and tried them out or just plain hired them cold, this is what happened:

1. Pregnant, she was put on bed rest.
2. Her existing employer decided she wanted her back full-time.
3. She never showed up.

4. A loving, Old World grandma did not comprehend the concept of gender neutrality. I couldn't get her to stop taking "boy" toys away from the girls and vice versa, or urging my son to be a little man and not cry, my girls to be more ladylike.

5. Her other employer insisted that any time their kid was sick, there was a snow day, or they needed extra help, they had dibs and I was up the creek.

6. I found her, more than once, curled up asleep on the couch with a blanket and pillow, with all three kids awake and playing.

7. A gentle, gracious woman who worked part-time in a doctor's office was with us a week when, noting how promising and unproblematic this one seemed, I cynically joked to Kirk, "You know that over the weekend she's going to be the victim of a drive-by shooting or something." I was wrong—it was her co-worker who died, making her needed full-time at the doctor's.

I had spent half a year on a round of nanny ads, references, interviews, hiring and orienting, scrambling, and starting all over again. There were few hours left in which to work. I bribed the kids with TV, cookies, hazardous toys, anything to get them to shut up when I had to take a work call. I did one interview in my closed closet with kids howling and pounding on the bedroom door. I was perpetually anxious, harried, and irritated; the kids were in constant upheaval.

Around NF (nanny fiasco) number four or five, the concept of taking care of the kids full-time myself started to brush up against my consciousness. I swatted it away. Being a professional writer and editor had long constituted a pillar of my identity, and pulling my own weight had always been a point of pride and honor. The idea of not bringing in any money felt as radical as "I'm going to become Wiccan" or "I want to try surviving on a diet of bugs."

With NF number six, I started making pointed comments to Kirk about how *impossible* it was to find a sitter. He would respond with reassuring optimism and helpful suggestions for new approaches. One drizzly November Wednesday shortly after NF number seven, I sat down to go through the weekly want ads again and instead put my head down on the table. I had just turned forty-four. I had been working for twenty-two years. Trying to find and keep a sitter was creating prizewinning stress and misery. Child care was not working, which meant work was not working. I wanted out.

That night I said to Kirk, "Um . . . what would you think about my just staying home and taking care of the kids?"

"You mean you'd *want* to?" he answered.

His biggest concerns were not about financial security, they were about me. How would I feel about giving up the stimulation, the contact with other writers? Would I have regrets about the long-term impact on my career?

I pondered the latter issue the longest and came to this conclusion: If the most impressive thing my obit could say about me professionally was that I had been a senior writer and editor at a big-time women's magazine and deputy editor at a small health one, good enough. Yes, I would miss some aspects of my professional life. But I'd enjoyed these perks for years. What I hadn't had for long, and wouldn't have too much longer, was young kids.

I'd already missed more of their childhood than I realized.

As with kissing off any detested job, tossing out the child-care classifieds brought dance-around-the-kitchen relief, followed by the hangover of being, technically at least, unemployed. I felt happy, yes, but also confused, guilty, and only half myself. For their part, the kids were thrilled to be done with Nanny of the Month. When Darcy said, "Really? You mean *you're* going to take care of us all the time?" there was more than excitement and incredulity in her voice. She sounded . . . grateful and, I don't know, *flattered* that she was worth my time and attention. Oh, right: The currency of love is time. I knew firsthand how wounding it felt to have someone say he loved me, but sorry, he had more important things to do. I don't think it would have helped my first marriage if Nick had hired someone to eat dinner and watch TV with me, either. (Well, maybe a little.)

With the kids the only big item on my agenda, I could be a better mother, too. For the first time, I could roll with the stomach flus, the potty accidents, the tantrums, without my head exploding. I got to say yes and let my kids be in charge more. Sure, let's go ride the Metro. Yeah, we can stop and look at backhoes in action for half an hour. Okay, how about we skip errands and read another chapter. Saccharine or not, those spontaneous yeses resulted in some of our most memorable, intimate times.

More than anything, I felt how powerfully my kids wanted, had always wanted, their *mother*. And though it was hard to explain or justify, I, in turn, felt an awakened, primal, animal instinct that babies and little kids and even bigger kids need and deserve their mother. This created big problems for my brain.

Do kids need their fathers too?

Brain: Of course, equally.

Gut: Yes, but not as much. Not in the same ways.

Does that mean women shouldn't work after they've had a baby?

Brain: Bite your tongue!!

Gut: Basically, yes.

Are kids better off having their mothers take care of them?

Brain: There's no real evidence that children benefit in any measurable way.

Gut: In some immeasurable way, children will know in their hearts that they are more important to their mothers than anything else, and that knowledge is invaluable. When a child isn't mothered by her mother, something precious and irreplaceable is lost to both of them. It strikes me as downright bizarre that studies assessing the benefits of maternal versus other care express it in terms of IQ, academic achievement, professional status later in life, quantifiable socialization. This is love we're talking about, not an LSAT-prep course.

It soon became clear that a qualitative chasm existed between being my children's caregiver part or even most of the time versus being there all the time. Now, before working mothers throw rocks at my house, let me state strongly: I don't think that nonmom child care damages kids. However, I found that there simply is no substitute for hours upon hours with my children.

What a working mother misses is often portrayed in terms of angst over not being there when the baby takes his first step, utters her first word. Yeah, there's that. But what I really missed were many run-of-the-mill hours surrounding those milestones. Letting Darcy put twenty-three barrettes in my hair, watching Liam turn a Tupperware container into a top hat, seeking Marron when she has hidden in the same spot five times straight—each constituted one more shared experience and chance to know each of them a little better. I'm at school, so I know my kids' teachers, their classmates, the bullies, and how my children interact with them; I know what their friends really are like, when it's the friend who's a pain, when it's my kid who is.

I don't understand why taking care of one's own children is considered hopelessly tedious or brain-deadening. I know well how quickly a new cocktail-party acquaintance needs a fresh drink when he finds out I'm a stay-at-home mother. I find it odd that I'd generate far more interest if I said I raised dogs or horses or chinchillas, but saying, in effect, "I raise human beings" is a huge yawn.

It might, in fact, be that boring if child care were simply a series of pink-collar tasks—bathe, dress, feed, repeat. But observing and participating in a little Homo sapiens's development is fascinating to me. Furthermore, being a mother isn't just a "job" any more than being a wife or a daughter is; it's a relationship. A self-described feminist friend was astonished that I wouldn't hire the Old World grandmother just because of her antiquated view of gender roles. I was astonished that my friend thought it didn't matter. The feminist in me is grateful to every mother who remains in the workplace, but it's partly because I am so fiercely, proudly feminist that I want to raise my own kids. Sexist messages still abound, and I want to make sure that, day in, day out, *I* get to counter with Kirk's and my view of things.

Likewise for sex and drugs, war and violence, beauty and body image. Having hours together every day gives us time to talk at the fleeting moment when the kids' interest is piqued and they're open to listening, reflecting, responding. Of what my kids absorb from me, they'll probably reject half if not all, which is fine. I'm not looking to loose three mini-me's on the world. I just want to foster their (and my) capacity for reasoned, independent thinking, and tolerance for other views.

Flush with fervor for the mother-child bond, I felt my tolerance for other types of mothers, ironically, shrinking. I started casting a more critical eye on mothers who worked, especially ones like the physician (I know because she mentioned her oh-so-important title) I phoned to ask if she wanted to read to her daughter's preschool class for fifteen minutes any time, any morning, during the next eight months. She was indignant that

I would even ask—had she mentioned how important her job was? I wasn't about to criticize women who must work in order to provide a decent standard of living for themselves and their families. However, I looked a lot harder at, for instance, the mom who groused jealously that she couldn't afford not to work, then grabbed her Kate Spade bag and headed off in her new Mercedes SUV.

The idea that parents should put kids first, things second, sounds right, and if I were a child whose mother cared more about collecting Manolos than cuddling with me, I'd save my tooth-fairy money for therapy. I must admit, though, that the trade-offs are often tougher calls. Our furniture is just a level or two above grad-student group house. Next year we have to get a new car, and it's the Corolla with 175,000 miles that we're *keeping*. I like to think that what we give up are just silly, materialistic frills. But sometimes I have to face that we sacrifice things that might genuinely make me happier—having a car with air-conditioning that actually works, or the money to travel back to places that mean a great deal to me. There aren't many *things* that I think our kids have suffered for the lack of, but when families take their children to the theater, to offbeat restaurants, to ski resorts, I admit it would be pretty cool to be able to do that with ours. Along with the stock-market fall went much of our college fund. Will they still be glad they had a mom at home if they have to work their way through college?

Next I began to notice that it wasn't just working mothers whose kids sometimes got shortchanged. When I stopped working, I arranged one day every other week when I had two to three hours free. Other than that, I had kids with me always (except when Kirk relieved me on weekends, that is). If we were richer, I undoubtedly would have tried to buy a little more breathing room. I had to consciously uncurl my lip, however, listening to an acquaintance expound on her experience as a full-time mother, when she might as well have worked for all the time and attention she spent on her kids. What with babysitters, classes, camps, preschool, and enrichment programs, her kids put in a good nine-to-five themselves, while she occupied herself with shopping, playing tennis, reading decorating magazines. I fantasized about saying, "Nooooo . . . you don't *work,* but you're not a full-time mother." One nonworking friend with 24/7 help epitomized the syndrome when her Saturday babysitter didn't show up, and she complained that she and her husband had to babysit the kids themselves. That's the word she used: *babysit*.

Over the years, I've watched friends I know to be loving, unselfish mothers return to work for reasons ranging from their own sanity to financial need, and seen at-home mothers try to live as if they don't have kids. It finally dawned on me that I'd been judging the wrong thing all along. I have come almost full-circle back to respecting the child-care choice each woman makes—to the extent that I respect the woman herself. A good mother is a good mother, working or not, just as a crummy one is crummy whether she's home all the time or hardly at all. Parenting cannot be reduced to a simple formula, but I have noticed one consistent element with all the moms I designate "good": When there's a significant conflict, the kids come first.

I can hear some of you muttering that I have some nerve criticizing anyone, that I'm indulged, judgmental, and selfish, trying to make out that I'm doing something Good when the truth is merely that I love being home with my kids, and that it is, frankly, um . . . kind of nice not to work.

I wish I could deny that wholesale. I recognize that I have advantages others don't: I am lucky that we can live, albeit with sizeable skimping, on one salary. I'm fortunate to have a husband who does as much housework as I do, not only lives for his kids (and me) but is also a full partner in raising and wrangling them. If I were a single mother, or married to someone who thought his role was to (maybe) take the kids Saturday morning, I'd probably resent a job with only three hours off a week. Lastly, God knows it wasn't by choice that I didn't have my first baby until almost forty. But because of that, I got to log a good chunk of career time and to make at least a very small name for myself, so I can hardly blame a woman who became a mom in her twenties for thinking, "Sure, work isn't that important—easy for you to say."

Fair enough. The question I still raise, though, is whether staying home might be right for more women if more women truly considered it.

I am exceedingly glad that I was not able to find a nanny. Within weeks of becoming a stay-at-home mom, I wished I could have had back all those Candy Land and playground mornings from the kids' earlier years—even though there are few things in life more boring than Candy

Land and playgrounds. I'm happy that I had years remaining to make up for lost time. For six years, I have loved my life as a stay-at-home mom, accidental or not.

This year was the first in which all three kids were in school a full day; my job is being partially downsized. Now I have more time to catch up on long-postponed projects, to do more paid writing and volunteer work. I have no intention, however, of trying to find a very time-consuming or structured job for a few years at least. When Liam is sick, I'm the one who gets him from school, sets up pillows and blankets on the couch, and stays nearby. A few days ago, Marron clearly needed a mental-health day off from school. I love that I can allow her to stay home and that, far from being a crisis, it can be a time for us to hang out and chat and gradually unravel why she needed a day off.

As I write this now, I'm feet-up on the couch while my kids play just across the room, all three of them absorbed in some game involving stuffed animals, flashlights, umbrellas, and billowing clouds of talcum powder. In between requests for help with the umbrella catch or warnings about the mess they'll have to clean up, I'm getting thoughts together and sentences written. I'm struck by how adaptable we humans are, how much theoretically discrete parts of our lives can blend together if we're flexible about readjusting our sights. It is mystifying in retrospect why I felt I had to keep working even while it was creating minor income and major havoc. Now, as the kids get older, I want to watch out for being so wedded to my self-definition as full-time mom that I overlook openings for broadening my life again, professionally or personally.

If I had it to do over, I'm not sure that I would do things very differently. My working-mom years meant money that got us important things—a good neighborhood, good schools, good doctors. But I'm endlessly grateful that I ended up quitting, too. I might have a hard time getting back a job that interests me and pays enough money to support me and three kids if I need to work again. But I know I will never get this time with my kids if I don't take it now.

When questions of working versus at-home moms come up with my kids, I always cover the pros and cons, explaining how complex childcare decisions are, and how tricky it gets second-guessing others' choices. Nonetheless, recently the kids and I were all settled into the family room watching a movie in which a wealthy mother chokes up over how much she loves her son.

Darcy, now ten, snorted to the TV, "Yeah, you love him so much, how come you leave him with some nanny person all the time?"

And while I geared up to do a quick consider-all-sides speech, what I was feeling was, "Damn right."

Good Enough

Beth Brophy

Beth Brophy is the author of *My Ex–Best Friend,* a murder mystery about estranged working and stay-at-home moms set in the hotbed of the D.C. suburbs. Beth was a senior editor at *U.S. News & World Report* for twelve years. She is now a freelance writer living in Chevy Chase, Maryland, with her husband and two teenage daughters.

When my seventeen-year-old-daughter, Ariel, was little, I used to drop her off at school on my way to work. From my place in the car-pool line, I'd watch her miniature jean jacket and gray backpack recede into the distance while my mind churned with what awaited me at the office: meetings, interviews, writing, editing, deadlines. I barely noticed the cars ahead of me and behind me, full of other parents, heads similarly reeling as they headed to their offices.

Instead, my eyes would rest on the other mothers making their way to school on foot. Wearing jeans and T-shirts, their hands clutching children, strollers, lunch boxes, and dogs on leashes, they clustered in the school yard in little groups, smiling and relaxed, as if they had all the time in the world. I'd watch them for a few seconds before stepping on the gas.

If mothers are divided into two camps—and women usually are split into some form of "us" versus "them"—I never doubted where I belonged. I worked. Always did. Always would. Just like my mother had before me.

When I was growing up on the South Shore of Long Island in the 1960s and 1970s, my mother, an elementary-school teacher, was one of the few mothers in our middle-class neighborhood with a job. She went back to work after my sister and two brothers were born, partly because she didn't enjoy being at home, and also because she and my father, a newspaper reporter, needed the money. I remember wishing she was home at lunchtime to fix my sandwiches like my friends' mothers. I was embarrassed when my father, who often worked nights but was around during the day, showed up for school plays, the only male in a sea of women. Like most kids, I wanted my family to be like everyone else's: Dad at the office, Mom at home. I didn't appreciate having parents who were ahead of the curve.

Then, when I was eight, my father died of a heart attack. Suddenly my mother was the sole support of our family. It was 1962 and most women were still perfecting tuna casseroles. But my pull-up-your-socks-and-get-on-with-it mother made being a single parent look easy. She liked her job. She did it well, and only complained when the principal dumped the most troubled kids in her classroom for straightening out. Besides, teaching is family-friendly, as jobs go. She was home after school to cart us to the dentist and run errands. We went on nice vacations and to summer camp. If she had financial worries, I was oblivious to them. My sister, brothers, and I had everything our friends did, except for a father.

And we had one thing our friends did not: a full-time housekeeper. Even before my father died, my parents were big believers in help. Barbara lived with us for eighteen years and became like our second mother. She babysat, made dinner, and yelled at us to do our homework. In return, we loved her.

What I learned from my mother was that you could be a good mom and have a job, as long as you didn't make the mistake of trying to do both without outside help. She showed us, quite literally, that in motherhood it doesn't hurt to have a career to fall back on. In fact, when you have kids to provide for, a good plan B just might save your life if your partner keels over or otherwise disappears.

Neither does it hurt to be an optimist. She was unrelenting in that department, reminding us day and night that "you can do anything you set your mind to, if you work hard enough." Some of her other advice was quirky: Don't aspire to be teachers, she told my sister and me. We didn't have to be like the smart women of her generation who were herded into the classroom. We had other career options.

I assumed that if my mother, alone with four kids, could combine work and motherhood, without any of us falling through the cracks, then so could I. My plan had a few upgrades, of course. For starters, I would have what was known in the early eighties as a "supportive spouse," preferably one who earned a decent living and was willing to unload the dishwasher. I'd cut the kid count to two. Through college and graduate school, through my twenties and early thirties, as I built my career as a magazine reporter, I believed the propaganda about "having it all" that women's magazines and TV shows shoveled at women of my generation. I even wrote some of those stories myself.

By the time I was thirty-seven, I was on my way. I'd met a man, a successful management consultant, on an airplane when I was a business reporter at *Forbes* and he'd gotten the mistaken impression that I was a hard-core economics person. He turned into my husband. We had two adorable children. I had pretty close to my dream job: senior editor of a national newsmagazine in Washington, D.C.

In Washington, work is the primary focus of life. Having an impressive job is essential, like having an impressive income in Manhattan, or an impressive car in L.A. A woman who has a low-prestige job or, God forbid, no job at all, may as well just stick her head in the oven and be done with it. In D.C. what you do isn't more important than who you are. It *is* who you are. Everyone here, including the guy who delivers your pizza, believes he influences the fate of the nation. I had terrific credentials to toss around at dinner parties. ("Yes, a magazine writer . . . Yes, my first book, nonfiction, was published a while ago, when I was thirty . . . Yes, I am working on another one now, a novel.")

And a weekly newsmagazine isn't exactly the gulag. Sure, there were hellish weeks of crazy hours, countless rewrites, and unreasonable demands by editors who had their own egos to feed. But there were also cushy stretches of hallway gossiping, reading newspapers with my feet up, and lunches with adults who could read their own menus. Every job has frustrations, but mine were easily erased by the sight of my story on the cover of a magazine that was front and center on the supermarket racks and would be read by two million people. At least until the next hellish week. Work boosted my self-esteem and kept my mind active. Not incidentally, it also paid well. I loved making money and I loved spending it.

I also relished being out of reach of my demanding little children for several hours a day. I adored them, of course, and found them endlessly fascinating. But they were determined to devour me. And I wasn't a baby person. Or a toddler person. (I'm just now adjusting to being a teenager person.) For me, writing even the most boring and tedious story was preferable to crawling around on a plastic mat, poofing up a parachute in a circle with cloyingly enthusiastic new mothers, or reading *Thomas the Tank Engine* for the six hundredth time.

At least that's what I told myself.

In truth, ambivalence was my constant companion. I alternated counting my blessings with whining about fatigue. My husband, supportive in theory, was actually never home and rarely in the same time zone. His job as a management consultant with an international practice owned him. For the first eight years of our marriage, until our second daughter, Lily, turned one and he changed jobs, his primary residence was the airport.

And for me, having it all quickly morphed into doing it all.

Even with our wonderful live-in nanny, who stayed for seven years, parenthood required major adjustments. I did most of the adjusting. I scheduled playdates and strep tests, researched camps, went to work late and left early so that at least one parent showed up at school plays and teacher conferences.

It didn't matter that I *wanted* to do all those things. I still resented it. I wanted my job but wished there were less of it. Eventually I asked to work a four-day week, which no one else at the magazine had, and got it. That one extra day at home made all the difference. I hardly noticed how one foot was slowly creeping toward the jeans-and-T-shirt camp.

Once my husband stopped traveling to foreign countries on a regular basis, things got better at home. I didn't need to go solo anymore during the predinner meltdown *and* the postdinner bath-bedtime crunch. And the long nights, which I had spent every day dreading, weren't nearly as tough with someone to help. Lily, just one, didn't believe in sleep, and only fitfully cooperated in our bed. Until she was four.

To others, I looked like one of those women "having it all." Actually, I had more. I also had guilt and self-doubt. My children wanted more mommy. My office wanted more writer. My husband could have used a little more wife.

"Nora is so lucky," Ariel announced one day when she was three.

"Why?" I asked, thinking of her friend Nora's life-sized pink Barbie car and her backyard swimming pool.

"Because her mom stays home with her," Ariel answered. "When I grow up, I'm going to be a homewife, too."

Home wasn't the only place the at-home moms ruled. At my children's preschool, it felt like the program was always weighted toward the nonworking mothers. Little details: the unspoken assumption that mothers were available to chaperone frequent field trips, or attend art shows and teachers' conferences scheduled smack in the middle of the morning exactly when it is impossible to slip away from the office unnoticed for an hour or two.

In the classroom one morning during drop-off, Ariel's preschool teacher, looking concerned, pulled me aside. "Were you out of town on a business trip last week?" she asked in that perfectly sweet but passive-aggressive way teachers are so good at these days.

"No," I said. "Why?"

"Oh, she"—her head nodding toward my daughter—"seemed a little out of sorts. I thought maybe she was missing you."

"No," I repeated. "I was home all week."

I wanted to snap her head off. She probably meant well. But I felt judged, found deficient in the good-mothering department. Yes, I had been at home the week before. But what if I hadn't been?

Before having kids, I had never had to balance anything. Married to a workaholic, I could sleep at the office, if that's what it took. Now, late nights at work meant disappointing my children, missing bedtime stories and tucking them in.

Like anyone trying to serve two masters, I had divided loyalties. I felt like I was screwing up, doing neither job well. Did I spend enough time with my kids? Was I a good-enough mother? Was I doing enough at work, or was I too distracted by my kids? Having it all doesn't mean much when you don't have time to enjoy any of it.

For years, life sped by, as if on fast-forward. I lived in the *next* moment. At dinner, instead of enjoying precious family time, mentally I'd be packing the next day's school lunches. Queen of the Multitaskers, I was always trying to cross the next item or two off my to-do list. With my husband or friends, after a few drinks, I might bring up the idea of quitting my job. It was the main topic of conversation among my working women friends. But I never seriously considered it. I had those brief school-yard moments, when I imagined that those other mothers, focused solely on their children, were doing a better job than me. They looked calmer, less conflicted. But I wasn't ready, yet, to try it their way.

From the couch in the den, where I was resting, I heard the voices of my husband and daughters playing in the next room. I tried to summon the strength to join them, but I couldn't move. Chemotherapy had zapped me into submission, made a mockery of the endless stream of errands that defined my daily existence. A simple task, like showering or making a cup of tea, defeated me. I stayed prone, feet up, rationalizing my inability to join my family. They were having fun, they were doing fine, they were going to have to learn to manage without me. The sound of their laughter prompted an unbidden reminder of my certain fate. I remember thinking: This is what the house will sound like when I'm gone.

Cancer is the line that divides my life. Before and After. Before, I was a forty-one-year-old mother of two, ages five and eight, a wife, and a full-time journalist.

Then cancer became my full-time job. I took a medical leave from work, and for the next eight months I barely left my house except for the endless round of doctors' appointments and medical treatments. Weak and dispirited, convinced of my impending death—this was nearly nine years ago and I appear to have been wrong, thankfully—I pared my once-crammed schedule down to the essentials. I had plenty of time to sit and think.

Behind closed doors, I cried enough to overflow the Potomac River. Then I'd wipe my eyes and issue detailed instructions to my husband and best friend. How my daughters' bat mitzvahs should be handled (no schmaltzy candle-lighting). Which of my single friends might make acceptable stepmothers (none). Who should take my children clothes shopping (anyone except their father).

I gave a lot of thought to my children. To say that it broke my heart that they might grow up without me doesn't quite capture my agony. My husband, my sister, and my friends stepped in to fill the child-care gaps caused by my illness. The kids' lives went on uninterrupted, or at least that's what I told myself. Around them, I was stoic and optimistic. I wore a wig everywhere so they wouldn't be traumatized by my appearance or embarrassed to bring their friends home.

Although I began viewing everything through the telescoped lens of a person with limited time—five years, tops, was my pessimistic translation of what the research and the doctors were saying—the treatments ended. I hated dwelling in the Land of the Sick. I cringed when people referred to me as "a survivor."

As soon as I felt better and my hair started to grow in, I went back to the office. But the old calculations about my job—pleasant, well-paying, four days a week—weren't adding up the same way. Many of my old and beloved colleagues were gone. There was a new editor running the magazine. The sixth in ten years. The first one I couldn't stand.

But other, bigger things had changed too. I had stopped living according to how my life looked (perfect, until cancer) and started paying much closer attention to how it felt (a little on the empty side). Cancer had kicked my ambivalence into oblivion. I saw my life with a new clarity.

The magazine could easily replace me. My children have only one mother. "Having it all" is an absurd concept after fighting for your life. My new definition of "all" was simpler: being healthy. Spending more time at home, to give my children an extra measure of comfort and security, was worth more than any salary. After my brush with death, the hours spent away from my kids seemed too much to sacrifice. They had gotten used to having me around during the day, and I had gotten used to being around. Even in my diminished state, my children preferred a bald, nauseous mother, home all day, to a healthy mother who went to work. This was hard to ignore.

Also, cancer had released my inner hedonism. My new mantra was "Life is short; live for today; it's all you've got." I felt pretty damn entitled. For a while I bought the expensive version of everything. Chanel makeup. Monthly full-body massages. Hardback books at twenty-five dollars a pop instead of waiting for the paperback.

I stuck it out at the office for a year. I quit on a day like all my other workdays. It really wasn't a difficult decision, even if it was based on a faulty premise: that my days were numbered. I wanted to spend my remaining time with my family and friends, not my new, irritating coworkers. My underlying assumption, however, was correct: Enjoy each day. Make the most of it. It's all anyone has, cancer or not. It's the human condition. My close call, decades before confronting mortality was penciled into my Filofax, proved the catalyst I had lacked.

Anyway, I had a plan, or more like a fantasy. I wouldn't give up my career, just slow it down by becoming a freelance writer and editor. I'd work until my children came home. I'd greet them with milk and cookies and ferry them to dance and soccer and piano. They'd tell me about their day. I'd prepare home-cooked dinners, and we would linger at the table, with plenty of time to spare for homework.

Another part of the dream was to finish the half-written novel I'd been dickering around with for years and get it published. When it became a bestseller, all the lost income from my magazine job would magically be restored to the family coffers. My husband rolled his eyes at that last part but signed on for the plan, provided we cut back our spending to reflect my new lack of income. We're still working on that one. I gave up my Chanel makeup but not much else.

There were humbling aspects to my new life. Children, mine included, can be noisy, messy, stubborn. The bickering, the endless demands for rides and snacks, brought on intense longings for the peace of my old office. I'm patient, up to a point, which usually coincides with ten minutes before my husband gets home from work. He strides in, briefcase in hand, at eight in the evening, with Gandhi-like calm, and wonders why I am losing it.

Outside of my home, I noticed that I got less respect from strangers. After decades of feeling superior to women who answered the eternal D.C. cocktail-party query with "I'm home with my kids" or "I work part-time from home," I was now on the receiving end of the snobbery. People would flee from my side, looking for someone else to talk to, someone with a better job with more promising networking opportunities.

"Instead of going to school, do you want to go to Daddy's office tomorrow for Take Your Daughter to Work Day?" I asked Lily.

She considered it for a moment, weighing the opportunity to miss school against the memory of last year's program of guest speakers and workshops, which she deemed kind of boring.

She offered an alternative. "Why don't I go to your work tomorrow? I can stay in my pajamas, lie on the couch in the study, and read magazines all day."

My daughter's view of my new career—which didn't always require me to be dressed—was funny. But it did give me pause, at least for a few seconds. When you work from home, location is everything. To most of the world, including your loved ones, you look like an impostor.

My kids barely notice that I'm still a working mom because I no longer wear pantyhose or rush around like a speed freak. Since I've "retired"—as my brother once called it—I've written a novel, started two others, had scores of articles published in national magazines, and taught journalism at three universities. Yet I often feel slothful compared with the years when I worked harder and longer and earned more. Novelist Anne Tyler, author of more than a dozen books and recipient of a Pulitzer Prize, once wrote that when she picked up her children after school, she was asked by another parent: "You still just writing?" Working at home and only on projects of my choosing has been so liberating, I feel almost fraudulent. Maybe I'm mistaking a hobby for my so-called career. After all, what kind of career would allow me to spend lots of time with my children, go to the gym every morning, and ride around in my convertible because it's a beautiful day?

It's been eight years since I quit my job. I've never looked back. My husband has glanced back, usually with a calculator in one hand and a stack of mortgage and orthodontia bills in the other. He misses my paycheck and I do too. When I had a steady one and I wanted something, I usually bought it. Now I can't. Or if I do buy it, I feel guilty. This is a new feeling and I don't like it. My novel was published, but it was no cash cow. For me, it's a choice between working more and earning more or working less and enjoying life more. I haven't cracked how to do both.

While I'm feeling a lot more relaxed with the new world order, my husband is developing an ulcer. As I've made abundantly clear to him and anyone else who asks, I hope never again to work full-time in an office. I hate to sound like Dr. Laura, or some other antifeminist throwback, but our household runs more smoothly with me at home to pick up the slack and the dry cleaning and the groceries. It makes more sense for me to run the household because my husband tends not to focus much on domestic details.

For example, I don't share his liberal view of dinner—a bowl of dry cereal is fine if the cupboards are bare. When our children were little, I always removed their sneakers before putting them to bed for the night—a detail he once overlooked when I was out of town. And, sure, he was overtired that time he forgot Lily was asleep in her seat in the unlocked car while he ran into CVS.

It takes a strong ego to stay home with your kids. Motherhood is, in many ways, a dead-end job. Do it right, your kids leave home, you're redundant. There's no external validation, no pats on the back or annual raises. No one invites you onto their radio or TV show for a chat. What I do at home, the things that benefit my kids or my husband, are largely invisible to them. No one thanks me for cleaning out the bookshelves or making healthy dinners or driving them everywhere. My daughters are thirteen and seventeen, and they're doing great. I like to think that my being around so much during their formative years, a constant reliable presence (rather than a nagging banshee), has contributed to their well-being. But I can't prove it.

Every so often I get offered a job that would take me out of the house and into an office. When I ask my children about how they would feel if I weren't around so much, the conversation usually goes something like this:

"Would we have more money to spend?" asks Lily, sounding enthusiastic.

"Whatever," says Ariel, already bored. "But how will I get to dance class?"

With one foot in each camp, I still identify with the mothers who work. I've also had years to observe the school-yard mothers up close. I was wrong about a few things. The inner peace I used to attribute to them may have been an illusion. Some of them are great mothers; some aren't. The same goes for working mothers. Personality, temperament, values, and wisdom are more reliable indicators of maternal ability than whether a mom works or not.

Being home doesn't always translate into being with your kids. Some at-home moms spend as much time at the gym, at the hairdresser, or on other hobbies as they do with their children. Or they're home but emotionally distant. Then there are those who could do with some distance, those "helicopter moms" who hover over their children twenty-four hours a day, micromanaging their worlds, turning the elementary school play into auditions for Juilliard or Saturday soccer into the pre-Olympics.

What makes someone a good mother is purely subjective, and largely the province of the subject's children. It's a good thing I don't think of being home as a noble sacrifice I made for my children. Today, my two teenage girls, absorbed in their social lives and schoolwork, are likely to describe me as the stupidest person in the universe. They couldn't care less where I am, as long as I'm available to be their personal ATM/driver/cook. Staying home was my choice. I did it for me, not for them.

I'm standing at a podium in a room filled with women, most of them a decade or so younger than me. They're former professionals now at home with their children. Once a month they invite a speaker to address their group. I read an excerpt from my novel, talk about being a Washington journalist, and answer all kinds of questions. I'm no parenting expert, but they seem eager for advice.

"What's the most important quality you need to be a good mother?" asks one earnest woman, visibly pregnant.

I answer, without hesitation: "A driver's license."

My mother used to say that her proudest accomplishment was her four children. For years, but especially as a teenager, I would cringe every time I heard this remark. "The poor woman needs to get a life," I'd think.

In hindsight, I realize I couldn't understand what my mother meant until I became a mother myself. My mother wasn't devaluing her other notable accomplishments as a talented, dedicated teacher, or as a loving wife (she remarried, very happily, eight years after my father's death). She was expressing a simple truth: There is no greater joy in life than your children.

The feeling is not universal among parents. Others might find their greatest joy elsewhere—at the office or on the golf course. But I'm like my mother, at least in that sense. My children are the whole ball game. Nothing I do is ever going to be as important as being their mother. Which doesn't necessarily make me the best mother in the world. Or even a good mother.

But am I good enough? I hope so.

In some ways, my children and I have come full circle. They've grown into interesting young women. We like many of the same things: hanging around bookstores, coffee shops, and beaches. Going to the movies and out to eat. Curling up on the couch with a book or TV show. But here's the paradox: Now that I can't get enough of them, they can't get enough of their friends. I've seen their future, and I'm being phased out.

Which isn't necessarily bad. I can always work more when my kids move away from home. Or not. I've noticed that the older I get, the less ambition I have. My work, while important, doesn't mean as much to me as enjoying my daily life.

One of my friends quit a similar job when I did, also to freelance and spend more time with her daughter. She speaks longingly, at times, about the prestige of her old job. Another friend, with children the same age as mine, had her own horrific cancer experience. Now back at work, she took a promotion that involved extensive international travel. She couldn't be happier. These women are among my closest friends. As far as I can tell, all moms, working or not, inhabit their own personal planets.

On my planet, I'm not sure what the future holds. If there's one thing I've learned, it's that I constantly have to adapt to shifting circumstances. I'm always searching for the perfect balance between work and my family. I've discovered that I probably will never lock in to that elusive perfection. What I have found, though, brings me a certain satisfaction, most of the time. And for me, that's good enough.

Big House, Little House,
Back House, Barn

Lois R. Shea

Lois R. Shea is an award-winning journalist and former *Boston Globe* staff writer. Her essay chronicling a mommies' road trip to a Bruce Springsteen concert won the 2004 Public Radio News Directors' first place award for commentary. She lives on a mountainside in New Hampshire with her husband and daughter.

was in a journalistic crisis. So I called Shirley.

Shirley is nearly two generations older than I am. She went to Capitol Hill as a reporter for *The Washington Star* during the Johnson administration and stayed through five presidents, one war, three political assassinations, the triumph of the Voting Rights Act, and repeated failures of the Equal Rights Amendment. She worked her way into the upper echelons of the *Star* when most women in the newsroom were relegated to the ladies' page. During the upward trajectory of her career, she was not married, nor did she care to be. In those years, she said, men wanted their wives home making babies and casseroles. She intended to make neither. She intended to cover Congress. She has neither children nor regrets.

I was all of twenty-nine—still fairly green and young and slightly stunned at having scored a staff writer's job at *The Boston Globe*. Shirley had retired to New England by then, but retirement didn't take; she still wrote occasional stories for the *Globe* and had taken me, for whatever lucky reason, under her journalistic wing.

Six years later a book project landed in my lap, and I was agonizing. The book represented the opportunity to work with a nationally renowned sociologist and author, to break into a whole new world of letters and publishing. It also represented a crushing deadline, frequent meetings in Boston (a two-hour drive from home), and a series of weeklong stints in places as far-flung as Chicago and Southern California.

I had recently left the *Globe* so I could devote more of myself to parenting—my daughter, Fiona, was five at the time—and (ludicrous as it seems in hindsight) I was actually considering taking on the book project. I was thirty-five, suffering with this notion that if I didn't do this book thing RIGHT NOW, TODAY, THIS MINUTE, *the opportunity may never come again! I would lose out! Be left behind! Even worse: Waste my talent!!*

Shirley listened, paused briefly, and said: "You can write a book when Fiona's in college."

I had never considered that.

I was still operating in the imperative.

The concept of you could do that *later,* that there will be time *later,* had literally never occurred to me.

Shirley's perfect sentence comes back to me every single day. *You can write a book when Fiona's in college.*

My imperatives have shifted.

In rural New Hampshire, winters are long, "downtown" means four stores and the post office, and municipal business is still conducted at town meeting. My town of 2,883 has a high measure of what sociologists call social capital: those connections that make communities safer, people healthier, and democracies vibrant. The town clerk calls to remind me to renew my dog's $6.50 license, the bookstore holds barn dances, we still vote on paper ballots, and you hardly ever see a NO TRESPASSING sign. It's still possible to know one another out here.

I live on the side of a mountain on one parcel of a historic hill farm, far enough up that we can watch the sun rise through the trees on the eastern horizon and set again over Mount Sunapee and the western hills. Out here, it still feels sometimes possible to retreat from the passage of time.

In northern New England, traditional house construction goes like this: big house, little house, back house, barn. The buildings are all attached, the better not to have to trudge through a January blizzard to fill the wood box or feed the sheep. Additions are built when babies are born or in-laws show up; woodsheds are added and subtracted, porches tacked on, mudrooms expanded. When houses are cobbled together until they bear no identifiable style—cape, say, or Georgian—we call them "New Englanders."

My life is cobbled together in much the same way now: paid work and unpaid work, teaching fractions by making pancakes, writing for radio and for magazines, teaching geography while baking apple pies, doing communications work for charitable and environmental groups, attempting to gather a book's worth of essays, caring for my daughter through a bout of the chicken pox. It's a New Englander.

When people ask me how it's going, I say: "Well, now I can arrange my work around my life . . . instead of arranging my life around my work." This makes people, especially other moms, envious. I don't mean it to, but it does.

I am told that in places like Manhattan and Connecticut (and among women who reside in a higher tax bracket than I do) working moms and stay-at-home moms are pitted against one another as fiercely as the Red Sox and Yankees in a late-September pennant race. Out here, those tensions seem less apparent.

In these little towns, identity is not all about how you earn money. "And what do you *do*?" is not always the second question people ask. I have stood around maple-sap evaporators with people for many Marches without learning how others sharing that sweet steam earned a living. I am (and was, even when I worked full-time) best known in my town as the pitcher on the women's softball team, a passionate Red Sox fan, and Coach Shea of the nine- and ten-year-olds' softball team.

Part of the reason for the egalitarian social order, I'm sure, is linked to town meeting, our late-winter act of ritual democracy. At town meeting, where we get together to debate and decide the town's business for the year (Should we buy a new fire truck? Do we really need to pave Bean Road?), the road agent's opinion holds as much or more sway than the lawyer's. How you make money, or how much you make, matters little. No Ivy League school ever handed out a degree in regular old common sense.

In higher-power pockets in New Hampshire—the larger cities and towns where social strata are built almost entirely on career—the second question people ask is *always* what you do for a living, and the reply "I stay home with my kids" gives you social cooties. But in this rural New Englander life, with its not-so-distant agricultural past, being home doesn't mean not working. It means quite the opposite: cutting wood and feeding chickens and mending fence and the ten thousand other tasks that a rural homestead demands.

Our house is part of what had been a much larger farm. The shorn-off parcel we own includes the hired man's cabin (an expanded version of which we now occupy), a section of the old orchard, and a couple of outbuildings. Taking care of even this small chunk of historic farm is no small task. Those outbuildings need roofs, and the brush grows back as fast as you can clear it. I yearn to bring the old apple trees back into the light and into production, to convert the small outbuilding into a sugar-house. The woodstove and its insatiable appetite for oak logs must be fed from November to April. Someone literally has to keep the home fires burning. There is always work to do. It is not "practical" in the modern economic sense for me to do that work. I can make more money wielding a pen than a hammer or a chainsaw (and I wield the pen with greater authority). But there is a satisfaction that transcends practicality in cutting firewood and roofing the barn.

Out here, I have cobbled together a framework of friends and neighbors who live similarly "New Englander" lives. Lauren works as a lawyer some days and stays home others. Kristin sells real estate and works out of her house. Laura, another lawyer, is home raising her two boys and doing unpaid work for Planned Parenthood and for the Coalition Against Domestic Violence. Deborah manages to make Halloween costumes and read bedtime stories and to work a thirty-hour-a-week job, inhabiting that maddening place where her co-workers think of her as "the mom" and her friends think of her as "the worker." Karen is home with her son and does unpaid work at the local school and library. David takes care of his two kids while his wife works as an environmental lawyer.

None of us are of the class of people who could blithely "choose" not to work. Women on both sides of my family have been in the workforce as far back as anyone can recall—many of them stepping off the boat from County Cork and directly into Massachusetts textile mills. They worked in bakeries and schools and offices and hospitals and supported their families through the Great Depression.

I have more choices than they did, but I sure as heck don't have a trust fund. For most of us, the paid work we do pays the mortgage. For some of us, the salary cut has cut very deep. (A journalism professor from my alma mater invited me to take part in a symposium on "How to Survive as a Freelancer." The best advice I could think of was: "Be married to someone with health insurance.")

We have created a New Englander system of shared child care and pinch-hit parenting. All of us have occasional last-minute demands (a meeting, a deadline, a closing, a postponed hearing, a sick sibling). And when we do, another of us steps in. It's an elaborate bartering system with no real accounting. We all deposit hours parenting one another's kids, we all withdraw hours when we need them. In nine years, I think I have paid for child care twice. The concept is simple, even if the logistics are not. It works pretty well. None of us could make it work alone.

I realize this all operates smoothly because our lives and work fit similar patterns.

The system gets clunky when women with different sets of demands and priorities step in. Kristin's unwillingness to say no led her to provide endless hours of child care and shuttle-bus service to a single mom who was working full-time as a lawyer and earning a second degree. Perhaps we are "enabling"—enabling that mother's choices, enabling the corporate beast, enabling the entire freaking patriarchy—by folding those women's kids into this system. Maybe we're just a bunch of weak-kneed, countrified, kid-centered Whole Villagers. But the consensus seems to be: Well, she's trying to do this on her own. And it's not the kid's fault, right? If one of us doesn't help, how can we call ourselves a community? We have all, at one time, had both feet firmly planted in the workforce, so our reaction is less "What a pain in the neck that mom is" than "There but for the grace of God . . ."

Being nonjudgmental, for me, is a learned behavior. And I'm not the world's fastest learner.

One morning in June, I pulled on shorts, a wrinkled T-shirt, and a pair of Tevas and went out to walk the dog. June is the dark heart of bug season in New Hampshire, and the air was uncommonly still. In an effort to retain some portion of our blood, we walked the mountain road instead of the forest trail that circles a wetland.

A car pulled up and its power window buzzed down. A woman I know—a high-powered lawyer whose husband is also a high-powered lawyer—was at the wheel. She was dressed in a crisp suit, her jewelry precise, cellular phone at the ready. Her eight-year-old son sat beside her in the passenger seat, eating breakfast from McDonald's. She was driving him to day camp on her way to work. As we discussed the possibility of a playdate for the kids, her cell phone rang. She cut me off midsentence. "I have to take it," she said. "It's work." She drove up the mountain road talking, her son eating beside her in silence.

And I had many judgmental thoughts: "What the hell is she doing? She doesn't even *have* to work. If *I* felt cut off when her phone rang, how invisible does her kid feel, how secondary to the cell phone? It's *summer,* for Christ's sake. Her kids are getting rushed out the door in the morning *all summer*. That can't be good. *McDonald's?* Yuck."

And had she a moment to think about it, I'm sure she would have driven off with an opposite but equally visceral set of judgments about me: *Isn't she bored? No real job. How irresponsible. They probably can't even save for college. Their house really needs paint. Doesn't she own an iron?*

I often catch myself teetering on a tirade (I'm Irish; tirades are an important part of my heritage) about, say, how rushing kids out the door in July and August robs them of the slow deliciousness of summer. I force myself to stop. And say, instead: "That wouldn't work for me. The way she does it wouldn't work for me. And it wouldn't work for my kid."

Part of that is true. I stand in awe of people who can leave work at the office door. No matter how hard I tried, I was never great at leaving work at work or leaving home comfortably at home. At work, I would long to be with my kid. I would steal ten minutes and type furious entries into her baby journal—attempting to seize and document, from a distance, every detail of her little being. At home I would be preoccupied with work, stressed, unable to be present. There were storybooks I read aloud fifty times that I never really *heard*. I would be silently writing and rewriting about, say, welfare reform while reading *Guess How Much I Love You* aloud. I remember driving home, already later than I should have been, but finally with my daughter and her little pal Iris singing happily in the backseat, when an editor called from the city desk. I had to take it; the local crime story of the day had my name on it. And so I had to call the New Hampshire attorney general, at 65 mph, and attempt to clarify details of a crime with Fiona and Iris in the backseat bellowing "Thunder Road" for all their little lungs were worth.

That didn't work for me.

No matter how hard my editors and supervisors tried to help—and they did try, for which I will be forever grateful—I could not strike a balance that worked for me. Fiona would not do well going from camp to camp to camp all summer. She would not be happy in after-school care. If she had afternoon activities stacked like cordwood—ballet and swimming and soccer and drama—she would be an overtired little wretch. Some kids thrive on this stuff. (David's, for instance.) Mine doesn't.

And, yeah, "That wouldn't work for me" is also sometimes part code. Laura knows that when I say "That wouldn't work for me" it's a safe bet that what I mean, at least in part, is "I think she's nuts for doing it that way." But here's what is also true about the lawyer on the cell phone: Her son is a wonderful, smart, engaged, and kind little person. He seems to benefit from time spent with his parents. He doesn't seem stressed out. The family can afford a nanny, one they have chosen very carefully. And I'm sure their college savings fund is already equal to an Ivy League price tag.

My daughter is also a smart, kind, engaged-with-the-world little person. She benefits from time spent with her parents. She's not stressed out. She gets plenty of fresh air and exercise. She knows that her mom is available. When it comes to college, we may have to drop back and punt. That last bit gets scary.

I'm learning, if slowly. More often, "That wouldn't work for me" masks a shrug, not a tirade. Sometimes there's genuine awe added in— awe at another mother's ability to rise at four-thirty, exercise, get her clothes on frontward, take the kids to school, work all day at something as consuming as lawyering, manage to be present for her kids in the evenings—and not have huge black bags under her eyes. That wouldn't work for me. But if it works for her and for her kid—well, great.

In Shirley's generation, my mother's generation, there were two models: Women worked or stayed home. Women who worked, it seems, often looked down their noses at women who stayed home. My father used to rail about a friend who had earned a master's degree—but had chosen to stay home and raise her three kids. "What a waste of a college degree," he would say. "What a waste of intellect." This was the 1970s, and I'm sure my dad was fumbling around in the new social order, trying to help raise a strong, independent daughter—and using his friend as an example of how not to be.

Though my dad has since revised his stance, plenty of people still hold that view.

Fiona was five months old, riding high in my backpack while we did errands in the state capitol. We ran into a friend on Main Street. He asked if I was eager to go back to work. I loved my work, but I was not particularly eager to go back. "I could stay home with my kid," I said, "and be perfectly content in the knowledge that I make an excellent grilled-cheese sandwich."

I might as well have been speaking Croatian. He smiled faintly and gave me one of those looks like a dog does when it hears a sound it can't identify—head cocked sideways, baffled. The conversation ended there.

But in our generation the two models—the full-time worker and the full-time grilled-cheese-perfecting mother—are just opposite end posts on a spectrum. Nearly every woman I know has created a life that falls somewhere in between.

There is no model for this. There isn't even a decent set of instructions. We're flying blind, gang. Making it up as we go along. We're creating a menu of options from which I hope our daughters and sons will be able to choose when they come of age. It's a major feat of social engineering without a blueprint. So you'd think we'd be a little easier on ourselves. Maybe even a *tiny little bit* self-congratulatory. But we are relentlessly self-critical.

I work at home. Why the hell can't I find time to paint the house? So I did cut and haul a winter's worth of firewood, and that's pretty good, but the bathrooms are dirty! The kitchen-floor crud is fossilized. Am I some kind of slacker, practicing for the dole? What's wrong with me?

We have an awful tendency to see our own failings as mothers—real or not—in one another's strengths. Deborah calls this phenomenon, only half-jokingly, the inner "you stink" voice. When Deborah arrives at school one morning before work with a basket of hot muffins, I think, "What a great, nurturing mom—but how the hell did she find time to bake muffins this morning? And she has more than one kid and she clearly ironed her clothes. What's wrong with me? I put on dryer-rumpled blue jeans straight from the laundry basket and sure as hell didn't bake muffins. You stink. You stink."

Deborah reads an article I've written about a trip I took with my daughter to Monhegan Island in Maine to build fairy houses. She sighs and thinks, "She's such a great mom. I wish I did things like that with my kid. You stink. You stink."

David's upright freezer is filled with organic, local produce that he put up all summer long. Deborah opens the freezer and thinks, "If I made different choices, if I were more efficient with my time, we could have frozen edamame beans too, and be eating better all winter. You stink."

Karen has created a life for her son that is comfortable and safe. In which adventure and strength and compassion and kindness are equally valued. In which there is time for reflection and silliness and Mom has time for Cub Scouts and to cook a good supper and just *be* there. Her ten-year-old son is empathic, strong, fun, and really smart. The kind of boy a feminist would approve of for her daughter. But Karen worries that by modeling "traditional" gender roles, by giving up her professional identity, she is being a bad feminist. *You stink.*

When I worked in newspapers as a news and feature writer, I never faulted myself for not being the best business writer or the best editorial writer or best film critic at my paper. None of that was what I *did.* None of it was my area of expertise. But I do fault myself for not being as able to take on as much as Deborah does, for not being as good at art projects as Lauren. For not being as calm as Karen, as freewheeling as Kristin, as mindful as Laura. *You stink. You stink. Stink. Stink.*

This is brutal stuff.

One August day, while sitting on my front porch, Laura and I made a pact.

She was surprised to hear how much I admired her parenting skills. I was surprised to hear how much she admired mine. Neither of us had ever said so—despite the fact that we met when our nine-year-olds were infants. We agreed, from that point on, to compliment each other's work as parents, as specifically and as often as we could. And to ask each other for feedback as often as we needed to.

And then we promptly didn't.

Every member of my mommy group (David being an honorary mommy) was once a full-time professional. We all used to go to those annual awards dinners—the Press Association, the Bar Association, the Realtors Association. The troops would chow down on appetizers; the dignitaries would make speeches and hand out awards. It was a tedious business undertaken in uncomfortable shoes. But maybe it was more important than we realized.

There is no Mommy Association to hand out annual awards. When your primary work is parenting, your peers (never mind your kids or spouse) rarely find ways—formal or informal—to articulate admiration for your work. There is no regular feedback, no "Hey, nice work today" from a boss or colleague. There is also no definition to the workday. It starts when you wake and ends when you sleep. You are on call 24/7, with no bonus or comp time.

We don't compliment parenting, I suppose, because parenting is supposed to be an innate skill, like breathing or digesting food. You should be rewarded for knowing how to breathe?

Maybe we need something as colossally contrived as Mommy Association Awards. We could give out awards for patience, for explaining complexities, for being the best at hauling kids up mountains and teaching them the names of flowers, or at encouraging kids to do artwork. It could turn into a *Saturday Night Live*–style farce (best mac-and-cheese cook, best snot wiper, best car-pool driver). But maybe it's an important exercise. Maybe if we had those trinkets of peer admiration, we'd be less likely to see our failings in one another's strengths. Maybe we'd be reminded, in our moments of self-doubt and struggle, that we're really damn good at what we do. Maybe we'd be reminded that the project we have taken on takes creativity, and brains, and guts—and an ego either so huge or so modest and secure that it can be sated with a perfect grilled-cheese sandwich.

Sometimes this "new social order" my friends and I are creating looks, well, suspiciously prefeminist. And sometimes that makes us edgy. Okay, more than sometimes.

Laura had to go to New York, so her boys came home with us. The kids were playing Lincoln Logs happily by the fire, the sun was setting over the western hills, pumpkin soup was simmering on the stove. I had worked on a radio essay while the kids were in school and had picked them up at three. The dads were still working in Concord. When they came through the door in tandem and sat down to supper, Laura's husband, Mark, thanked me almost sheepishly. "You didn't need to feed us," he said, in a way that both apologized for my apron and asserted his own ability to make pizza.

I knew I didn't *have* to feed them. But let's see . . . two of the three available adults were stuck working in offices twenty miles away until at least five-thirty. One of the adults was home with the three kids. And all six of these people needed to eat. So the adult at home with time available and access to the kitchen would, what, not cook? That just seems stupid to me.

A newspaper publisher I know called the other day—a perfectly amiable guy, and a righteously unapologetic social conservative. He asked what I was doing, and I launched into my hyphenated litany, wrapping up with my oft-recited phrase about being able to arrange my work around my life instead of my life around my work.

And he said: "Lois, what you're doing is not only good for your daughter—it's good for the country!"

Which sounded to me an awful lot like: Women belong in the home, and I knew you'd see it my way eventually.

My husband is still getting mileage out of that one.

"*Lois Shea,*" he proclaims in the tone of a political ad announcer: "*Good for the country!*"

The fact is, though, it is good at least for the kids in my town—if not for the state of our union—that I am available to coach Little League. It is good for the country that David had time to help John Kerry win New Hampshire in 2004. It's good that Laura has time to help combat domestic violence; that Karen helps keep the library running. It is also good for the country that we are all making some version of the same value statement: Kids matter, and the work of raising them is a good use of our energy and intellect and, yeah, our multiple college degrees. My instincts are more maternal than patriotic on this. But our country can use whatever help it can get. Are we *better* for the country than the women—like my friend on the cell phone—who work full-time in boardrooms and operating rooms and newsrooms and universities and government? *Of bloody course not.*

Here is my admittedly utopian definition of feminism: self-determination for women. I am doing exactly what I want to be doing in this fleeting chapter of life that includes my daughter's childhood. I am lucky enough to have the support of a partner who helps make this life possible; lucky enough to have a trade that I can ply sans pantyhose and independent of the nine-to-five world.

Plus, it's good for the country.

The other day I took an old oil lamp down from a high shelf. It is a favorite thing of mine, a gift from my mother. I used to light it in the kitchen when the days grew short. My kitchen is tiny and cramped, with warped countertops, chipped floor tiles, and cabinets that somebody built on the cheap around 1945. The oil lamp throws a circle of light wide enough and bright enough to eat by, a circle that relegates clutter to the shadows, in which everything appears golden and warm, softened of its twenty-first-century edge.

I remember the day I put the lamp away. Fiona was an infant, swaddled, asleep in a cradle. I put it up high on a deep shelf, far from where a curious toddler might reach it. I remember thinking that day—a little sadly, because I would miss that warm light—that I would probably not take the lamp down again until Fiona was well beyond the perils of toddlerhood.

That day was nine years ago. *Nine years* have gone by, a full half of the time that Fiona can reasonably be expected to live with us.

And I thought, again, of Shirley.

I will write that book when Fiona's in college.

That works for me.

What Goes Unsaid

Sydney Trent

Sydney Trent is deputy editor of *The Washington Post Maga-zine*. Her essays and articles have appeared in *The Washington Post, The Miami Herald,* and *The Philadelphia Inquirer.* She lives in Maryland with her husband and two young daughters. An active volunteer in her daughters' school, she is secretary of the board of the parent-teacher organization and chairs the annual fund-raising committee. Here she tackles the subter-ranean tensions between career and stay-at-home moms, through the lens of an African American working mom who married into a traditional middle-class white family.

I send out the invitations, pretty little pastel butterfly cutouts beckoning the cousins to a tea party during our vacation at the beach. "Fancy dress welcome," I pen on the bottom. Their mothers reply quickly and with enthusiasm, and the show is on.

On the appointed day in June, my husband and I, our two daughters, and my mother arrive at our rented beach house on the coast near Charleston. We leave our girls with my mother, and I drag my husband, Bruce, to the local Target to look for just the right tea-party accoutrements. To my dismay, there are no children's tea sets to be found. I begin to mull the grown-up china, and Bruce looks at me wearily. "Sydney, they're *children*," he says.

In the end, I have to agree that china would be foolish for a group of mostly toddlers. And besides, wouldn't that immediately peg me as a clueless working mom? About an hour and seventy-five dollars later, we emerge with four thick plastic Disney Princess plates for the girls and one Clifford plate for the two-year-old boy, matching cups and napkins, several festive fuchsia plastic bowls to hold the appetizers, and a generous party favor for each small guest.

A couple of hours before the party, my five-year-old daughter, Alexandra, and I get to work on making the main course: sugar cookies from scratch and cut in the shape of large circus animals. This mostly consists of my fussing at Alex, as follows:

"Honey, please don't eat the flour."

"Stop eating the sugar, sweetie."

"Alex, if you keep eating the butter, the cookies aren't going to taste good."

"Alex, you're getting the sprinkles all over the place."

I repeat it, with a smile. Then without smile. And again, with clenched jaw. All along I'm thinking that another, cheerier, more patient, and undoubtedly stay-at-home mother would smoothly engineer it without the edge in her voice.

Alex stuffs herself on leftover dough and, now bored, goes off to shimmy into her princess dress. I shove the cookies into the oven and survey the room. The table is set with the Disney Princess and Cliffordware. The scattered fuchsia bowls brim with Goldfish and strawberries. The gifts are swathed in cheery paper. My mother cradles our nine-month-old daughter, Olivia, on the couch.

Bruce is right: This *is* a lot of effort for a bunch of kids. And why am I so nervous, anyway?

Of course, I *know* why. It isn't the children I'm trying to impress. It's their mothers and grandmother, that close-knit clutch of traditional women I call my in-laws.

I'd been nervously awaiting this trip since my sister-in-law Carole* suggested a family reunion at the beach with her husband, their two daughters and four grandchildren. Many years ago, the beach reunions had been grand affairs filling a luxurious rented house on the Outer Banks of North Carolina. Family tensions gradually eroded enthusiasm for the gatherings and after a few years halted them altogether. But Carole and I still hoped to get at least some of the clan together during vacation. Last summer, as the others gradually opted out, we went ahead with our mini-reunion. Bruce, my mother, the girls, and I had spent a delightful week at the Wild Dunes resort on the Isle of Palms the year before, and so we booked the same house, and another for Carole and Co. nearby. My love of family gatherings eclipsed my reservations at first— but as the vacation approached, my anxieties began to take over.

You see, Carole and I are very different. That's partly, although not entirely, because she is white and I am African American. But it's not as simple as a lot of people seem to imagine.

Nobody denounced the relationship when Bruce and I started dating eighteen years ago. No one refused to attend our wedding five years later. In fact, our families have shown an enduring fondness for one another, and the memories of them mingling are some of my most treasured. Why

*Some of the names in this essay have been changed.

should this be so unexpected between two middle-class families from eastern suburbs who mostly share the same politics and social values?

When Bruce and I were dating and during the early part of our marriage, Carole and I hit it off. I was twenty-four when we met, and she was almost forty, but she is the most outgoing of Bruce's three sisters. I basked in her ebullient good cheer and found her easy to talk to. During those early vacations to the Outer Banks, she'd confide in me about how hard her husband worked and the challenges of raising Melissa, then a smart and serious teenager, and Jennifer, three years younger and as extroverted and fearless as her mother.

Years passed. At Melissa's wedding, long after the reunions stopped, Carole pressed a ring of rough-cut diamonds into my hand. She told me she loved me. The ring was, as it turned out, a family heirloom more than two centuries old.

I now think of that unexpected act of generosity as a symbol of our relationship at its best. It was before I became a mother and kept forging ahead full-time with my work as a journalist. And before Carole became a grandmother and encouraged her daughters to stay at home as she had. The stay-at-home way of life had been advocated by Bruce and Carole's mother, whom Carole told me once chided her for even considering part-time work after she had children. I've since felt Carole has eyed me somewhat suspiciously, almost as though I were a female of a different species. Why else would she ask me whether I attend my daughter's tee-ball games, or suggest that my mother does more for my children than I do?

Of course, I knew when I married Bruce that his childhood had been, in many ways, the mirror opposite of mine. My mother, a divorced social worker, moonlighted selling handbags at Bloomingdale's to keep us going. I'd let myself into our apartment after school and pretty much roam unsupervised wherever I wished. His mother stayed at home with her five children, and their house was a happy Grand Central for all the neighborhood. In the evening when his father, a railroad executive, returned to the family's large stone home in an affluent Philadelphia suburb, his mom would put a steaming meal on the dining room table and they'd all gather in what I imagine was Rockwellian splendor.

No doubt the idea of joining that perfect portrait of an American family was part of what attracted me to Bruce. I still maintain that there was much that united us that had little to do with race. But years later

I've also come to see that the difference between his upbringing with a stay-at-home mom and mine with a doubly employed mother had as much to do with race as anything. As well as the tension I felt develop between Carole and me once I became a working mother myself.

After nervously inspecting my handiwork at the beach house, I join my mother on the couch. Alex, in her dress of peach tulle and ivory velvet and her white plastic heels, keeps peering out the window to catch the cousins' arrival. "Mommy, when are they going to get here?" she asks.

"Any minute now," I reply.

A minute later she says: "They're never going to get here, Mommy!" An interminable few minutes later, she shrieks, "Mommy! They're here! They're heeere!"

Now I can see them through the blinds too, four tiny cousins and their parents traipsing down the driveway. Bruce grabs the video camera and starts chronicling the procession. Jennifer and Melissa's older girls, both three, totter in their play satin and plastic heels. Bobbing after them are their baby brother and sister. Their thirty-something parents, Carole's grown children, trail respectfully behind.

Peppy and outgoing Jennifer exclaims appreciatively over my elaborate handiwork. The more reserved Melissa seems somewhat taken aback. "Wow," she says.

Something in her voice makes me begin to wonder if this whole effort isn't subliminally trumpeting "This working mom is in desperate need of affirmation!" An hour later, amid cookies and Goldfish and strawberries selectively eaten in that small-child way, gifts torn open and wrapping paper decorating the floor, the procession returns to whence it came. Not one to let the lack of an invitation interfere with fun, Alex wastes no time in joining the cousins at their house.

A couple of hours later, when I arrive to pick up Alex, Carole compliments my sugar-cookie animals. "Did you make these, or did your mother?" she asks.

When I tell other mothers that my mother lives with us during the week to take care of our two children while we work, then goes home on the weekend, I usually get some variation of these responses:

"You don't know how lucky you are!"

"What an ideal arrangement!"

"There's nothing like a relative who loves your children!"

Some working moms are clearly envious about what I've come to think of as my child-care safety hatch. One embittered stay-at-home mom declared acidly: "Well, you just have it all, don't you?" For others, the news seems to provide a kind of endorsement of their own choices: They do what they do because they don't have what I have.

My mother came down to Miami to help after Alex was born, staying until we all moved back north about a year later. Olivia came along about three years after that. My mother is my secret weapon against the daily assaults of life.

Have to work a little late? No problem—Mom will give the kids dinner.

Can't be there when the plumber comes? Mom can.

Another birthday party is looming and you haven't gotten the gift? Mom will pick just the right thing.

She is warm and energetic and loves children, ours most of all. She challenges them intellectually and delights in playing fish or blocks or Sorry and in just about everything they say and do. We are lucky and we know it. But it has sometimes seemed to me that Carole just likes to make sure.

"You are *so* fortunate to have Enid!" she has often said, both when Mom is around and when she's not. "She is *so* wonderful." In the way that women have of saying things without speaking them, and knowing things that go unsaid, I am certain she is really saying: *Your mother is raising your children, and doing all of the things you should be doing.* Hence, "Did you make these or did your mother?"

But despite how long we've known each other, Carole doesn't really know my mother, or me.

She doesn't know that when I've wondered whether I'm doing the right thing by working full-time, my mother has always been there to shore me up. "Do you really think all these women who stay at home have great relationships with their children?" she says. "Some of those kids would be better off if their mother weren't at home with them all the time. A lot of those women are miserable. They're bored out of their minds."

When my mother had her first child in 1957 at twenty-one, she did a very nontraditional thing for a middle-class African American woman:

She stayed home. She'd already graduated from college, and her father had hoped she would continue on to graduate school. She figured that as a military wife it would be hard for her to stay in a job anyway, so she might as well stay home. But she retains many memories of being one of the few stay-at-home mothers among her black peers during those first twelve years of motherhood. There were silent questions about why a woman like her would waste her talents and education, which was seen then, as now, as the Holy Grail that would uplift the race. Of course, most black women did it all because they had to. Black men, if they were hired, did not earn the kind of money that white men did, and black women were compelled to enter the workforce to help support their families. Today we continue to work, mostly out of need but also out of proud tradition and because there is no taboo among blacks against a woman saying that she wants to work, that she likes to work.

When I was about six, my father started running around. My parents stayed together, but my mother figured it was time to enter the workforce so she could leave him if she needed to. Four years and several of my father's affairs later, she did. I often wonder what would have happened to us if my mother hadn't gotten her college degree and begun her career as a social worker. Her work allowed us to rent an apartment in a suburb with good schools, but we almost never ate red meat because it was too expensive. My father paid minimal child support. When we ran out of money we sometimes had to ask for gasoline on credit. The threat of hardship lingered around the edges of our daily lives. We never lived in poverty, but we lived in fear that one day we would. Just as Bruce's mother and Carole had many white, middle-class stay-at-home counterparts, my mother was one of many like her—struggling, single black women trying to do their best by their children. I always knew that like my mother I would work to support myself and my children, whether I was single or not. It never even occurred to me that I would stop working when I had children.

Living as I do between cultures—bicultural, I call myself—I'm privy to it all. My white friends agonize with me over whether their work is damaging their children. My black friends almost never do. As a working mother, I often feel judged by whites and rarely by blacks. I sometimes agonize because I miss my children, and at the same time I hold on to my work for dear life.

I've considered cutting back to part-time and once came so close that I was accepting congratulations. But I couldn't do it. It's about shameless love of work and what I've built over eighteen years. And, yes, it's about money—about having enough for college tuition and retirement and just living. The fear is deep-seated, primal. What if I find myself without a job and my husband loses his and our children live with my childhood fear of a deep plunge with no net?

Later on the day after the tea party, we walk next door to have dinner with Carole and the others. "I'm sure Sydney has to work late a lot," Carole's husband says at one point.

I start to say something.

"Actually, Sydney's almost always home to make dinner since she started working at the magazine," my mother fills in quickly.

It won't be the last time Carole's husband mentions my long work hours. I notice it seems to happen when one or both of his daughters are around. I wonder if he's trying to underscore the wisdom of their choice for them.

Later, as we all sit in the living room, I get the distinct feeling Carole is watching out of the corner of her eye to see whether my baby crawls to me or my mother. Olivia starts to make her way to me, and I give my baby a big smile.

As time goes on, the reunion's center of gravity seems to shift to Carole's house. They don't seek us out much, and when they do it's always on their schedule. Dinner is there, because the house is bigger, which makes sense. But it's always at six. Carole's husband has been conditioned to get hungry at six on the nose and apparently must be indulged. Melissa and Jennifer already have their children in their nighties by then, ready to go to bed at eight. After all, nobody's rushing home from work to get dinner on the table.

My family does not function this way. Bruce and I get home fairly early. We've gotten pretty good at planning meals in advance and putting the meat out to thaw, but we usually don't sit down until after eight. Then we get the girls in their jammies and they're usually sleeping by nine-thirty or ten. It's supremely important to me that they get at least ten hours of shut-eye—no doubt projecting my own desperate need for at least seven—but since Alex doesn't have to get up for school until eight, it works out just fine. I mean, this stuff about kids needing a schedule can be carried too far. Now we're on vacation and flexing the bedtime rules, since the girls can sleep as late as they want to. By the end of the week, we are eating at our house so we can be as loose as we want.

Then one afternoon, unbeknownst to us, Carole organizes a T-shirt-painting session with her grandkids. Alex and I stop by impromptu, and I feel that kind of hurt mixed with anger a mother feels when her child has been left out. I guess the tea party or cookie-baking sessions with Carole's grandkids don't count, I tell myself. So much for my idea of warm family gatherings.

Carole does the right thing and invites Alex to join them. But now I'm feeling that my family and I are being rejected, or at least not embraced, in some significant, unspoken way. And I begin to steam. Later in the week my mother buys T-shirts for all Carole's grandchildren, and I make sure Carole is nearby when I laud my mother's generous spirit. I remember reading once that all manner of selfishness is excused under the banner of focusing on one's family, and it strikes me now as penetratingly true. How many of us don't do for others because we're supposedly saving it for our families? And how valuable is staying at home if you're not teaching your children how much other people (and their feelings) matter?

Let me pause a minute to say that I am objective enough, even in my anger, to realize that I can't be entirely objective. Who can be, walking around in this silent, dark space that is modern motherhood, all of us afraid to speak and unsure if what we perceive is real or imagined? Why *do* I care so much about how they view me and my family? Isn't this ridiculous behavior for a woman who just turned forty and has built a life that really works? Alex and Olivia are turning out just great, happy and sweet and generous and remarkably outgoing. We have a beautiful marriage. And I am crazy about my job as a magazine editor, which is challenging and creative and invigorating.

Why do I care? Why *do* I care?

One slightly overcast but still-warm afternoon, we spread the old brown quilt out on the sand and pitch our sun tent and everyone is there, frolicking in the sand or surf, or reading or walking on the beach. Olivia is in the house for a nap, and I can see Alex out there in her pink Gap swimsuit with her cousins, laughing loudly as they all work on creating a moat of ocean water in the sand. Jennifer is sitting next to me in a beach chair, a floppy hat shielding her freckled face. She asks me how I like my new job.

"It's the best job I've ever had, and the hours are the best too," I tell her.

"That's great," she says, with what sounds like true enthusiasm. Then she tells me how she's earning extra money entering data for the moving company where she used to work. She says the work isn't thrilling but the money is nice. There's no tone of self-belittlement that I sometimes detect from stay-at-home moms when they talk about their paid work or the lack thereof.

"Alex is so great," Jennifer tells me. "She's so outgoing and so good with little kids."

Jennifer strikes me then as comfortable with her decision to stay at home. I feel myself really admiring her for it. I think of my resentment at the way I think my family and I are being treated, and I wonder again how much of this is really about me. Have I been seeing things that aren't really there?

Later in the week, we make dinner plans with Jennifer's sister, Melissa, and her husband. The last time we'd hung out with them was years ago, before they had children. We always liked Melissa's independence, creativity, and dry sense of humor. Tom was her perfect match, smart and funny and open-minded. After marrying, they moved to Tom's native London, where Melissa got a job marketing for a website and Tom began his law career.

At brunch the morning after Jennifer's wedding, it was clear to me that Melissa was struggling with how she would manage a career and children. She kept asking me how I did it. After the first baby came along, she worked part-time from home. I remember her saying to me on the phone that with two children "you have no choice but to quit working." I still had just one at the time, but I thought of my working friends with two kids and how just fine they seemed and how different her experience was from mine. I also wondered how comfortable she would be as a working mom when her mother believed so deeply in staying home, or how happy she'd be staying home because she had so much intellectual energy.

She does not seem very happy at dinner. She doesn't smile much, and there are lots of lulls in the conversation. She talks about a playdate her three-year-old had in which she'd tried to make conversation with the little girl's nanny. Very boring, she says, in fact looking bored at the thought. I tell her that Alex is thrilled to have a baby sister.

"Just watching her, I can see why having a sibling would be good for her," she says. There's an edge there.

"What do you mean?" I counter.

She mumbles something I don't understand, and an awkward silence settles over the table. Has she been scrutinizing my children or my mothering? Later during dinner she asks me how it feels to have children and work full-time. I tell her I love my job but it's hard trying to do so much well. Still, I tell her I feel like I'm managing to do it.

"Really?" she says. Again, an edge, like she thinks I can't be telling the truth.

On the way home, I tell my husband how negative she seemed. I'm not upset or offended; I feel concerned, like a mother. These are such personal decisions, in which we weigh what is right for us and our families, and no one has the right to judge them. Which one of us can't understand that mammalian urge to be with our children, or that terrible missing when we're away? I wonder if Melissa is giving enough consideration to her own needs. Mothers' lives count too. Don't they?

Like the tide, the mood turns later in the week, as though we have fully come into our own as people away on vacation, shedding for a time the burdens of home.

It is another afternoon on the brown beach quilt, the children in the surf looking like a beach artist's watercolor. Melissa confides to me that she is using the photography skills she honed in college to begin taking portraits of children.

"Nobody's paying me," she says, sounding tentative. "I'm mainly just shooting my own kids and my friends' kids. But I'd like to do more."

"That's wonderful," I say. "You're such a good photographer."

That evening at dinner, her father says to all of us, "Melissa is trying to start a children's portraiture business."

What parents don't want to brag about their children? In this work-obsessed culture, it must be hard to boast about your smart daughter's loving decision to stay at home. It occurs to me that everyone is struggling here, trying to justify what we oughtn't need to. I remember my talks with Jennifer and Melissa and my anxiety-ridden tea party and the importance of being comfortable with our choices, and the wearying self-erosion of not.

It's about eight on Friday night, our last night, as Mom, Bruce and I, and the kids settle down to eat out on the screened porch at our cottage. Bruce has popped open a few beers, and we can see the foam on the low waves and hear the faint crash of the surf in the distance. The doorbell rings and it is Melissa and Tom. They've put the kids to bed and have come over to chat. We offer them beers and Melissa talks about the difference between the schools in London and the schools here and how they plan to move back to the States in a few years. Her hair is caught back in a barrette, tendrils spilling around her face, and she looks relaxed, open. They seem younger and more carefree, like they did when we used to go to bars together in the years before all the children arrived.

The next morning, before Carole and her family take off, I invite everybody over for some of my famous buttermilk pancakes. I make seconds, then thirds. After I serve everyone else and prepare to cook my own, I turn to look at my relatives gathered around the kitchen table and close by on the screened porch, sitting and eating and chatting. And I think: Why is it only now, when we are about to say good-bye, that we are finally able to be ourselves? Why can't it always be this way—all of us so close and satisfied, looking into one another's eyes and talking, head on?

I Hate Everybody

Leslie Lehr

Leslie Lehr won the Pirates Alley Faulkner Prize for her first novel, *66 Laps.* She is also the author of *The Long Way Home, Nesting, Welcome to Club Mom, Club Grandma,* and the screenplay for *Heartless,* produced by Santa Monica Pictures in 1997. She grew up in Ohio and now lives in Southern California with her two daughters, a dog, a cat, and a white picket fence in need of painting. Does she really hate everybody? Don't we all sometimes?

The first person I ever hated was a car salesman. My urge to strangle the guy, however, had nothing to do with his job. It was the way he described mine.

I can still feel the California sun blazing through the windows of the Honda dealership that day, half a mile from our cozy starter house in Woodland Hills. This was soon after the birth of my first baby, Juliette. I hadn't gone back to work yet. Since abandoning my Buckeye roots for the University of Southern California film school, I had shimmied up the film ladder to become the West Coast production manager at a busy TV-commercial company, then jumped off into the fire of freelance film production. I had every intention of climbing out of the flames at the top rung to strut down the red carpet for a gold statuette. I even had the perfect Oscar dress: a beaded, backless blue vision I kept wrapped in tissue paper on the top shelf of my bedroom closet.

Confronted with the blank space next to "Occupation" on the car-loan application, I panicked. The word *housewife* flashed to mind. My husband, Jon, checked his watch on the arm cradling our sleeping bundle of joy. The spit-up on the shoulder of his denim shirt was a badge of honor, but breast milk leaking through my blouse was not. I racked my brain for a title to print on the form. In the freelance film business, if you aren't working, you are unemployed. There is no maternity leave, no vacation pay, no guarantee of work after your current job wraps.

When I broke into a sweat, the salesman retrieved his pen, smiled, and scribbled something beneath my signature as if he were doing me a favor. Upside down, I read the words "Domestic Engineer." Before I could respond, my husband passed me the baby and wrote "Daddy" beneath his own name. "It's my proudest title," he said, this Romeo with whom I'd had sex on a balcony overlooking San Tropez.

Juliette started crying.

"Excuse me," I said. I snatched the new car key to jangle in front of her. "Mommy has the higher credit rating."

During the decade that followed, I drove that Honda through winding canyons and crowded freeways with Juliette, and then her sister, Caty Joy, strapped in safely. Every time I turned the key in the ignition I felt infuriated by the world's double standard when it comes to motherhood and work. I still do.

I started hating my husband when Juliette was six months old. Many wives start in the hospital delivery room, so maybe I was a late bloomer. But I had never imagined using *hate* and *husband* in the same sentence.

I first noticed Jon at the end of a long day spent estimating the budget for an upcoming commercial shoot. He was the property assistant, working with a director famous for beer shoots and videos like "I Love L.A." He walked in the door with his petty-cash envelope and took my breath away. On our first date, I learned he was a Vietnam veteran, and that he'd rejected the politics of a cushy studio job to start over as a broom pusher in the art department. While the receptionist screened my soon-to-be-ex-boyfriend's calls, I daydreamed about the movies I could make with this amazing man, movies that would change the world and give me a chance to wear my beaded blue dress.

On my twenty-fifth birthday, Jon surprised me with a set of Winslow Homer prints during a sunset picnic overlooking the Pacific Ocean. I knew he was "the one" the night I overheard him brag to a friend on the phone that he had burned his little black book for a woman who read *The Wall Street Journal*. How many men in the California film industry would reject a casting call of buxom blondes for a flat-chested brunette like me? Over dinner at Chez Jay, a legendary Santa Monica dive, he told me he wanted to "take care of me" and make me "happy for the rest of my life."

I always figured I'd take care of myself, thank you very much. But no one had ever said that before. It struck me as a lovely thought.

Once we were married and the white roses from my bouquet were pressed inside my unused gift of *The Joy of Cooking,* I quit commercial production to work with several film-school friends on a low-budget thriller called *Witchboard*. I felt bad while my former boss searched for a replacement, until two months later when he hired a man at triple my salary. I freelanced on more movies and music videos and wrote screenplays in between.

Life was glamorous and exciting, and I anticipated running Paramount Pictures someday. Sure, I was from Ohio, wasn't related to a soul in Hollywood, and wasn't getting any help from the male buddy system. But I was smart and eager to work eighteen-hour days. A mansion in Malibu seemed inevitable. My husband agreed; he told me so during romantic rendezvous when our schedules brought us both through Memphis or Chicago or once in a while our own apartment.

When you freelance, like all film- and TV-production crews do, jobs last a few days or a few months. Since there are so many people vying for jobs that often change, overlap, or get canceled with little notice, you can't afford to be choosy. "One day chicken, one day feathers," my great-grandfather, Sliding Billy Watson, a vaudevillian from the 1920s, used to say. Unfortunately, I didn't know I had show business in my blood until I started working in Hollywood. I learned the hard way that during production, your life is not your own. For instance, my father flew from Columbus to Los Angeles specifically to meet Jon shortly after we got engaged. Jon was working on a Budweiser beer commercial. The shoot continued through dinner, breakfast, and lunch the next day, then past the departure time of my father's return flight. The two men in my life didn't meet until the night before our wedding.

One rainy January evening when Juliette was six months old, the phone rang in our cottage in the Valley. It was Dave (not his real name—I might need the contact someday), a producer I had worked for before Juliette was born. He knew that while I was pregnant, I had line-produced a million-dollar Dodge truck commercial for a British music-video director on one of Hollywood's largest soundstages. While Juliette slept in her white ruffled bassinet in the pink nursery down the hall, Dave offered me a huge opportunity: to take over a big-budget national commercial campaign for which I'd make two months' salary in twelve days, a real job with a real title for real money. I did have to start at six A.M. the next day, but I'd already stayed home far longer than I'd intended. Jon, who had sworn off movie projects after missing six months of my pregnancy for the Jerry Lee Lewis biopic *Great Balls of Fire* (that's Juliette playing Dennis Quaid and Winona Ryder's baby at seventeen days old), happened to be hired for the same job, so we'd get to work together, too.

Due to the ungodly hour I had to report to work—or rather, have people report to me—the commute to the location in Pasadena would take a mere hour. I called nanny hot lines all over L.A. and lined up three shifts of babysitters (none of whom spoke English or had a car). Then I packed my dusty briefcase and brushed the lint off my black blazer. When Jon heard the fax machine spitting out storyboards and budget forms, he came in from the bedroom and caught the end of my conversation.

When I hung up, he asked me one question. "What would you do if something happened to Juliette while you were away?"

"I would call 911," I said. "What would you do?"

"I would never forgive you," he said.

Fuck you, I wanted to say. Instead I called him a sexist pig and crawled into bed. And stared at our cottage-cheese ceiling for six hours.

My mother, a college professor, was the first woman in our midwestern community to work, so my sister and I were the only kids ruled by a housekeeper. I don't remember spending time with my mother when I was young, except for those nights when my sister and I watched *Laugh-In* on her bed, pretending to understand the jokes while she studied or graded papers. But I didn't resent her work. I waited proudly by the window every night, watching for her Toronado headlights to shine down McCoy Hill. My mother was inspired by Gloria Steinem, who didn't have children—a critical detail—and, it was rumored, was aided by a wealthy boyfriend.

My mother was beautiful and brainy, an early trophy wife. My father loved when people telephoned for Dr. Lehr and we had to ask, "Which one?" After grueling years spent earning her doctorate in child development, publishing excerpts of her thesis in *TV Guide* and *McCall's,* and teaching at Ohio State University, my mother quit work and fired the housekeeper so she could stay home with my sister and me. My father promptly rehired the housekeeper and got my mother's job back for her.

Frustrated, my mother called her father long-distance for advice.

"Obey your husband," my grandfather said.

So she did. In the early 1970s, even a working mother lacked the power to make her own choices.

Not only was my mom the first career woman in our neighborhood, she was also the first to be divorced—and it wasn't from a desire to be liberated. That was my father's idea. Divorce was so appalling back then that some friends weren't allowed to play at my "broken home." My mother's modest income somehow proved to the Ohio family court that she didn't need alimony, so now she had no choice; she had to work.

Mom was an amazing role model. I spent my childhood counting her Teacher of the Year certificates, watching her local TV talk-show appearances, and polishing her plaques from Planned Parenthood. As far as I could tell, staying home was for wimps.

Naturally, I figured I would follow in my mother's high heels and my kids would have a housekeeper, too. But I fell in love with the wrong industry—a business so competitive you have to work for peanuts until you really make it. Despite my growing résumé, I hadn't quite made it. Peanuts couldn't cover a housekeeper or decent day care, and on-site child care barely existed even for studio executives, and certainly not for freelance producers like me.

That night, after Dave's call, I lay in bed for hours, as far across the mattress from my pigheaded husband as possible without risking a fall off the bed. He snored blissfully while I debated my options. Like most women who grew up in the shadow of divorce—and that means most women of childbearing age—I knew better than to rely on a man for the mortgage, no matter what he said while courting. It was far safer to be strong, to protect myself from heartbreak and handouts. I could take care of myself, dammit. I certainly intended to.

Then the baby cried.

I ran down the slippery hall to the pink room with fluffy lambs on the wallpaper border and rocked Juliette until she slept. Sure, I could take care of myself. But who would take care of my baby? My maternal instinct crystallized my lack of faith in men, my lack of faith in Uncle Sam for not offering child care or help finding any, and my lack of faith in those early feminists who forgot the profound reason why we could never be truly equal. Thanks to reproductive science, women can now be more than equal: We can take the test tube and run. Yet motherhood's basic issue remains unresolved: Who can our children count on?

I kept rocking, listening to the rise and fall of Juliette's soft breath. I imagined her rolling off the changing table and cracking her head on the wooden floor while I was gone. In my mind, I knew it wouldn't be my fault. In my heart, I was sick. I didn't care whether my husband would forgive me; I would never forgive myself.

After carrying her so carefully for nine long and nauseous months, how could I abandon her so quickly? It began raining harder outside the eyelet curtains. Juliette woke up, so I unbuttoned the top of my flowered nightgown. She latched on and sucked at my breast, watching me, so serious, with her big brown eyes, as if to see what I would do. I would find the umbrella in the garage, I thought, and leave early for Pasadena to avoid the rainy-day traffic. Then she wrapped her little fingers around my thumb and held on.

When dawn broke I called Dave and bailed out of the job. He was angry, not only that I left him without a key player on short notice, but also at me, personally. We had worked together before I was married and several times since. He had spent many hours teaching me his computer program for budget estimates; now he would have to train someone new. Plus, he respected me. He fully expected me to produce Oscar-winning movies one day, not to crawl along the mommy track after producing one measly little baby.

I understood completely. I felt the same way. My beaded blue dress was still wrapped in tissue, on the top shelf of my bedroom closet. But Juliette was blowing bubbles at me, so sweet and helpless and *mine*.

I went into the den and emptied my briefcase with one hand while I held Juliette with the other. Then I sat with her by the window and watched Jon back his car out of the driveway and head to the place I wanted to go, to the job I'd worked my butt off to earn.

Juliette is a teenager now. I still hate her father for making me stay home, for trapping me inside those pink walls. Of course, he didn't actually make me. It was my choice. If only that was how it felt. Maybe I can't bear to take responsibility for betraying my dreams, my destiny, my sense of self. But my husband's words caught me at my most vulnerable place. Often, I sit at my desk and wonder where I would be today, right this second, if they hadn't.

One week after ruining my reputation in Hollywood, I started hating my father, too. There was reason to hate him already, but that had more to do with my mother. On my thirtieth birthday, after I'd been up all night with Juliette, he called from Ohio. Still handsome and fit from training for yet another Ironman triathlon, he had appeared as an extra in all the movies I had worked on and was eager for another gig. He expressed birthday wishes, then asked when I was going back to work.

"I have no idea," I said with a yawn.

"A girl as bright as you?" he asked. I could practically hear him shake his head. "What do you do all day?"

I looked across the messy kitchen as the clothes dryer buzzed. My reflection shot back at me from the window: dirty hair plastered to my head, strained peas sticking to my cheek, a croupy baby squirming in my arms. "I could write a book," I told him.

So I did. I scrimped to hire a babysitter three mornings a week while I wrote wisecracking essays that turned into *Welcome to Club Mom: The End of Life as You Know It*. Get this: The publisher thought the subtitle was so scary they made me change it to *The Adventure Begins*. Who were they trying to fool? Fortunately, the short chapters proved to be ideal for sleep-deprived mothers and the book sold well. I followed up with *Club Grandma*, and by the next Mother's Day, the paperback rights were bought by yet another well-meaning publisher, who changed it to *The Happy Helpful Grandma Guide*, a title so nauseating I no longer list it on my résumé. Mostly, the book reminds me of how sore my nipples felt from nursing newborn Caty Joy to keep her quiet during dozens of radio interviews. The irony didn't escape me that, as an author, I was known mainly for being a mom.

I started to hate myself. The success of the new book gave me a good enough excuse to stay home with the girls. But with a second child to feed and clothe, we couldn't afford any help at all. I didn't pick up a pencil for nearly a year, until the day I realized Toys "R" Us had become my Disneyland. Each week the girls and I played for hours with brightly colored toys in the temperature-controlled climate. Every cart had a baby seat. Every bathroom had a diaper changer. For a few bucks, we could even buy a souvenir. Then, one day, I found myself arguing with two other moms over the merits of Pampers versus Luvs. Around me kids were screaming for toys, mothers were sloppy from self-neglect, Caty Joy was teething on my filthy Honda key, and Juliette had diarrhea leaking from her *Little Mermaid* panties onto the tile floor. "Anyone could be a mother," I thought. I wanted to be more.

When I looked in the mirror, I had no idea who was looking back. I

had never had a thing for Donna Reed. I'd never learned to cook beyond
scrambled eggs, or to clean beyond emergency toilet maintenance. Since
I was the one home all day, however, guess who got to cook and clean?
Once my husband was saddled with the four of us, he got religious. "By
God," he proclaimed, "a working man deserves a hot meal on the table."
He wasn't as liberated as either of us had thought. Maybe no man truly
is; I have yet to hear anyone with a penis worry about combining kids
and a career. I hadn't worried about it either, until Juliette stared me in
the face.

With two small children, even the household chores were more than I
could handle. Here I was, a lifelong overachiever with a shelf of prestigious awards. I'd fantasized about ruling a film studio and bringing
home a royal paycheck, with my genius husband plying his art and playing with the children while the nanny cooked dinner. Why the hell was I
home doing the laundry?

On the other hand—the dirty one—I knew going back to a "real job"
in the film industry would mean missing every baby step I cared about. I
couldn't walk out on my girls now that they were one and four any more
than I could leave Juliette when she was only a few months old. So I decided to keep writing until the girls were in school. Unfortunately, I
needed their nap time for chores, and I was brain-dead by nightfall. Caring for two small children and our household left me with little energy to
write.

So I spent the next year doing the only thing I could think of: I pushed
all my ambition on my husband. I clipped the "Films in Development"
column from *Variety* and taped it to the refrigerator. I made a list of producers he should meet for lunch. I booked a video editor to make sample
reels for agents who could get him bigger jobs. He was talented; I was
impatient.

Soon he hated me too. Things got ugly. The house got noisy. We both
got lonely. My mother, who was now a licensed therapist, warned that I
was in no position to leave.

It was time to get a job.

I splurged on linen stationery, got out my old crew lists, and updated
my references. Then I took the girls on one last weekday beach outing
and brought my résumé along to proofread while they napped. The
beach was perfect: sunny, warm, and nearly empty at 10 A.M. on a

Thursday. A few white sails dotted the horizon. I put up our shade umbrella and spread out the sand toys.

As soon as I turned to put sunblock on Juliette, her naked little sister ran straight down toward the ocean. When I raced after her, she just looked back at me and giggled. Run-look-giggle, run-look-giggle, until she fell over a clump of seaweed and somersaulted into the surf. I picked her up, took both girls' hands, and on the count of three, we jumped over the frothy waves. Caty Joy never stopped giggling. "Again!" Juliette cried. Then she spotted two dolphins leaping across the shimmering water just beyond the break. We watched until they disappeared from sight. When the girls fell asleep on our blanket beneath the umbrella, I watched their little chests rise and fall, as ceaseless as the tide.

I pulled out my résumé. And ripped it up.

Soon Juliette was in kindergarten, Caty Joy was in preschool, and I was working on a novel. I'd drop off the children, throw a load of laundry into the washer, nuke some popcorn, and get my butt into the chair. I literally strapped myself in with a back-support device that buckled around the knees. My husband was working as steadily as one does in the chicken-or-feathers freelance life, often out of town.

There I was, working two unpaid jobs with no time off, no getting away from the office, no one getting me coffee, and no guarantee of future returns. How could I justify my life without a paycheck? I had made my bed, and now I had to change it every fucking week. I kept writing, tearing myself apart over volunteering at kindergarten versus wasting valuable hours to write a book that might never get published. I couldn't hire help with intermittent money and an intermittent husband. When I bought a new computer, I felt guilty about spending my husband's money on a gamble that might not pay off. The only password I could think of for the software was "Mommy."

I was always exhausted.

That's when I started hating stay-at-home mothers. Every school morning, I said hello to a toned woman in tennis togs who dropped her kids off at school en route to an early match. Then I waved to the friendly group who met in front of the auditorium to hike to Starbucks and chat about yesterday's *Oprah*. Even though I was lucky enough to choose my lifestyle, I resented that these women had lives that included leisure. Why did I have to work so hard to feel good about myself?

One morning, when Caty Joy was sick, we went to the pediatrician and ran into Bonnie, the mother of a preschool classmate. She was there with her new baby, the third new baby since Caty Joy had been born. I tried to scoot away quickly to avoid getting her baby sick, but also because Bonnie was so damned happy. She shouted across the waiting room that she'd always wanted four children and was having a ball. I felt so inferior. How could she coo over baby number four while I struggled so much with only two?

I didn't commit to two as the magic number until the Northridge earthquake in 1994. Jon was in Georgia working on a Visa commercial. That night I awoke to a cacophony of deafening booms. I rushed through our dark hallway, which shook like a rope bridge at a carnival funhouse, scooped up my baby and my toddler, and held them safe in my arms beneath the beamed doorway off the front hall as the house crashed down around us. There was no sound after all the glass shattered and furniture fell, no electricity to see what surrounded us, no phone service to call Jon—and no way to determine when the aftershocks would stop. To calm the girls I sang "Baby Beluga" until dawn, accompanied by emergency sirens and the dark smoke of not-so-distant fires. The first rays of light revealed how small our safety zone was, surrounded by piles of books from our shelves and broken glass from the front window and chunks of plaster from the gaping walls. I carried both children through the debris in search of shoes and finally reached my closet after climbing over the upturned television that had barely missed me as I leapt out of bed.

Two arms. Two kids. It just made sense.

Watching Bonnie made me reconsider. I was tempted to pop out another baby just to prove I could. Then I heard the names of her kids: They all started with B. I suddenly remembered how much I'd hated babysitting.

Bonnie took another look at my sick child and recommended fresh juice, something I could provide with one of the amazing juicers she sold from home just for fun. I smiled and wrote down the date of her next party, but I'd be damned if I was going to waste hours of work time at Pampered Chef/Tupperware/Faux Fashion parties, even if there was free food. Bonnie hugged me good-bye as if we were best friends. How could she be so nice? I could never be that nice. Sue me.

I hate Supermoms too, because they trigger my greatest guilt. I was a proud member of the PTA, but some of those women are volunteer vampires on a mission to suck other moms dry. I wrote a column for the newsletter, coordinated holiday parties, worked the weekend book fair, sold entertainment books, took tickets at Back-to-School Pizza Night, and sliced and baked cookies by the score. My work hours, beginning when the school bell rang at 8:10, were off limits; it was distracting enough that I had to pass Target on my way home. But when the PTA president cornered me in the school parking lot and I was still in my pajama bottoms, it was obvious that I wasn't in a rush to get to work downtown. I didn't have a real job: no boss, no clock to punch. No, I answered, I can't stay to count sales from the candy drive. I have to finish chapter 2. That little voice of insecurity in my head rang out like God or at least Barbara Walters: Who even cared about chapter 2? Besides me. I waved good-bye and dug in my purse for Tums. Then Tylenol. Then any traces of chocolate I could scrounge.

In *Welcome to Club Mom,* I wrote that there was no such thing as having it all, not at the same time. But damned if I didn't try, anyway. Last month, *Vogue* ran an ad for diamonds that read, "Your left hand rocks the cradle. Your right hand rules the world." But there were no children with the elegant model in the photograph, no hint of how to rock that cradle while ruling the world. During that same week, *Newsweek* touted Ivy League–educated young mothers who planned their lives in stages: work, kids, back to work, as if life were a puzzle women could figure out if they were sufficiently smart.

Whether those women succeed or not remains to be seen. But to my generation at the end of the baby boom, taking turns was not an option. Career women had to break through the glass ceiling or die with blood on their heads. Anything less was a sustenance job, not a career: failure. I had failed to break through before my biological alarm buzzed. Now I felt unqualified as either a working mom or a stay-at-home one.

Life improved when my screenplay, *Heartless,* went into production, even though it had taken seven years to find a producer and director and funding. Now that I was legitimate in the eyes of Hollywood, there were places to go and people to see about my next screenplay. Once again, I was more than just a mom. No one needed to know that it took me a week to coordinate the car pool, the babysitter, and exactly the right trendy (but affordable) outfit for each meeting. I pitched my spec script to production companies headed by A-list actresses, but not one could finance an original story that lacked a male lead. I met with one agent, an older woman who wanted to know if I wrote the script "all by myself." Yup, hated her. Younger female studio executives were even worse: They recognized *Welcome to Club Mom* from the website that bought the book rights, so no matter how close I was to them in age, I was a mother. Like their mother. Boring. (Don't even mention those privileged movie-star moms gracing magazine covers these days. Just don't.)

In the nick of time, as the buzz from being a produced screenwriter ebbed, my first novel won a prize. *66 Laps* is the story of a young career woman turned stay-at-home mom who slaps the bitch who points out her first gray hair and then starts to suspect her husband of infidelity with a young blonde. Sound familiar? Except for the affair part, I kept writing the what-ifs of my insecure life. Was I a real writer, or someone so frustrated that she had to write? Either way, the Pirates Alley Faulkner Society flew me to New Orleans, where I was wined and dined with the glittering southern literati and put up in a penthouse room overlooking the Mississippi. Unfortunately, a hurricane struck, the awards ceremony was postponed for a year, and I found myself back in the pumpkin patch by nightfall, doing the fucking laundry.

By the time I returned the following year to accept the prize, suddenly, after three books and a movie, I was a real author. I bought a real chair, did book signings in New York and PTA fund-raisers at my local bookstore. When I rejoiced internally, it was mostly a sense of *whew.* Finally, the stay-at-home moms stopped inviting me to make Popsicle Pilgrims. I had a real job, and I was happy to contribute anything except my time. Even my father stopped asking when I was going back to work. Instead he asked when I would have a bestseller.

Jon reached the top of the ladder as production designer (which means he designed the sets and somebody else actually climbed the ladder), but there was still no guarantee of the next job until he was in the car or, more likely, on a plane. Uncertainty was our only constant. Forget about planning vacations—I couldn't count on my husband to do anything except feel exhausted and left out when he finally came home. First he'd sleep for a few days while the girls tiptoed around, then he'd interrupt our intricate family schedule of softball practice and study dates and expect a steak dinner with sex on the side. If he was working in L.A., we wouldn't see him during daylight. When he wasn't working, sometimes we saw him too much. When the two of us did find time to go out to dinner every couple of months, there was enormous pressure for everything to be perfect, from my manicure to the meal to the mutual orgasms.

When Jon was working, I was like a single mom who isn't allowed to date. I'd take care of the kids, the pets, the bills, the house, and count the days until Friday. If I had time between writing, laundry, and chauffeuring, I could take Caty Joy and her preteen friends to an early PG movie (and pretend not to be with them). Then we'd pick up Juliette, now fifteen, from art class, stop to buy her favorite frozen yogurt, and zoom home to watch *What Not to Wear* together. If she emptied the dishwasher, I could fold laundry during commercial breaks.

On Saturday mornings, I would clutch my ClubMom coffee carafe, drag my folding chair across the softball field, and pray I could itemize our credit-card bill and get a peek at my horoscope in the *Los Angeles Times* without appearing rude. When finished, I'd reward myself by chatting with the other moms. It was often the social highlight of my week, the only time I didn't feel guilty about not getting any work or laundry done.

After 9/11, when my husband's work resumed, most of the jobs were in New York. He was gone for nine months last year. If he were home more often, maybe I would be less inclined to guard the fort. While I once worried about diaper rash, now I'm concerned about drugs. As for my work, I used to worry about finishing a page. Now I wonder if my readers will like it. Each day can still be interrupted by a phone call from the school nurse or the dishwasher flooding the kitchen. For three hours every Tuesday I have a maid who loves me because I don't care if she skips dusting—I'm so goddamned grateful just to have her scrub the toilets. I'm looking for a college coed to buy milk and pick up the girls from their respective schools, so I can fiddle with a few more paragraphs and delay the onslaught of softball practice, study sessions, and playdates. I wait all day for my children to come home and tell me who they sat with at lunch and how they did on their math tests. But if the words are still flowing, I shut the door to steal another hour. Often, I am farther away than they can imagine.

Last week after she was dropped off from school by Karen, the stay-at-home mom/afternoon car-pool driver, Caty Joy barged into my home office and plopped down on the love seat. "What does Karen do all day?" she asked.

I hit Save on my computer while I frantically racked my brain for an answer appropriate for a twelve-year-old. She waved a photocopy from Career Day in front of my face as an explanation for her query. I scanned the career categories. "Mother" wasn't on the list.

Caty Joy had to know that Karen was PTA vice president, Brownie-troop leader, and Room Mother every year. How could she forget that Karen gave her a ride home whenever I ran late? What about all the times I stashed her at Karen's house for an hour or two when I had to drive her sister somewhere? How could she take Karen so utterly for granted?

I had to think of an answer that would show how important stay-at-home moms are, but not so important that Caty Joy would think of becoming one. She needed to multiply fractions so she could stay on the honor roll, get into an Ivy League college, and choose a good career. Something with an employment contract and stock options. Then, like a zap from Mother Nature, I remembered that Karen also did the books for her husband's small company. But if I mentioned that, would it take away the value of Karen's time at home and in the school? My brain seized from the mental whiplash. "You know she volunteers a lot," I began. "Plus, she's a mom."

My daughter thought about this for a moment. She wiped cookie crumbs from her mouth and nodded.

"She's a good one," she said.

I smiled and blinked back tears. Did that mean I was not a good one? Should I have skipped that business call, and picked her up with a plate of warm cookies perched on top of the steering wheel? Then Caty Joy took a pencil from my desk and printed "Mother" on her list. I felt better.

Would I have ripped up my résumé that day on the beach if I'd foreseen the challenges of my lifestyle? Probably not. I could be at the Cannes Film Festival right now or in an office where people who wanted my job fetched me fancy coffee. But I wouldn't be home to have these impromptu conversations, to offer a hand or a hug. How can any woman predict her reaction to motherhood? By then, of course, it's too late to backtrack and make changes. Like picking a family-friendly career, waiting five more years to get pregnant, or being born a man instead of a woman.

I had never changed a diaper until Juliette was born. But when she made those sweet gurgling noises in her crib every morning, it was me she was calling to, me who made her world complete. I was surprised to find that she completed mine, too, as much as another human being could.

Every year, I've found another excuse—in the form of a story or a script or a tween's transition to middle school—to stay home. But I've also needed to keep working to prove I wasn't wasting my time by being only a mom. As a work-at-home mom, I have bits of "it all." I don't have all of any one thing. I have neither time to bake cookies nor an employer-matched retirement plan. No golden parachute has landed in my front yard.

Yet there's another kind of parachute that rides low enough for me to appreciate the view. After five years of combining motherhood and writing, I bought myself a beautiful desk, antique white with clear knobs and a glass top to protect my photos of the girls. After ten years, we moved and I chose this house, affordable enough that I wouldn't worry about the mortgage if I decided to scrap a hundred pages, yet with enough bedrooms that I could have my own office. I painted it periwinkle and planted pink roses outside the French door . . . that opens to the pool . . . so I can supervise the girls on hot days while I work. I teach weekly writing classes so my girls actually recognize me in high heels and makeup. Sometimes they bring me coffee, but unlike my former assistants, I can pay them with a kiss. Still, the doubt returns each time I sit down to work. I suspect that deep down in every mother, with or without a paycheck, there is an element of self-doubt that never goes away.

I hate moms who choose to work most of all, because I could have been one of them. My friend Stephanie, who buys and sells companies, is devoted to dugout duty Thursday nights and weekends. At our daughters' softball games, she always knows the score. Busy with my bills, I ask her when Catherine will be at bat. Not only does Stephanie know the difference between shortstop and second base, but she cleans out the ice cream truck to treat the team, then drives her Lexus to buy fancy kid clothes while her nanny stocks the fridge. She doesn't have to go to the dry cleaner or the car mechanic or wait four hours for the plumber. She wears baggy sweatpants to the same events I get excited about dressing up for. She invites me to her beautiful home for barbecues and serves better wine than I bring as a gift. On holidays, she locks her office and drives away. She is tired but happy, with her Prada purse full of restaurant receipts and first-class airline tickets to meetings in China. As a work-at-home mom, I don't ever get a day off and I can't possibly measure up. Glimpses of her life make me feel I've chosen the worst of both worlds.

It seems only fair that my girls should be better off for my staying home: smarter, more polite, better adjusted than other children. Oddly enough, my sacrifice doesn't seem to have made this kind of difference. Having a stay-at-home mother isn't an achievement they can put on their college applications. *I could be running Paramount Pictures,* I want to tell them. They could have bedrooms that overlook the Pacific Ocean, and real ponies to ride on the beach every afternoon. I would never be around to make them pick their panties off the floor or finish their broccoli.

They are surely big enough now for me to go back to work, to get a real job. But what would I do? My husband insists I can't possibly understand his job stress, because everything has changed, and he's right. Hollywood has moved on without me.

After four books and a movie, I haven't earned enough money to impress anyone in this town. Sure, my family is proud, but Daddy is the one standing on a concrete floor fifteen hours a day. I thought I could provide for myself. Could I now? My production skills come in handy managing a household, but in a business known for networking, I have no contacts to trade.

I hate working women without kids, too. A few months ago, I had lunch with Tina, whom I last saw at my wedding. After a decade of working for Sony in New York, traveling far and wide to open up foreign markets for distribution, she has a new job with an office overlooking Rockefeller Center. She has an apartment on Central Park South, a "cottage" in La Jolla, a well-dressed husband, no kids, and no stretch marks. She is my alternate reality. It was the strangest lunch I've ever had, because I tried to talk for two hours without mentioning my children. I wanted to tell her about Juliette's poetry prize and Caty Joy's all-star softball games, but it felt too much like bragging. I wanted to share my frustration over adolescent cliques and academic pressure, but it felt like a complaint. I brought pictures but never pulled them out of my purse. Pictures can't make Tina understand my life. She had lunch with only part of me. Motherhood is my reality.

One night, after wrapping a particularly long and tiresome job, my husband invited me to have a glass of wine with him and watch the sunset from the back porch. The orange sky and his glass of Merlot looked tempting. "Sorry," I bitched. "I have to finish the taxes and pay the bills."

"I'm the one paying the bills," he said. "We made a deal when Juliette was born that you would do everything else."

I nodded; it was true. Unfortunately, "everything else" grew even faster than Juliette, who is now three inches taller than me. That night, I was on my fourth load of laundry, exhausted and resentful that he had time to relax. He had walked right past a pile of dirty clothes to get to the back porch, as if his paycheck gave him a pass. So I got mad and we did that ugly dance of work versus value and how he pressed me to unpack my briefcase that fateful night when Juliette was six months old and the phone rang. As he sat on the porch, alone with his Merlot, I finished the taxes and paid the bills and then slipped into bed across from where he snored on the other side, just like that night long ago. I stared at the ceiling—Navajo white this time instead of cottage cheese—and wondered how much of the argument we believed and how much we still held on to because we felt so incredibly helpless in what would seem to be—what should have been—an ideal situation.

My life is a trap of my own creation. Basically, I am at peace with my choice. Some days more than others. On the days I feel insecure, I kiss my girls *and* look at the line of books in my office that bear my name. One or the other is just not enough. I still want it all, dammit.

You could say I owe my career to my children. I always wrote, but I never took it seriously until I was a mother. Maybe needing a job I could do from home was the excuse I'd been waiting for. Motherhood has certainly provided rich material. I am endlessly inspired by the what-ifs. Perhaps one day I'll still get to wear that beaded blue dress. But as our girls face adolescence, I can't bear to abandon them. I trust no one but myself.

Now that my mother has retired, she spends a lot of time with my sister's young children. Last night she called to tell me that she was dancing with my ten-month-old niece, Daisy, in her arms, singing to a Rod Stewart album (that she liked a rocker from my rebellious youth freaked me out all by itself). Then she described how Daisy sang along. When the song ended, the baby said "Nana" and rested her head on my mother's shoulder. "It was better than an orgasm," my mother told me.

I laughed. I understood. I recognized that magical moment from when my girls were young. Even from tonight, when Caty Joy refused to sleep without my good-night kiss stamping her cheek.

"I wish you had time to dance when my girls were little," I said.

My mother was silent for a moment. "I wish I'd had time to dance with you," she said in a quiet voice.

There was another pause. I was too stunned to speak.

"You've done the right thing with your girls," she said.

I hung up the phone and went across the hall to where Juliette was sleeping, her lanky form sprawled across her bed. In three short years, this child will be gone. Six more, and both will be gone. Then I can work all I want. For the first time, the thought made me cry. When did I blink? I am the same woman, but now there are two more.

I wonder what choices my daughters will make. They have witnessed my struggle to be a work-at-home mom. I hope they will benefit from my compromises as much as I have. I also hope they'll respect all women, no matter what choices are made in terms of work and motherhood.

Most of all, I want my daughters to be happy. They know that I don't really hate anybody. And they know that I love them most of all.

Before; After

Molly Jong-Fast

Molly Jong-Fast lives in New York City with her husband, their son, Max, their cocker spaniel, Godzuki, and Pete, the world's fattest cat. She is the author of the quasi-autobiographical novels *Normal Girl* and *Girl [Maladjusted]*. She is the only child of famed author Erica Jong and screenwriter Howard Fast. Molly's accidental pregnancy at age twenty-four reads like a good postfeminist TV script—famous feminist mom, unwed pregnant daughter . . . feminism today finds itself set against a new backdrop: Molly's generation of women has more choices, and new doors to open.

"You don't have to be a hero here," my friend Jane said, stroking my arm. "You don't have to have the baby. There's no reason to put yourself through this. This is your future, this is the rest of your life, don't throw it all away!" It was a scene that must have played itself out in a hundred Lifetime movies: the pregnant teen and her older, wiser friend.

Except I wasn't a teenager. I was twenty-four.

It was a few months ago and I was in my apartment drinking lemonade with my beautiful thirty-something friend Jane. She had brought the galleys of her novel over for me to look at, and the pages were spread across my huge black dining room table.

She looked at me consolingly. "I mean come on, Moll, think of your parents, of your family!"

I thought of my mother, who had joyously bought me a maternity wedding dress at Mom's Night Out, a store on the Upper East Side. I thought of my dad, who had walked around the house all day asking my little half-brothers if they thought he had what it took to be a good grandpa.

But I understood where Jane was coming from. She has few friends with children, let alone eight-year-olds, like the one I'll have when I'm her age. She had spent the last decade finishing graduate school, pursuing a freelance career, working on getting her books published, and holding down an oppressive nine-to-nine job at an impressive magazine.

The reaction of my other thirty-something friends to the news of my pregnancy was the same: shock, shame, pity. My gorgeous globe-hopping friend Kim, childless and recently divorced, explained to me on the phone that "children ruin your life. It's never going to be about you again. Your relationship will change, everything will change." Kim believed you weren't supposed to have children until you had made at least your first million, had a nanny lined up, and had at least one book on the *Times* bestseller list.

Kim's beliefs were more than right; everyone knows having a book on the *Times* bestseller list makes you an amazing mom. Speaking of the land of amazing moms (or amazing illegal nannies), where I grew up on the Botoxed Upper East Side no one ever dropped out to have a baby. And no one found herself pregnant, as I had, by accident. I actually thought that people didn't get pregnant by accident anymore—I thought it had gone the way of polio and iron lungs. Of course, that's always what you think right before you get pregnant by accident. But where I grew up, if, God forbid, you'd ever need an abortion (and I never heard of anyone in my high school, the Riverdale Country School, needing one), Mommy would take you to Paris to stay in a suite at the Crillon, shop, and get RU-486. Besides that, everyone I knew saw (and still sees) one brilliant gynecologist who specializes in adolescents, Dr. A, who doesn't take insurance and is a birth-control Nazi. When I was growing up, condoms, the pill, and diaphragms were pushed on us before we even knew what sex was. In grade eight (before I had ever kissed a boy) our teachers at the Day School (where I went after getting kicked out of Dalton) made us go out to the drugstore and buy condoms. I think it's fair to say that almost no product of the winning combination of Dr. A and the Manhattan private-school system gets pregnant by accident, except, of course, for me.

My visions of pregnancy always involved that pilgrimage to Paris with my mother. I always saw myself as someone who would have an abortion if my pregnancy were the least bit inconvenient. But when I got pregnant after my fiancé and I had been engaged a few months, I became a Jewish Pat Buchanan (except without the radical right-wing beliefs or the talk show or the weird shellacked hair). Suddenly I knew I couldn't have an abortion.

We decided to get married a bit earlier and have little Max Greenfield. It was a very easy choice. Pretty much from the moment I knew I was pregnant I was sure I was going to keep Max. Even though I had never seen myself as the mother type and I was (and still am) totally grossed out by all the stretching, tearing, and bleeding associated with childbirth, when I saw those two red lines on the pregnancy-test stick, my whole attitude toward motherhood changed. I knew I had to do this.

Of course I hate children. Recently when a baby that was sitting in my lap spat up, I almost threw up on it. I'm beyond terrified by the prospect of going to Mommy and Me classes and meeting so many earnest women with Prada diaper bags.

There are also, however, some things I don't worry about. I don't worry about missing my youth. I don't want to go to Lotus every night. Sadly, there's almost no kind of wild youthful misdeed that I didn't commit before I was nineteen (and then document in my highly autobiographical first novel). Besides, I belong to a generation of people mortally afraid of becoming what the generation before it became so proudly (and documented in many ambitious and wildly amusing "women-looking-for-love novels"): thirty-something workaholics desperate to have children but quickly losing the battle with time.

The fear of being over thirty and desperately roaming the city looking for disease-free more-or-less heterosexual men to breed with is far greater for me than the fear of not being able to pick up and head for Atlantic City for a night of debauchery.

Maybe there's something wrong with me, maybe I'm heading for disaster, but I'm just not that scared. Sure, I worry that I'll have a miscarriage or that the baby will have a collapsed lung, but I'm not afraid of a baby slowing down my career. I'm not afraid of a baby ruining my upcoming marriage. I'm not afraid of a baby. Of course part of the reason I'm not that afraid is because I have no idea what having a child entails. I recently learned they don't go to school until they're three. I was thinking maybe six months. I have only recently learned what babies eat. But perhaps it's better that way; maybe Generation X's big problem is that they've had too much time to worry about baby. Or maybe in four months I'm going to be in a lot of trouble.

Either way, I am in no way a pioneer.

I am pregnant at twenty-four and I'm not the only one. I've got friends who've had babies younger than I. My friend Nichole married a movie star, moved to L.A., and promptly had two sons, all before she was twenty-three. My friend Sarah had a child at twenty-three. Now he's three, and when she pushes him around Park Slope she is constantly asked if she's the nanny.

No one ever asked my mom if she was the nanny. In many ways my mom, feminist author Erica Jong, anticipated the Generation X ideal of motherhood. She was successful, in her late thirties, and had both a book on the *Times* bestseller list and a nanny all lined up. She had already published two novels and four books of poetry and had earned a master's degree from Columbia. My mom was a wonderful mother, but did having a book on the *Times* list help with her mothering skills? I would say no.

There are huge differences between my mom's experience and mine. When Mom got pregnant, she was afraid to tell her publisher because she was sure they'd cancel her book. When I got pregnant, I called up *Modern Bride* (which I was writing for at the time) and they didn't bat an eyelash. When Mom finally told her publisher that she was pregnant, NAL took out a million-dollar life-insurance policy on her. When I told my publisher that I was pregnant, he warmly congratulated me and asked when the shower was. The difference between my mom's circumstances and mine is the passage of a quarter of a century (and that my editor is a darling saint).

I thought I would have my first child at forty-one. I thought I would have abortions in Paris. But the truth is that I just didn't know myself at all. I hate Paris. I've never had an abortion. I'll have my first child way before thirty, and I'll probably go to play group with earnest women carrying Prada diaper bags. Am I a reaction to piles and piles of chick lit focusing on the difficulty of mating after thirty? I would say absolutely. Will my life be better than those women in the generation before who waited? I don't particularly think so. Sure, I won't be writing a sex column, but fertility won't top my worry list.

Ultimately this Generation X ideal of motherhood would make sense if you were going to die during childbirth or if childbirth rendered you hopelessly stupid. But if you don't die, if you can still make money and be successful after you have your baby, then why do you have to wait until you're forty? I mean sure, you do get drugs for in vitro fertilization, but I don't think they're the fun kind.

After: August 2004

Motherhood makes you crazy. If there is one thing I can glean from the hopelessly naïve essay you just read, which more than a million people also read when it was published in *The New York Times*, it is that the insanity starts even before birth, during those ten months of chunky pre-motherhood known as pregnancy.

I was twenty-five years old when my son, Max, was born. By Upper East Side standards I was a very young mom, flexible in my habits and in excellent physical health, but let's face it, I had been going to a shrink since I was a zygote, and I had a huge number of neuroses about merely keeping myself alive.

I superciliously blundered into motherhood, sure I'd make my own organic baby food while writing the great American novel. But when Max was born I would just put him in his little bassinet and cry. A month postpartum I wasn't making baby food or writing or even taking care of my child. I was too busy crying and eating quarts of ice cream. Yes, my own unique personal form of insanity involved paranoia, lethargy, self-pity, and overeating.

Sometimes I would cry because I wasn't going to be able to protect him in this horrible world.

Sometimes I would cry because I was worried he was going to die.

Sometimes I would cry because it was January, it was snowing, and I had stopped taking my Effexor.

Sometimes I would cry because of the decline of Western civilization and the difficulty of finding Kobe beef.

My mother-in-law hired a baby nurse. Miss Phyllis took care of my child as I cried. Slowly I came back from the edge of total insanity. Slowly I became sane enough to worry about my condition. I had (through a quest to sample every flavor of pound cake on the isle of Manhattan) touched the wobbly hand of obesity and topped the scales at 250 pounds. It was not the way I thought I would start motherhood, but anyone who is a mother knows that motherhood is like Chuck E. Cheese's (hours of fun punctuated by moments of ravenous bingeing followed by sheer terror and boredom or vice versa), where every preconceived notion must be immediately tossed out the window (and where a Diet Coke is no longer a balanced lunch).

Part of my craziness/stupidity was an obsession with being a better working mom than my own mother. We all want to be better than our parents. My mother was a pretty wonderful mother, but my attitude had nothing to do with the facts of her parenting. I (like all adolescents) judged harshly something I had no experience with. Now that I stand on the other side of motherhood, I find myself profoundly humbled by the huge emotional and physical work of it. If I end up being half as good a mother as my own was, I'll be thrilled.

My mother always felt bad. Either she felt like a bad parent or she felt like she wasn't spending enough time writing. Part of my confusion growing up in a single-parent household was the belief that Mom was always having a great time. What I could not see was that Mom was deeply conflicted. Once Mom was leaving for a monthlong book tour in Europe and I lay in the doorway and held her legs so she literally had to step over me to get out the door. She had to step over my tiny feet. Now I understand how she felt, how most working moms feel, because I also always feel bad.

It is the great lie and the great truth of feminism that you simply can't be both at home and at work. It's the schizophrenia of modern-day motherhood. It's the schizophrenia of affluence and more pointedly the schizophrenia of feminism. Why can't we admit that life is about sacrifices? I work at home but I work. I don't get to sit in the park all day with the other mothers, but I also don't have to explain to patronizing people at cocktail parties that motherhood was for many centuries considered a full-time job. I don't spend as much time with my son as my friends who don't work spend with their children. I don't "have it all." I have mornings, weekends, and some evenings. But my whole life I was sure that I'd never have to sacrifice anything at all. I didn't understand that life, feminism, and parenting are all about compromise. I can't be at the Central Park Zoo with my son and here at my desk writing this piece. Even the most ambitious mom can still be in only one place at a time.

When I talk about the schizophrenia of affluence I am thinking of the difference between the working-class and the comfortably middle-class (or what is left of them). Max's nanny, Audrey, doesn't obsess about working or not working because she knows she has to—not because of self-esteem but for the old-fashioned reason, for the money. Audrey is a first-generation American, and she does not have the luxury of grappling with identity and self-esteem. The idea of working purely for self-esteem gives rise to countless problems. First of all, it trivializes the whole institution of work. Building one's self-esteem smacks of narcissism and self-obsession. Although ultimately my generation is probably as self-obsessed as the one that precedes it, we certainly don't see ourselves that way. Many older feminists have alienated members of my generation by appearing narcissistic or disinterested in the plight of anyone outside of their own socioeconomic class.

When I talk about the schizophrenia of modern motherhood I am referring to my own and my mother's situation. I was told as a child that I would blaze my way through the world, that I could be anything I wanted. It was expected that I make something of my life (e.g., become famous or successful in the arts—that was my family's particular insanity, but that is another story). My mom told me I'd be a bestselling author (like her) or a famous painter (like Helen Frankenthaler). At the same time I knew that being a good child (which required, I understood, being a good Jew) was about giving your parents what every parent wanted—grandchildren. So I understood that I'd just have to do both.

When my son was born I was one lecture away from finishing my master's degree. So I brought the baby, my husband, and (gasp) our nanny with us to a relatively inexpensive B&B near campus for ten days. But I was worried that Audrey wouldn't have a good time, so I brought my sister-in-law (and her car) too. I was also worried that Audrey wouldn't have the right luggage, so I bought her some LeSportsac bags. I was also worried that she wouldn't have the right cosmetics, so I went with her to the Whole Body store and bought her sundry items. All this reminds me of a story about how my mom used to fly my nanny, Margaret, and me with her on the Concorde. Get where I'm going with this? I felt really horrible about my son having a nanny, really horrible about bringing her, and really horrible about the fact that she herself had three young children living on Saint Vincent with her ex-mother-in-law, a diabetic.

I was really embarrassed about the fact that we had a nanny, so I got a big room in the B&B for the nanny and another room for my sister-in-law. I proceeded to spend the rest of the week playing "hide the nanny" with my fellow students.

My week of trying to hide our illegal nanny without letting her know that I was trying to hide her was going well, until one day I came out of my bedroom with the baby and stumbled upon my nemesis, a student in my MFA program who loathed me. She was chatting with Max's nanny and my sister-in-law, and she didn't see me (at first). "So you're Molly

Jong-Fast's nanny," she said to Audrey, smiling. "What a lot of work you must have."

Oy vey.

In the end I got my degree, but I spent most of my time worrying and too little of it working. My lecture wasn't nearly as good as it should have been. I had to work twice as hard to produce half as much.

The last pope recently accused feminism of trying to destroy the American family. One can only hope that his translator got what he was trying to say totally wrong. Perhaps he was trying to say that he didn't think it was fair that popes couldn't marry beautiful feminists like Naomi Wolf and Katie Roiphe. But if the American family is in jeopardy, it's the idea of "having it all" that will be our unraveling. The children of the baby boomers, Generation X, waited to have children because they didn't want to make the hard choices. They didn't want to choose between children and a bigger apartment. They didn't want to have to pick between having a good job and being at PTA meetings. Generation X wanted to run the world, and they planned to marry and have children later. But when was later? And did they ever consider that "later" might bring its own devilish compromises?

I myself was sure having a baby would only make me more productive. What I found was that I really had to fight for myself and for my work. I remember my mom fighting like that when I was a kid. There was a joke in our house: You could be bleeding, but you didn't go into Mom's office. Sometimes my nanny would literally hold me back from trying to go in there. Sometimes I would wonder how Mom could love me and not want me with her. Somehow having Mom at home made the situation all the more explosive. I knew that on the other side of her office door she sat doing nothing much. Often she was just staring at a piece of paper. I didn't understand what was so special or important about staring at a piece of paper.

When I was growing up, my mom would always do interviews about how she "had it all." She won a Mother of the Year Award in 1984. Perhaps she was overcompensating, afraid that she was so busy having it all she'd end up with nothing. But in some ways we lived in a sandcastle in the sky. During the first eleven years of my life my mother was astonishingly lonely. We ate pasta, we watched TV, we went to Europe—Mom, my nanny, Margaret, and me. Publicly, she might have been the poster child for a working single mom, but the truth is she was very conflicted about having to work. I could tell her I loved her a million times, but it would never ease that feeling she had—guilt. She would frequently launch into impassioned speeches about how she wasn't like the other moms, how she really did need to earn a living. She made these speeches to convince herself, not me, because I had no clue what she was talking about.

Mom's obsession with me getting kidnapped—she made my nanny walk me to school when I lived three blocks away; she didn't let me take the subway until I graduated from college—was a palpable manifestation of her ambivalence. Her constant worrying that she would die in a plane crash and leave me forever was another way that her subconscious guilt leaked out. It was only when I got older and I could travel on book tours with her that she felt truly comfortable. When I was a teenager and we started promoting her books together, she stopped feeling conflicted for the first time in her life and started feeling good about working and about the example she set for me.

I have it easier because of my mother's struggles. I am able to sit down at my desk with the knowledge that in the end I turned out fine even if my mom didn't watch me every second of every day. When I wake up and my husband and I have two pure hours alone with the baby before our nanny arrives, I feel a kind of pressure to work harder at parenting, to make extra-special muscle-stretching funny faces, to make up for those hours between 10 A.M. and 4 P.M. when I am working. Of course, these are the problems of the affluent; my less well-to-do friends worry about getting adequate time for maternity leave and kids catching colds at day care and keeping stifling jobs because of the good health-care benefits.

I know the truth. I know that I have it better than 99.9 percent of all working and stay-at-home mothers. But I still have a very hard time closing the office door on those little fingers, fingers I love more than anything in the world . . . although my home office actually doesn't have a door yet.

I Do Know How She Does It

Ann Misiaszek Sarnoff

Ann Misiaszek Sarnoff graduated from Harvard Business School in 1987, and subsequently worked in consulting, media, and sports, with her most recent position as the chief operating officer at the Women's National Basketball Association. She lives in New York City with her husband and two children. Her story embodies what many working moms have cinched already: Despite the negative hype, it is entirely possible to combine motherhood and ambition.

'm a working mom. I'm not a procrastinator. I'm just the opposite. I pride myself on getting things done—including this essay. Yet, despite the fact that I have lived the issues of working motherhood for the past thirteen years, I've found it a struggle to capture in words the keys to my happiness as a working mom.

So I started talking to my friends to get their perspective on this topic and me. The best advice came from a male classmate from Harvard Business School who's known me for nearly twenty years. "Ann, don't over-think this," he told me. "You're not conflicted. That's what's so great about you. Just write about that."

So there's the beginning. I am not conflicted; I love working. I've navigated my career through jobs in management consulting, at Viacom, Nickelodeon, and VH1, and now as chief operating officer at the WNBA—fascinating jobs I've been able to do well while being a mom. I have two children, Rachel and Peter, and a husband, Richard, who despite his own career pressures makes it a priority to be home for dinner and bedtime with our kids unless he is traveling.

How have I managed it all? A few lessons, learned early on, have served me very well.

I recently had breakfast with my friend Becky, who has been at home with her three kids for the past seven years. She'd just gotten an offer to return to office work and was feeling the cut of a double-edged sword: thrilled to feel valued and to be able to reenter the workplace at a fairly high level, worried about her kids and their reaction to her not being around as much. "How do you do it, Ann?" she asked me.

"Buckets," I told her. Becky looked at me like I was crazy.

When my daughter, Rachel, was born, I was working at an intense strategy-consulting firm where the average workweek was sixty-plus hours. I commuted an hour each way to work, so my weeks were seventy-plus hours long. Do I need to tell you I had no time to spare? So I figured out what I wanted and needed to do as a working mom, what I would ask my husband to do, and what our nanny could do. Basically, I organized my life into three buckets—essential for me to do myself, possible for my husband to do in my stead, and things our nanny could do and do well. The three of us divided and conquered the chaos of caring for one tiny baby. And we did it a few years later with another tiny baby and a toddler, accompanied by my career change to the media business. And we're still doing it these days with two almost-teenagers and another career change.

"Bucket number one: things I absolutely cannot miss and don't want to miss," I told Becky. "I won't miss Rachel performing her first solo in the school talent show or Peter's first goal of the season on his travel soccer team. Those are life's most precious, lasting moments across all dimensions. In the second bucket are the things that Richard and I can take turns covering—class dinners, ad hoc doctor appointments, safety patrol at school. Before the kids were in school, he would sometimes wait for the nanny to arrive in the morning so I could get a head start to work. In the third bucket are things that are completely delegable: grocery shopping, dry cleaning, cooking dinner, buying birthday presents for my kids' friends."

Becky laughed at this one. "I spend so much time shopping for exactly the right present every time one of the kids gets invited to a birthday party."

I took a sip of coffee. "Why don't you give the money to your nanny and have her take Adam to the store to pick out a present for his friend? It's a win/win. You're teaching him to take the responsibility to think about what his friend might like. And it frees up your time."

Becky wholeheartedly agreed.

Of course, there's a P.S. to this story. Becky is back at work and has established her buckets, but her kids initially had a tough time. She had been immersed in their lives for seven years—picking up, dropping off, attending to their every need. Now someone else is doing some of that, and it's been hard for all of them to adjust. In the first few weeks of her new job, each of her kids seemed to pick a week to act up, so she had her hands full. On the flip side, I've never seen her happier. At work, she hit the ground running and is feeling appreciated and fulfilled.

And therein lies one of the issues of being a working mom. Trade-offs.

Certainly no one wants to trade her child's happiness for anything. And I think it's particularly hard to take something away from kids. The buckets help me to be the kind of mother I want to be.

How did I come up with this buckets idea?

Early on in my career, I attended many working-women's-issue forums and listened hard to those who came before me. At one unforgettable lunch, a female executive fifteen years my senior talked about trailblazing in the corporate world and the sacrifices she'd made to get ahead. I sat in my red velvet chair along with the other women guests, impressed by the speaker's track record of achievement and the strength and charisma she exuded. Then she launched into a story about one incident that she deeply regretted. I thought she was going to talk about a promotion that had gone to someone else or a mistake in judgment that had taught her an indelible business lesson. Instead she told a story about an event at her daughter's school. She referred to it gravely as "the dinosaur lunch." She had intended to go, but something important came up at the last minute and she decided to miss the lunch. Her daughter was the only child without a parent present; the little girl was devastated, hysterical even hours later when retelling the story after her mother got home. As this strong, capable senior executive finished the story, she got teary-eyed. "Don't miss the dinosaur lunches" was her final advice, advice I've taken throughout my career.

So when did I begin to work? When I was nine years old I got my first job babysitting for two toddlers after school in my small hometown in western Massachusetts. The family lived across the street from my grandmother, so there was an adult nearby who could help in case of an emergency. Although I was only nine, this experience gave me a sense of what it took to earn a dollar (literally) and inserted into my otherwise carefree life a true external responsibility.

I also worked around the house. By the time I was seven my siblings, who were much older, had moved out of the house. I was effectively an only child and a latchkey kid of two working parents. I cut the lawn every week. I cleaned our house. I heated up dinner most nights. Compared with kids growing up now, I had a lot of responsibility.

When I was fourteen, I obtained a work permit and got a job as a sports counselor at a nearby day camp. At sixteen, in addition to the camp job, I began waitressing at the local Friendly's in the summer evenings. Although I loved the people and could scoop a Fribble like no-body's business, working there certainly gave me a sense of what I didn't want to do for a living.

I have never not worked. Frankly, I don't know if that's good or bad. It's just the way it's been.

My mom, like most of the moms in our Polish Catholic neighbor-hood, worked because my parents needed two incomes to support our family. There wasn't any choice in the matter. But Mom liked what she did and was good at it. She worked for twenty-five years at the local Sears, Roebuck, for the last few in the catalog pickup department. I'd mention to someone where my mom worked and they'd say, "Your mom is Vera in Catalog? I love her!" I saw Mom get tremendous fulfillment from her work.

Dad had various jobs, sometimes two at a time, including house building, factory work, and greenskeeping. (He was also a scratch golfer and got the first hole in one at the club he helped build with his cousin.) Dad wanted more for me in life than he and my mom had. He would often take me out to the golf course and say, "Ann, if you want to be in business, you have to play a good golf game." I'm not sure that I knew anything about wanting to be in business at the time, but the point is that he didn't rule it out because I was a girl. And this is a guy whose Polish immigrant mother once said to me, "Annie, why you want to go to col-lege? You're just gonna get married."

During that breakfast with Becky I stressed how important stable child care is to the family of a working mom. We've had only two nannies in thirteen years. When I was pregnant with Rachel, Richard and I decided not to have a nanny live with us. We wanted one of us to be home every night with our kids despite our job demands. Having a live-out nanny ensured that we put a limit on time in the office.

Our first nanny worked for us for three years, and we loved her. She left when I was pregnant with Peter, because she also became pregnant and no longer wanted to be a nanny. The lovely woman who's been with us since then is extremely reliable and kind, and she loves our children as if they were her own.

One of the keys to our symbiotic relationship is that I don't tell her what to do all the time. I trust her and let her make most of the day's decisions about playdates, what to cook for dinner, and who needs a bath. A *Wall Street Journal* article a couple of years ago argued that women's focus and energy at work is bifurcated compared with that of their male colleagues, unless they delegate daily housekeeping and child-care responsibilities. Assigning certain zones of child care to my nanny helps us both in our work: I have far less to worry about, and she's happier not being micromanaged.

Richard's support in parenting is also key. Like me, Richard balances being successful at work with being a great dad. So much of the work/life balance discourse focuses on working moms, and the push for change centers on corporations becoming more mom-friendly. But from my perspective, working dads who are involved in their children's daily lives don't get enough credit, and they don't get much flexibility from the companies they work for. Most of my female friends who have left the workforce after having children have done so because, for the most part, their husband's work schedule is too demanding for the family overall to keep a balance between work and kids. I've seen many men use the pressure of being the single breadwinner as an excuse for not seeing their kids enough, creating an even greater imbalance in the household. I could not be happy in a marriage with that imbalance, and certainly I couldn't be successful at work without my husband's partnership at home.

That's not to say that either of us only puts in an eight-hour workday. We work hard in the office, get home in the evening to be with the kids, and then get back to e-mail, the in-box, or whatever else has to be attended to after the kids go to bed. When the kids were younger, I used to feel guilty leaving the office at times, especially if others were still there. I always got the work done—called in from home, worked on presentations after dinner, whatever it took. Some of that guilt evaporated several years ago when my male boss directed a woman interviewing for a job to talk to me about work/life balance because I did it better than anyone else. A little affirmation goes a long way.

Things do go wrong, though. Home sometimes takes priority no matter what's happening at work. One morning two summers ago, we woke up to smoke in the apartment. "Mommy, is this a bad dream?" Peter asked when I roused him. I wish it had been. Walking down fourteen flights of stairs, I had no idea whether we would all be walking back up again to the same apartment. It turned out that an elevator fire had created huge plumes of smoke that oozed into the apartments. Luckily, the New York City firefighters put out the fire quickly and the apartments suffered only smoke damage. I spent the day mopping, wiping, and arranging for fire-damage professionals to clean the most serious spoilage. The meetings I missed at work never seemed so inconsequential.

Things slip through the cracks. One morning on the way to school I asked Rachel what day it was. "Thursday," she told me. "Oh no," I replied. The prior evening had been hectic, and I simply forgot the parent/teacher conference that morning. At school, the teacher gave me one of those "You're a working mom, aren't you?" looks but was very nice about the half hour she'd sat waiting in the empty classroom. We rescheduled for the following week. I remembered that one.

Kids have accidents and of course get sick. My heart pounds when the school nurse calls me at work. Most of the time, the issue is minor and she's very good about recapping the situation in the first ten seconds so I can regain my breath. There was one time, though, when Rachel was just one, and Richard called while I was working late to say she had fallen and split open her lip. I ran out of the office, leaving the presentation I was working on strewn across my desk, and met Richard and Rachel at the doctor's office. I got into work at dawn the next morning and finished the presentation.

Sleep is a luxury for a working mom.

I dabbled briefly with a less-than-full-time schedule back when Rachel was a baby and I was struggling to juggle the demands of the consulting firm with new motherhood. I worked part-time for a couple of months and then moved to four days a week. The firm valued me and was trying hard to retain senior women (there were no female partners, and I was one of the more senior female managers). But I realized that the only way to really get ahead there was to work like everyone else was working— all the time.

Commuting was no longer for me. Maybe it was the time when I was pregnant and had to pull over on I-95 to vomit. Maybe it was the realization that I could be with Rachel for two more hours each day if I didn't commute. In any case, after about a year of being a new mom in consulting, I knew I needed to find a job closer to home with more manageable hours.

I also realized that I needed to work in a job I felt more passionate about. My time had suddenly become more precious; I measured more acutely what I was getting out of work. While I'd always loved the analytical rigor and challenge of consulting, I'd never felt terribly ardent about my specific clients or projects. My musical background and interest in pop culture led to a job at Viacom in the corporate-development department—an eight-minute taxi ride from our New York apartment. That job in turn led to an offer from a Viacom division, Nickelodeon.

The first time I sat in Nickelodeon's offices, I wanted to work there. Nickelodeon was filled with talented, creative people who "bled orange." Their passion was contagious. The staff was 60 percent female, many of the senior women had kids, and the president and founder, Geraldine Laybourne, was a working mom and former schoolteacher. Plus, they offered me a job when I was six months pregnant with Peter—a good sign that I'd hit the working-mom jackpot.

Soon after joining Nickelodeon, Gerry taught me an invaluable lesson about combining motherhood and work. I was helping to prepare the annual budget presentation to upper management. The week was filled with late nights. Friday morning came and I arrived at Gerry's office with the presentations in hand.

"You don't look so good, Ann. I bet you haven't seen your kids all week."

I said that I was pretty tired. No, I hadn't seen much of the kids that week.

"You need to bring your kids into the office, Ann," Gerry responded.

I asked her to repeat that.

"My kids have always been a part of what I do here. You need to make sure that Rachel and Peter understand what you do and feel a part of it. Bring them in."

So I did. Peter was still a baby, but I started bringing in three-year-old Rachel. Gerry wanted executives to understand kids, to think like kids. Nickelodeon's kidlike environment constantly reinforces the company's mission. The walls are painted bright green. Toys fill people's offices. Couches line the hallways. There is a Ping-Pong table in the programming department. Needless to say, Rachel was in heaven. She would sit in my office and draw pictures for my co-workers to hang on their doors. She would wander the halls and visit people. She would sit in the Blue's Clues Thinking Chair and watch television.

Rachel was almost eight when I got an offer to become chief operating officer at VH1.

"Why do you need to change jobs?" she wailed incredulously.

"It's a better job, honey," I tried to explain.

"Well, it's not better for me!" she angrily replied.

I thought hard. Finally, a way to calm her down came to me.

"Rach, have you heard of the Backstreet Boys and Britney Spears?"

"Yes," she said hesitantly.

"Well, you might get a chance to see them in Mommy's new job."

The tears dried up.

VH1 had a slightly less child-conducive culture. But Gerry's advice stayed with me; I occasionally brought Rachel and Peter into the office nonetheless. My boss had a drum set in his office. Virtually every executive had an instrument of some sort. So instead of toys and Ping-Pong tables, the kids would bang away and watch me work.

My current job at the WNBA has involved them too. I took the job in part to help grow the women's league to ensure that Rachel and other girls would grow up with female role models in sports. As an athlete growing up, I had none.

When the L.A. Sparks came to Madison Square Garden to play the New York Liberty this past summer, Rachel and I brought a few of her friends and their moms to the game. Just before the start of the second half, the girls screamed out center Lisa Leslie's name. Lisa turned to them and broke into a smile. The four girls squeaked with excitement, "Oh my God, Lisa Leslie smiled at us!"

One of the moms turned to me and said, "We need to come here more often."

Soon afterward, I took Peter and one of his nine-year-old friends to another game. Watching two boys wearing WNBA hats cheer for female players brought on a surprise set of goose bumps. I realized it's just as important to me that Peter look up to female role models in sports. I hope his generation of boys will not grow up with stereotypes about what women can and cannot do.

When Rachel was seven and I had been working at Nickelodeon for about four years, she entered a "Why My Mom Works" essay contest that was sponsored by Viacom and *Working Mother* magazine.

Why my mom ● werks By Rachel sarnoff
I am 7 yers old.   she likes it.
and she gets mony for it.
I like her werk to. the whol
famly Loves it. Becaus she
likes the brecfests. Becaus she
likes talking obout things in
metings and she likes the
pepole she werks with. She
likes what she dus. she likes
to wach ● TV. werking macs
her happy and I Love my mom

Rachel won third prize in the contest, but I was the real winner. That framed piece of paper hangs in my office, and I still get tears in my eyes when I read it. An older working mom who had sacrificed a lot of time with her kids to advance her career saw it one day. "Ann, you have no idea how lucky you are that she feels that way," she told me. She had tears in her eyes too.

Involving my kids in my work and finding ways to be involved in their lives have been critical to me, but making significant career progress is also crucial to my overall happiness. Some working moms willingly trade promotions and advancement for more balance with their home lives, but I enjoy a challenge and have not hesitated to venture into new areas and industries. Fortunately, I have had bosses along the way (most of them men) who have challenged me to demonstrate skills beyond my résumé qualifications. At Nickelodeon, for example, my boss lobbied for me to have operational responsibilities added to my strategic role. Doing well in that position helped me segue into another position building and running one of Nickelodeon's key businesses. Stretching myself at work has kept me interested and motivated.

Do I ever feel tugged in different directions? Do I ever wish there were more hours in the day to get everything done? Absolutely. All the time.

I have moments where I'd like nothing better than to take a day off and read a book in bed, or go on a field trip with my child's class, or meet a friend for lunch and shopping. I know, however, that if I strung a few of those days together, I'd start longing to be back at work again.

So instead, I try to weave those things into my life whenever I can. I do yoga before work and swim on weekends. I occasionally surprise Rachel or Peter by picking them up at school. I try to have a girls' night out every once in a while. I try to live life on my terms, at least most of the time.

Will it work forever? I don't honestly know. Forever is a long time. I know that it's worked for me so far, and that's good enough for now.

How can I sum up this essay?

"Working Mom Has It All"? Boring, self-righteous, and certainly not the way I feel.

"Working Mom Struggles to Strike the Right Balance"? More provocative but still inaccurate.

"One Mom's Working Works for Her—and for Her Kids." Well, it's not the snappiest title, but it probably best describes how I feel. The bottom line is that combining motherhood and work is an inherently complex and deeply personal matter. The key to being fulfilled is having work that both takes advantage of your talents and allows you to manage your life the way you need to. There is no formula for success, but there are many individual solutions, and I've found mine.

When Rachel was born, a fellow working mom told me not to ever leave the house in the morning with regret. She said that my kids would sense my conflict and be confused by it. So I've tried to follow that advice and leave and return every day with a big smile on my face. I want to show them, particularly my daughter, that you can and should enjoy work (and be successful at it) as a woman and as a mom. I want my kids to know that I'm happy going to work. Because I am.

Red Boots and Cole Haans

Monica Buckley Price

Monica Buckley Price has one child, a seven-year-old boy with autism. Monica had written and performed a one-woman show, *Spontaneous Vertigo,* in New York and was working for NBC in Los Angeles as assistant to the executive producers on *Unsolved Mysteries* when her son's diagnosis forced her to quit to care for him full-time. Many of us, even die-hard working mothers who find it hard imagining staying home alone with their children without losing their sanity, would make the same choice if we faced that dilemma. Monica is the author of a memoir, *Driving with Dead People.*

Motherhood is not what I expected. I didn't expect the infinite love I have for my child. I didn't expect to be a stay-at-home mom. I didn't expect to have an autistic child. Every day is what I didn't expect.

Before I met my son in the delivery room, slippery in the doctor's gloved hands, life was simple in a way I had never understood or appreciated. Before that moment I did not question maintaining my "freedom" as a thirty-five-year-old woman with a promising career and financial independence. I was going to have a child, true, but I was a modern woman. The baby would only add to my free and productive life, which had included being an actress in New York and, for the past two years, a thrilling (sometimes too much so) job working in Los Angeles on the television show *Unsolved Mysteries*.

My water broke at 6 A.M. one sunny California morning. *Stay calm,* I remembered our Lamaze instructor, Ida Byrd, saying. *Take a shower before going to the hospital. You won't be having one for a while, and you'll be glad to have had it.*

I climbed into the shower. I turned on the water and bumped into my husband, who had also climbed in.

"What are you doing here?" I said, my huge stomach pressing against his. Pink liquid was squishing out of me and onto our feet, which I could barely see.

"She said to take a shower," Michael replied.

"Me, not you! My God, what are you thinking?"

He climbed out. I could hear him banging around in the bedroom.

"Take my suitcase to the car and I'll be right there!" I shouted, trying to give him a purpose. "And wake up Mom."

My mother had come from Indiana for the birth of my first child. I hoped that sharing the experience would mend our long-fragmented relationship. I knew she loved me. She knew I loved her. Beyond that, we had zero between us.

Michael, Mom, and I drove to the hospital, winding down Benedict Canyon in Friday-morning rush-hour traffic, me sitting on a black plastic garbage bag as directed by Ida Byrd so that the amniotic fluid, which had not stopped gushing, would not ruin the crappy car seats.

My mom kept clapping her hands and saying, "Aren't we lucky?"

Apparently, her uterus was not doing what mine was.

At Cedars-Sinai Hospital, the nurse checked my blood pressure and reported it was abnormally high. They called my doctor, who decided to hook me up to a Pitocin drip. I protested. I wanted childbirth without medication; it said so in my chart. But due to eclampsia risk, the doctor said the baby should come sooner rather than later.

Within half an hour, the contractions slammed into my body. By 3:30 P.M. the pain had become unbearable. I asked for an epidural. This would not be a natural birth.

Finally, at 9:30 P.M., I felt like pushing.

The nurse wheeled me into the delivery suite and called for my ob-gyn. I had a great view of the twinkling lights of the Hollywood hills and the Hard Rock Cafe with the back end of a car artfully smashed into the façade. All I cared about was the empty bassinet to the right of my bed.

For three and a half hours I tried to thrust my nine-pound son into the world. With every push, his head would crown. The doctor and Michael would shout, "There he is, keep going, keep pushing!" Then his head would disappear and they would emit a collective groan.

At 1:15 A.M. the bassinet was still empty. I was exhausted and scared.

The only person in the room who had been through this before (four times) was hiding behind a little curtain near the door. I could see Mom's faded blue sneakers sticking out beneath the beige fabric. I tried to concentrate on my breathing. I focused on the empty bassinet.

At 1:45 A.M. the doctor announced, "This baby is coming now. We're taking him with suction. Hold completely still."

Not a small request when your body is contracting involuntarily. The doctor attached the wand to the top of Wills's head and pulled. The epidural had worn off hours before. Muscles tore and I felt every one as the doctor ripped the baby out of me.

I was in bloody shreds. But Wills was here.

The doctor held him up. There he was, in hushed perfection, the light silhouetting his head. He had soft black hair, no neck, and a turned-up nose. He looked just like Michael.

Burning pain in my crotch and abdomen jolted away the beauty of my son's arrival as the doctor began the process of pushing out the afterbirth and repairing the damage.

"This is a complicated episiotomy," he said. "I'm literally putting you back together in layers." My stomach turned over. It *felt* like he was putting me back together in layers. "You're torn all the way to the rectum. A fourth degree."

Michael brought Wills over to me. "Do you want to hold him?"

I looked into Michael's radiant face, feeling like I'd been in a car accident. My body shook uncontrollably. I took Wills in my arms.

I saw his perfect face. I felt the elbows and knees I had gently rubbed so many times inside me. As hard as the birth had been, it looked as if Wills had done beautifully. I was incredibly relieved as I handed him back to Michael.

"I thought you'd want to hold him longer," he said.

I didn't have the strength to scream, "Look at me! I'm a mess! Can't you see me shaking?" Michael took Wills down to the nursery without saying another word.

When my doctor was done stitching, he put my legs down and covered me with warm blankets. Mom was next to my bed when I felt hot, thick liquid rushing out of me. My crotch was so traumatized I couldn't tell where it was coming from. I said to the nurse, "I think I'm having a bowel movement."

Her face went white. She raced over, tossed the blankets off me, and I saw bright red blood streaming onto the crisp white sheet. The room began to fade.

I don't remember how the doctors stopped the bleeding. After five hours and another hemorrhage, they finally stabilized me and rolled me to a room in Intensive Care. I had lost so much blood I felt literally drained, deflated, despite the gas pumping into my lungs.

Mom had gone back to the house to get some sleep.

Michael came in during my second blood transfusion. He had Wills in his arms. I began to sob. *Your Pregnancy Day by Day* showed what this moment was supposed to look like. The picture looked nothing like this.

As someone else's blood dripped into my veins, Michael said, "You should try to nurse him. According to Ida Byrd, it should've happened last night."

Ida Byrd could kiss my swollen ass.

Michael raised the head of the bed. "You should try it, Monica. He really needs it."

He handed me Wills. I could barely raise my arms to hold him. After all I'd been through, as exhausted as I was, how could I nurse a baby? I didn't think I had any bodily fluid left.

I tried anyway. To my amazement, after three near-misses, Wills latched on. Seeing his tiny hand curl over my breast, and the clear light in his new eyes, I suddenly believed I would live and love him and that he would love me back.

I knew I would never leave this child. I wouldn't even go to the bathroom without him. He was my third arm. It was now my sacred obligation to keep him safe and fed and happy. My job at *Unsolved Mysteries* was a distant, laughable memory.

I had entered a perfect world, a world I didn't understand.

Day eight. Time to go home from the hospital. I had lost sixty pounds. I was ordered to take ten weeks of bed rest. I walked like a very old person looking for change on the ground. I didn't want to leave the hospital. Not because I feared another hemorrhage. Because I didn't want Wills out in the world.

Once home, I entered what my husband and I later referred to as Vietnam. I loved my son and felt completely consumed by caring for him. Yet he pooped yellow-green shit without pause, slept only during the day, and nursed until my nipples felt like they would crumble onto the carpet. Who was I now? And who was this baby so vulnerable that his paper-thin toenails could be peeled off without clippers?

The first week was buoyed by friends stopping by to see Wills and shower us with gifts and flowers and Styrofoam containers filled with chicken and butternut squash from Koo Koo Roo. My child was gorgeous and healthy. Having the house full of people who made me laugh helped me regroup. My husband's agent called to say Michael had gotten a job writing his first network-television sitcom. I wouldn't have to go back to work for financial reasons. For the first time since I was sixteen, I had a choice.

My mother flew back to Indiana that week without having cooked one meal or changed a single diaper. She did administer one nugget of motherly wisdom to comfort me. She held Wills in her arms and said, "I would never do this again. If I had it to do it over, I would never have children. You will never keep him safe—never, ever, ever."

Weeks passed and I started to feel physically stronger. My cheeks glowed pink and I no longer crawled around the house on my hands and knees. My crotch did still resemble torn meat left behind by a lion that you'd see on some National Geographic special. And there was night, when the logic-snatching ghouls came and my white shabby-chic rocker was transformed into an animal poised for attack and Michael's guitar became a ghost hovering by the stereo.

Once at 3 A.M., in an attempt to help out, Michael got up to change a diaper while I sat on the floor by the changing table, the breast pump wheezing and pulling both boobs. I was so tired and stretched and stitched, I didn't think it could get worse. Then I felt warm liquid splatter against the side of my face. I didn't move. "That better not be shit on my face," I snapped.

It was. Michael had forgotten to cover the baby's butt while he looked for another diaper, and, yes, I now had shit all over my head and could see it splattered on the wall behind me.

"Why is this so fucking hard?" I screamed. "I'm doing all the hard stuff and all you had to do was change a fucking diaper and now there's shit all over me. Can't you help me in some way? Any way?"

Daylight came and I woke without the sound of the baby crying. I looked at the clock: 9:30 A.M. I rushed toward the nursery expecting to find Wills lifeless.

In the crib was a note:

My Sweetheart,

I took Wills on a ride.
We hope you enjoyed finally getting rest.

We'll bring home Starbucks.
We love you Mommy.

Michael and Wills

It was the first time I had seen Wills's name written on anything. "Michael and Wills" looked foreign and exactly right to me. I felt overwhelmingly happy and schizophrenic.

The next day Michael went back to work. My friends went back to their busy schedules shooting TV pilots, designing Legos toys, and not nursing babies. I was home with National Geographic crotch, too terrified to take my son outside of the house. What if he needed to nurse in the middle of Target? What if an infertile woman knocked me on the head with her Hermès bag and abducted him? And there was the very real chance that my vagina would detach and fall onto the sidewalk.

By the seventh week, my husband's new job was demanding fourteen-hour days. I paced the house like a caged animal. I went from window to window to see if maybe the Arrowhead Water driver with that nice smile or maybe a Jehovah's Witness was coming up the drive.

In direct betrayal of my son, my third arm, I started thinking of going back to work. My bosses had left a message wanting to know when I was returning. I had avoided calling them because I was ambivalent. I had started to become unambivalent.

Nursing my son for the thirty-eighth time that day, squeaking back and forth in the mommy glider with greasy hair and pimples from hormones and lack of grooming, I noticed my squishy, sagging belly, which hadn't been nourished in at least ten hours, and my bizarrely uneven breasts. My right breast had grown to a C cup while my left remained an A. I had waited my entire life to have boobs. Now I had boob.

As I rocked, the phone rang. The answering machine picked up, and I heard Michael's voice apologizing for having to work late again and signing off with "I love you." I hated him for being bathed and out in the world, for not having to feed the baby from one or two of his body parts, for having a penis that wasn't stitched like Frankenstein's forehead. Remembering how relieved he looked walking out the door that morning and sprinting to his Honda, I began picturing ways to torture him.

I looked down at my sleeping son. He had no idea who was rocking him. Neither did I.

I rocked faster, fantasizing about my desk at work, my mail, and my office self for the first time since Wills's birth. He wouldn't die if I worked part-time, I reasoned. I could resurrect the old me, wherever she was. It might be good for both of us.

The evening before my first day back I had a nightmare. I'm sure it was aided by all the missing-children searches I had seen on *Unsolved Mysteries*. In the dream, Wills was abducted from Encino Park, near our home. I knew he had been killed. I woke up and ran to his crib. There he was, safe with his stuffed kitten tucked in beside him. I carried him to the rocker, cradling him close while tears rolled down my cheeks and onto my nightgown. I couldn't live without my son. Would going back to work mean losing him?

When the sun rose, I was still in the rocker with Wills on my lap. I got up, laid him in his crib, and walked to the bathroom. There in the mirror was a bedraggled woman with dried milk stains on the front of her shirt. I looked like I'd been dragged behind a car for the extent of my maternity leave. I was so anxious about leaving Wills that I had to nurse him sitting on the toilet, harpooned by diarrhea. When my sister arrived to babysit, thick beads of sweat rolled down the sides of my face from changing Wills's diaper, picking up the house, and laying out all his favorite toys, purple blanket, and Raffi CDs.

I was late my first morning back. Leaving Wills felt like having my skin flayed off. When I got to work I was happily surprised by how normal everything felt.

Thirty minutes later, my phone rang. When I picked up, I could hear Wills screaming in the background. My sister's voice shook. "I can't help him at all. I've tried everything. He won't take the bottle, and he's been screaming for almost half an hour. Really, I'm freaking out. He's inconsolable."

I raced home. That week we tried it four more times. Four more times my phone rang less than an hour after I got to my desk. I rushed home each time because I was incapable of seeing that working three mornings a week should be manageable and that Wills was probably more resilient than I gave him credit for. I raced because I had an irrational fear that he would die if I didn't get there in time.

I made one last-ditch effort. I brought my sister and Wills to work with me and had them hang out in the conference room near my desk. Wills started screaming as soon as I closed the door. I could hear him from my desk; everyone could.

In the few seconds it took to reach Wills, I remembered crying myself to sleep as a six-year-old; Dad ripping a closet door off its hinges and throwing it; the gun my mother kept under the front seat of her Buick; my grandmother killing her own cat; needing new shoes; Christmas night alone; the neglected cemetery behind our old house. I remembered everything about being a helpless child that I had worked for years to forget.

I scooped Wills up, grabbed my purse, and told my sister I was done. We all went home. That afternoon I called and quit.

I vowed to never leave Wills again, even if that meant giving up my work and my financial independence. He was *my* baby and he needed *me*. Despite my mother's prediction, I was going to keep my baby safe. If I had to build a fortress with my own flesh, I would.

At home the next morning, I was lost. I sat nursing Wills at the end of the couch, the rest of my life stretching endlessly in front of me like the road leading away from the Baghdad Cafe. It did not matter if I showered or not, if my eyebrows were plucked or my mind sharp. I was a dining cart, a waste-management system. Without a job, I had no idea who I was.

I pored over the Yellow Pages until I found a listing for Gymboree. The ad said, "Our fun, specially designed activities gently stimulate baby's senses with special props, songs and gentle parachute play. During group discussions, you'll share ideas and advice with other new parents." Translated, it might have said, "We torture babies with sound and color and then have a helpful discussion that you won't hear because your child will be screaming."

I dressed Wills in a fabulous blue-and-white-striped Petit Bateau outfit and myself in the smallest pants I'd had on in almost a year. We headed out to be welcomed in all our neediness and walked through glass doors with multicolored letters spelling out salvation. Wills started crying immediately. Other mothers were trying to introduce themselves. I was embarrassed and panicky.

Suddenly, Wills quit screaming. I was about to rejoin the church to thank the Lord, when Wills's face turned beet red. I could hear an enormous poop squirting into his diaper. Sweating, I fumbled for my Laura Ashley diaper bag as I saw brown stains appearing around the legs of his Petit Bateau outfit. I wanted to kiss and squeeze my beautiful baby and not let even a speck of dirt touch his perfect skin. I also wanted to throw his shitty, screaming ass against the wall.

The teacher suggested the mothers move into a large circle and sit with their babies lying in front of them. I finished the diaper change and carried him over to the circle with yellow poop stains on my hands.

"Mothers, gently pull the baby toward you on the blanket," she instructed. When I laid him down, Wills went insane, screaming so loudly we couldn't hear her directions. I picked him up.

"Lay him back down," the teacher ordered.

I laid him back down. The shrieking continued.

She tried to talk over him. "Gently massage the top of their legs." She began yelling. "GENTLE CIRCLES." Wills screamed louder. "TURN THEM ON THEIR SIDES AND . . ." She turned to me. "Pick him up if you need to," she suggested. If she'd said, "Put him in the freezer and then come back to the mat and stand on your head," I might have done it.

I picked up his tense little body, and he began writhing in my arms like the creature that broke out of John Hurt's stomach in *Alien*. I put him over my left shoulder. Then my right. I held him out in front of me like a football. It was hopeless. He was still screaming, and I was missing the discussion on caring for circumcisions. A mother next to me began nursing her tranquil son.

"I don't think my son's very happy," I said, attempting a smile. "What's your secret?"

Without looking at me, she whispered, "I know what I'm doing."

"Wow, I can see how that would help," I said.

The teacher advised that perhaps a bit of fresh air would help settle Wills down.

As I walked toward the door, I spotted my diaper bag and furtively grabbed the handle. I walked out into the sunshine, away from a circle where we did not belong. As soon as we cleared the building, I ran for the car.

When I strapped Wills into his car seat, he instantly fell asleep. He was perfect. I was alone.

On the way home, I drove through McDonald's and ordered a Quarter Pounder with Cheese and a super-sized Coke. It was decadent, it was unhealthy, and it was just for me.

A few weeks later, I was feeling more adventurous. Wills wasn't. Going to the market or stopping by the post office turned him into a shrieking, panting mess. On miracle days when I got Wills to sleep in his crib, I prayed for silence, knowing that even the sound of the refrigerator door closing could mean he was up for the day: eight more hours alone with a little guy who couldn't hold up his own neck.

One Friday when I had just gotten Wills tucked into his crib and had fantasies of a hot bath and a good book, our friend Cade stopped by to drop off a script for Michael. He innocently opened our front gate and walked up the sidewalk. Our dog started barking. I burst through the door, a lunatic in filthy sweatpants. "What the hell, Cade? You're going to wake Wills." I flung my arms in the air, eyes bugged out in disbelief.

Cade looked back at me, startled. "I'm sorry. I was just going to lay this on the porch. I wasn't going to knock or anything."

"You can't stop by between one and three P.M. because that's *nap time,* and if the dog hears the gate, she'll bark and wake up Wills."

"I'm sorry. I'll call next time."

"No! Don't call next time; the phone will wake up Wills."

"Okay, Monica, once again, I'm really sorry. See ya."

He backed out the gate, afraid to turn his back on me.

I stormed into the house and slammed the door, causing more barking.

"What a jerk," I muttered, and Wills started crying.

My friends eventually quit calling or stopping by. I didn't need friends. I was out of the world, having officially merged with Wills. It was suffocating and intoxicating. No one had ever needed me so much.

I tried not to think of my unemployed status because it only brought on "loser" stress. I put it out of my head and focused on Wills. Now thirteen months old, Wills still only wanted to be held by me in our house. There were new worries as well. He wasn't hitting the appropriate developmental marks: babbling, gesturing, crawling. At sixteen months, Wills was finally walking, but he wasn't talking and his stranger anxiety worsened. If someone at the park came up to us, he would bury his face in his hands and let out a high-pitched shriek or take off running in a wild panic.

One Sunday my sister, Wills, and I were standing outside a piano store in Santa Monica. Suddenly, Wills pointed to a spigot on the side of the building and said his first word, "Water." It startled us so much, we screamed. Wills started crying.

I picked him up and said, "Yes, water. You are exactly right, that is where water comes from."

He pointed toward the sky. "Sky."

I danced in place. "You want to see airplanes?" I asked him.

"Airplane," he said.

"Okay, let's go airplane watching." I would have taken him to Vegas if he'd asked.

From then on, almost every day, Wills and I sat alone in the lobby of the tiny Van Nuys Airport. He pressed his small face against the glass to watch the planes come and go. He was happy there. He was not happy anywhere else.

When Wills was eighteen months old, my friend Jenn called and asked if she could drop off a book she had borrowed. I hung up the phone and looked at Wills. He was playing with soft blocks. "Jenn's coming over," I said. He looked startled. "I know you don't like visitors, but she's really great."

A few minutes later, the doorbell rang and Jenn was waving at me through the glass. I felt the old me, the woman who loved company, rumbling beneath my sweaty T-shirt. I opened the door, and when I turned to introduce Wills, he was gone. He was so wise-eyed and glorious; I couldn't wait for her to see him. But the ache in my stomach reminded me that Wills might not feel the same way.

"Hang on, Jenn, I have to get Wills," I said, following the trail of dropped blocks. The trail ended near his closet, where two red leather boots were poking out the door.

"I see you," I teased. When I pulled back the door, he was sitting there, arms wrapped around his body, rocking back and forth. "Hey, buddy," I said kneeling down, "what's going on?"

I looked into two completely blank eyes. Wills was not there.

I tried to pick him up, but he scrambled farther back into his closet and clamped his hands over his ears.

"Hang on, honey, I'll be right back."

I ran out to the living room. "Jenn, I'm sorry, Wills isn't feeling well. Can we get together another day?"

"Sure," she said, heading for the door.

I forced a smile. "Thanks for stopping by."

I closed the door and ran back to Wills's room. He was behind a stack of boxes now, his soft blond head barely visible.

"Jenn is gone, buddy. Can you come out now?"

He couldn't.

I sat in front of the closet with my hand stuck behind the boxes touching his soft leg. "It's okay, buddy. Come out when you're ready. It's okay."

I could live with the shrieking in public. I could humor his obsession with airplanes. I could minimize his sensitivity to sound and texture. But I could not deny that he was vanishing from me. I knew if I let that happen, I might never get him back.

I called our pediatrician.

"I think he should see someone," he said over the phone. "Right away."

I was alone the day I received Wills's diagnosis: autistic spectrum disorder. A gun pressed against the side of my head. Bullets ripped through my skull: *autistic, autistic, autistic.*

Dazed, I walked slowly out of the Santa Monica child psychologist's office and down the stairs to Wilshire Boulevard. I leaned against the car door and stared down at the gutter. I couldn't cry. I couldn't breathe. I couldn't remember how long I had been standing there. People walked by as if nothing had happened, carrying sandwiches from the Quiznos down the street. Didn't they know the world had just ended?

I unlocked my car door and sat down in the driver's seat. I had to pull it together. I had to pick up Wills at my sister's house.

That afternoon was sunny and bright as I watched Wills playing Green Ball in Bush, a game he had invented. The diagnosis hadn't changed him at all. He was exactly the same child I'd left that morning. But now, a new word—*autism*—was part of him, our future.

That night I saw the excitement in his cobalt eyes as I read him *The Encyclopedia of Trains*. I knew he was in there.

Suddenly, I had a new career: rescuing Wills.

From the Internet and our neighborhood bookstore, I learned that autism is a complex brain disorder, a lifelong disability that usually manifests in delayed speech, an inability to relate to others, and resistance to disruptions in routine. This certainly described Wills. Autism is a spectrum disorder, meaning that there are varying degrees of affliction, ranging from profoundly affected (no speech, no eye contact, repetitive behaviors) to high functioning (language, an ability to learn, to acquire social skills, to make eye contact). Autistic children often have sensory integration problems. Ordinary sounds become unbearably loud to them. Certain textures, like the tag on the back of a shirt, become agonizingly painful. For Wills, even bubbles in the bathtub "hurt" his skin. Autistic children often develop a "topic of interest" that they compulsively research and analyze and talk about.

Wills's topic had changed from airplanes to trains. This meant I spent at least six hours a week reading to him about the history of trains and studying maps of railroad lines. We watched train videos. We rode the Los Angeles Metro System around the city and Amtrak up and down the West Coast.

His psychologist, in an attempt to help him face and possibly overcome some of his social anxieties, suggested a toddler group at the Early Years, a Santa Monica preschool where she was a consultant. This would be the first time—since Gymboree—that Wills would be among his peers and I would be among the Motherset.

On our first day of school, Wills walked reluctantly into the Early Years play yard and sat beside me on the blue iron bench. He slipped off his red boots and dropped them onto the ground, curling his bare feet up under his corduroy bottom. His teacher, Lynn, walked over, picked up the boots, and handed them to Wills. "We wear our shoes at school," she gently told him. Wills took a quick breath in. "Because of safety reasons," she explained, "we wouldn't want anyone to step on a bee or worse." She smiled and walked back toward the slide, not realizing what this rule would mean to him.

Wills almost never wore shoes. He sampled the textures of the world with his feet, and in particular his toes. His face became red and blotchy, and his chin started to quiver. He pointed toward the gate. "Home, Mommy, home now." I slipped my arm around his middle. "I'm sorry, Wills. You can take them off as soon as we get in the car." He scooted away from me, tears and snot wetting his face. I attempted to put on a boot. "NO!" he screamed, kicking his feet, "NO SHOES. HOME, MOMMY." He was sobbing.

"Wills, there are all kinds of new things to learn at school, and some of them will be great and some of them will feel terrible. I know it doesn't help now, but you will get used to leaving your boots on. I promise you will." He leaned his head on his knees and sat still for a long time.

Finally, he climbed up onto my lap and I laced first the right and then the left boot, asking him to uncurl his disappointed toes each time. His shoulders were rounded and sad. Slowly, we got off the bench and walked up the stairs and inside the school.

I looked around at the toddlers' happy faces and tiny hands, noting who was singing and who was clapping and who was doing both. My heart sank as I clearly saw what Wills could not do. It was one thing to read it in a book, quite another to see what other kids his age were capable of. Wills was not like these children. I held back tears. He was being diagnosed all over again.

And I was too. I was not like these mothers. The stay-at-home mothers wore capri khaki pants, the working moms had on business suits, and they all sat in the same circle, oblivious to their incredible good luck.

At playtime, Wills refused to get on a swing or tricycle. He wouldn't climb a structure or explore the water table. He refused to put his hands in sand or interact with other children. He stood frozen by the back gate. All of this made sense in light of his diagnosis. I was beginning to question why we had come.

Even though I knew Wills might not participate, I still wanted it to happen. I wanted us to learn ridiculous songs like "Rags the Dog," and I wanted to bounce him on my lap. I wanted my child to laugh and have fun. But Wills was under the art easel rocking back and forth. We were the twosome other mothers tried not to look at.

From the playground, I called the psychologist on my cell phone. "Can you remind me why we're here?"

"I think that Wills can come out of his cocoon, given the chance," she explained. "If we don't push him, it'll never happen. He needs to see other children interacting and playing. This will help and encourage him."

Hard as it was, I decided to believe her.

Three months later, Wills moved from the toddler group at the Early Years into the preschool program. Parents were expected to leave their children four afternoons a week. Most of the mothers stayed at school for the first two weeks, and some even stayed for three. But eight weeks later, I was still sitting on the steps of the little blue house, quietly having therapy sessions on my cell phone while the other mothers were forming a coffee klatch down at the Coffee Bean or rushing back to the office.

After ten weeks, Wills's psychologist told me I had to leave him at school because Wills needed to learn that he could function without me. So one day I walked out the gate and left him behind shrieking, "OH, NO, MOMMY, PLEASE COME BACK! MY MOMMY, COME BACK!" I didn't know if either of us would survive.

I sat in my car with my head on the steering wheel, sobbing. A mother I recognized from the parents' orientation meeting tapped my window. She seemed annoyed. "Wills is screaming," she said through the open window.

"I know," I confessed. "I'm trying to help him separate. His therapist says this is best for him in the long run. He needs to be able to separate from me."

"How could you let him scream like that?" she insisted. "If that was my child, I would march right in there and get him."

"I'm trying to do what's best for him," I begged. She shook her head and walked away.

As I sat there crying, I thought of how I would never hurt Wills, how I'd given up my work, my self, to devote my entire life to him. Yet here in public, one uninformed mother could make me feel totally exposed and completely unsure of myself and the psychologist's guidance. All I wanted, all I could think of, was rushing in to rescue Wills—and my-self—from the hell of trying to do what was best for him.

Wills and I were completely alone now. Michael was in Chicago working as co–executive producer on *The Joan Cusack Show* and com-muting back to us every other weekend. He worked long days and often much of the night. We needed the money, with therapy bills running seven hundred dollars a week, plus the expensive preschool tuition. Oddly enough, it was a relief to have Michael in Chicago because my un-realized expectation that he would come home before midnight was no longer an issue. He wasn't coming home. Our marriage, which had not been steady since Wills's birth, was in serious trouble.

I found myself in a position I had vowed never to be in during all the years I'd been a working woman, before I'd had Wills: the tight corner my mother, my grandmother, and my great-grandmother had found themselves in—dependent on a husband for money and children's finan-cial security. For the women in my family at least, the results had been universally disastrous.

But I had no choice. I could not leave my son. No one else could ad-equately supervise his developmental progress. I was Wills's emotional net; Michael had to be our financial net.

Over the next year and a half, Wills began to reach the promise his psychologist had dangled in front of us like keys to a Mercedes. Through her therapeutic skill, the help of his preschool teachers and classmates, and my work with him every day, Wills began to separate. He began telling me exactly what he felt. "Being here is making my stomach hurt" or "It's too loud in here." He made his first friend, a boy who drew pic-tures of himself and Wills playing on a Santa Monica beach, two stick figures, one with yellow hair (Wills) and one with brown hair (Jeremy), holding hands.

When Wills was four years old, his school held an end-of-the-year sing-along at a park overlooking the Pacific Ocean. Beyond anxious, Wills bit his thumbnail, hid behind my leg, and cleared his throat again and again. I wore a funky new Anthropologie outfit—a long beige jacket with brown bell-bottoms and chunky shoes—hoping that if I looked nice, the day would follow suit.

When the whistle blew and it was time for the kids to sit down in the circle, Wills began screaming. Trying to climb up my body, he pulled down the back of my pants, exposing the thick band of my Jockey underwear to the thong-wearing Beverly Hills crowd. The director of the school offered to let me sit in the circle with Wills. My feelings of dread mounted as I climbed over a field of small bodies with my thirty-two-pound son in my arms to a tiny spot on the quilt. There was no room for crossing legs, so my size 9 Cole Haan loafers stuck up among the tiny Stride Rites. Wills wrapped his arms and legs around my body and buried his face in my shirt. He tried to soothe himself by rocking back and forth and making small whimpering noises to drown out the world. I sat in the circle patting Wills's back and scanning the crowd, feeling intensely alone in the crowd of mothers and fathers and children. The love of my life was in Chicago writing jokes and breaking my heart.

The children began to sing "I Can See Clearly Now":

> *Gone are the dark clouds that had me down.*
> *It's going to be a bright, bright sunshiny day.*

I suppressed an urge to scream "FUCK YOU!" to all those little toddlers. Then something happened. It was so small that nobody in the crowd would have noticed it. But to me it was a miracle. Wills let his hands slip away from his ears, his body relaxed for just a moment, and I heard vibrations coming from his throat. I had never heard him sing or hum anything. Even in front of a huge group of people, his worst nightmare, Wills was finding his own way to be part of the sing-along. His psychologist was right. As anxious as Wills was, there was still a part of him that wanted to belong, to connect, as even I did, as we all do.

I put my cheek against his cheek. He squeezed my side, and I forgave the gods, a little, for everything they had put us through.

A year later, Michael returned from Chicago permanently. While he was gone, one of our neighbors had asked me out. When I thanked him for the compliment and explained that I was married, he blushed and said, "But I've never seen your husband."

"Exactly," I said, nodding.

I greeted Michael's homecoming with an ultimatum. "Be part of this family or get an apartment."

He did not get an apartment. We worked hard on our marriage, and he worked hard to regain my trust. He is now co–executive producer of a popular television show with reasonable hours. He takes Wills to school every day and is usually home in time to read him books at bedtime. Wills only wears shirts that "look like Daddy's" now.

We are finally a family of three.

Wills and I are driving back from his weekly psychologist appointment. The car climbs up a hilly, congested road. From the backseat Wills says, "There's a stomach-wide water shortage back here."

I look at him in the rearview mirror. His new golden retriever puppy sits next to him. He named her Cowboy Carol Lawrence. He softly bangs a Nike Velcro tennis shoe on the back of my seat.

"I can't do anything right now, buddy. Sorry."

He sighs and rolls down his window, letting the wind blow his thick brown hair off his forehead. His huge blue almond-shaped eyes look as if they're continuously contemplating the universe from their perch on top of his freckled nose.

"We need to spray 'Traffic Be Gone' out there." He cracks up at himself.

He has friends who love him. His friend Emily kisses him, holds his hand, and brings him into the circle of children at school. He does not hug her, but he smiles when she gives him a squeeze. At his request, we will have a Dinosaur and Fossil Hunt party to celebrate his seventh birthday next month. This will mark the first birthday party where he wants to hear the Happy Birthday song.

I worry about Wills's future. I worry I will never hear him say "I love you, Mommy." I worry he won't be able to read or handle a checking account or live on his own. Knowing what it means to have given up my own career, I wonder what a lifetime without financial independence will mean for my son.

And me? I'm glad I stayed home with my son. He needed me, and I needed to feel that I was there for him in a way my mother never was for me. And once I knew about the autism, the choice was crystal clear. I'll never know what I gave up to stay home with Wills. But I do know what I would have given up if I hadn't stayed home. I would have given up Wills.

Right now he wants water. "This is like the Mojave Desert, I'm telling you. I need rain back here."

"Wills, I can't move any faster with this traffic," I tell him. "We'll be home in ten minutes."

"In ten minutes, I'll have no body fluid. I'll be dust on the seat."

I look again and he attempts to wink at me. He's been learning to wink. I wink back.

He settles back into his seat and hauls the puppy onto his lap.

We are turning down our street when I hear, "I love you, Cowboy."

Maybe I'll be next.

Working Mother, Not Guilty

Sara Nelson

I first crossed paths with Sara Nelson, editor in chief of *Publishers Weekly,* when I was an intern at *Seventeen* in 1987 and Sara was the magazine's star writer, contributing a cover feature to nearly every issue, and also writing for several other national magazines. In 1988 Sara wrote a story for *Glamour* describing a week during which she and her sister, who had two children, traded places. Her sister came to New York to live the single life in Sara's SoHo apartment; Sara flew to Georgia to try motherhood. Even *Glamour*'s young readers, most of them years from motherhood, were fascinated by what Sara and her sister learned about trading single and motherhood lives.

Sara is now married and has a son, Charley. She has written for *The New York Times, The Wall Street Journal,* the *New York Post, Newsday, 7 Days, Glamour, Redbook,* and many other publications. She has taught at Columbia and New York University and the Radcliffe Publishing Course. She became editor in chief of *Publishers Weekly* in January 2005. Her most recent book is *So Many Books, So Little Time.*

When I called Sara to ask her to write an essay, she replied, "Sure, but I don't really have anything to write about. I never feel guilty about being a working mom." In that moment, I knew that she did have a story to tell. Here it is.

About a year ago, when I was working as a reviewer for a women's magazine, I was invited to a luncheon to launch a new book, a book about motherhood. Hosted by the publisher in a tony restaurant, it was slightly different from the typical publishing lunch. At most book launches, about 50 percent of the attendees are women; at this one, we all were. The publisher clearly hoped we'd bond with the author upon hearing her theories about how society sets unreasonable standards for those of us with children.

And they were right. Before we'd even touched the requisite field-greens course, the conversation had turned personal. By the time the salmon came, the assembled working moms were fully engaged in apparently joyous guilt one-upping. One woman, I remember, began talking about how she had missed her daughter's first word (nods and sighs all around). Another told us how agitated she got every time her boss even breathed the words "business trip" (ditto). And a third narrated a long, involved story about being dissed by the "nonworking" mothers at her son's school (scowls). Then a woman I knew better than the others delivered the guilt coup de grâce: "My daughter made a sign for our front door last week when I was at work," she revealed. "It said: 'Come home, Mom.'"

There was a collective gasp from all assembled, and I fully anticipated tears to fall.

Then a younger, childless working woman at the head of the table piped up. "You know what?" she said. "She's playing you. I used to leave notes like that for my mom, too. I missed her, but what I really liked was knowing I could make her feel guilty."

"Ooooh," moaned the crowd, stunned.

"Bingo!" went a voice in my head.

I have one child, Charley, age ten. I've recently taken over as editor in chief of a weekly magazine. For the last decade, I've held a variety of jobs. I've been a newspaper columnist, a freelance writer, a TV producer, a reporter, a magazine editor, a teacher, and an author. I've worked part-time for corporations and full-time for myself. I figure, on average, I've worked at least forty hours a week for the past ten years. Working motherhood has on various occasions made me feel tense, elated, exhausted, thrilled, bored, and, sometimes, angry.

What it hasn't made me is guilty. Or, let me put it this way: If being a working mother makes me feel guilty about anything, it's about not feeling guilty.

I always focused on work, even as a kid. In my family this made me a star. My father spent my childhood building our family furniture business. My mother, while not a member of the paid workforce, prided herself on her organizational abilities in volunteer work and household running. She was no Donna Reed or Mrs. Cleaver, but she wasn't exactly Hillary Clinton either. Definitely not a get-down-on-the-floor-with-the-kids kind of mom, she still made it to every school play, piano recital, and field day the four of us kids ever had.

Still, "Take care of it" was the watchword in our house. Achievement itself was prized, but the preparation for and road to success were nearly as important. As a ten-year-old running a temperature of 103, I begged to be allowed to go to school because I had a science test. It wouldn't have been responsible to miss it, I guess. Even today, at eighty-six, my mother considers the most bitter criticism she can make against someone is to say that they're "disorganized."

As a suburban kid, I dreamed of having a big-city life and an interesting job, more Brenda Starr than Donna Reed. It's not that I rejected the image of myself as a mother. It was simply not my emphasis. Or, more accurately, marriage and children were only part of what was expected of me, and what I expected of myself.

As I approached my thirties, husband- and babyless, my parents didn't pressure me about personal plans. My career was on track and I seemed happy enough; I didn't need marriage and babies, the then-popular panacea for all ills. *The Rules* had yet to come out, but the ideas behind it were bubbling up, even then. Find a man and get him to marry you and give you babies; that was the supposed ticket to happiness. But somehow I never bought that ticket. I'd been born just a little too late to experience the feminist movement, so I never knew there could be conflict between work and family. I was young and arrogant enough to ignore the articles I was reading (and writing) about infertility in "older" moms. Characteristically, I just went about my business: working and dating. For years, I was as passionate about both as I was unclear about where they'd lead.

Then, in my mid-thirties, I met Leo. For all his surface differences—he was older, he had a grown son from his first marriage, television was his career focus, he was a stickler for doing his own housework—Leo was a kindred spirit when it came to love and work. You can see the attraction; Leo was a man Brenda Starr would have really appreciated. And he wanted to have another child. With me. Somehow, it never occurred to him that I wouldn't want the same for myself. So we got married and set out to make our baby.

When I think back on it, I see now that the three years it took me to get pregnant were the first sign that God was laughing at our plans. When our healthy eight-pound, one-ounce boy was born, I was the happiest I'd ever been in my life. For a minute, all thoughts of work vanished.

"I don't care if I never leave the house again," I told a friend, who'd been back at work since her son turned six weeks.

"That'll pass," she replied.

She was right, of course, both about my desire to stay home with my son and about another idea of mine—stridently stated to anyone who would listen—that "nothing" would change once the baby came. Everything changed, of course, though we denied it for as long as we could. From birth, essentially, Charley went everywhere we went, strapped into the Snugli. And I mean everywhere: Leo's office at the TV studio, my various workplaces, restaurants and movies and parks and playdates and Mommy and Me classes. Evenings and weekends were spent searching our SoHo neighborhood for places that served breakfast at 7 A.M. or welcomed kids who couldn't sit up yet.

But within weeks Leo was back in the studio and I'd loaded up with several assignments. We hired a full-time babysitter, even though I was working at home. As much as possible, I rearranged my (thankfully flexible) schedule so that I could be home every day for lunch and a feeding. It was not lost on me—not for a second—that we were lucky to have an "easy" baby as well as the kind of careers that could be modified, without giving up much in the earnings or satisfaction departments.

But except for that brief postpartum period, I never once considered giving up work. I could just as easily have stopped breathing. I was thirty-seven when I had Charley, and while you don't read much about this in the late-pregnancy articles and books, I'm glad I was so old; by the time I became somebody's mother, I'd actually become a grown-up and I finally understood a few things, not least of which was what those airline emergency instructions meant. "Those traveling with small children should put the oxygen over their own nose and mouth before assisting other passengers." Suddenly, I got it: Work was my oxygen. Without it, there was no way I'd be able to teach my son to breathe.

By the time you're thirty-seven, you should know who you are. Fashionable or not, this is who I am: my mother's and father's daughter, a person who needs to get things done, who, for the sake of her sanity, needs to work. And while I know plenty of women who've turned their executive natures and high-powered work experience into planning the perfect one-year-old's birthday party, refining the yummiest chocolate chip cookie recipe, or maintaining the cleanest kids' clothes, I knew even ten years ago that I wasn't going to be one of them. Like Hillary Clinton, excoriated for announcing she was not going to "give teas and bake cookies," I was hell-bent on being who I was. I could only hope I'd get less criticism for it from my peers.

"But you don't need to work," some acquaintances would admonish, pointing out that I had a working husband and money in the bank. To which I would respond in the Clintonian (Bill, not Hillary, this time) manner. "Define *need*," I'd say.

I love my son and I love my work. (I also love my husband, at least most of the time, but that's another story.) I haven't had to make a choice between work and family. If I did, there's no question what I'd choose. All the published books or completed to-do lists in the world don't begin to equal the pleasure of the toddler falling asleep in my arms, or even the ten-year-old talking back when I ask him to put his plate in the sink. I may never have had specific rock-the-baby-in-the-yard-behind-the-picket-fence dreams, but Charley is everything I could have dreamed of, and more. He takes second place to no one and nothing.

As a working parent, I'm often frazzled. Working or not, I've never been particularly long on patience. But I am not—at least not often—resentful or depressed. And while I take both parenting and working seriously, I don't feel Obligated with a capital O. I'm lucky; I love to work and I love being with Charley. If each "obligation" spells me a bit from the other—gives me some breathing time, in other words—so be it. I've seen enough angry, depressed, and capital-O-Obligated mothers to convince me that staying home with your child all day, every day, because you think Mothers Are Supposed To doesn't do anybody any favors. An old friend of mine recently told me she'd gone on antidepressants because she was "just so mad" all the time. This was the same friend who up and left her promising career the minute the first of her four children was born—and hasn't been back since, despite a significant drop in income, a move to another state, and the invention of preschool.

"Do you think it might help if you had some other outlets, maybe new people to meet or some articles to write?" I asked, and I offered to set her up with both.

"That's got nothing to do with it," she snorted.

O-kay, as Charley would say. Whatever.

Now, before I go any further, I have to say I know my work life is not typical. I love what I do, first of all. What I call "work" 95 percent of America would call play, or at least hobby. I don't punch a time clock, and despite plenty of deadlines and annoying editors, I can pretty much make my own schedule. It also helps that Charley has an interested father with a flexible schedule, and that we have enough money and luck to have found a spectacular, loving babysitter, Hazel, who has called in sick about three times in eight years. I couldn't do what I do alone—and I know there are women who are far less fortunate. But it seems to me that we hear a lot less complaining from those women, the ones who need, in the traditional sense, to work, than we do from the overeducated professionals on the 8:30 A.M. from Ardsley. I guess when you don't have a choice, you don't have the luxury of agonizing about it.

I remember an episode of *Murphy Brown* a decade ago, in which Murphy—the high-powered, seemingly cold-blooded TV personality—had to decide whether to pursue an important story or go to her son's first birthday party. There was a lot of Sturm und Drang around the decision, and finally Murphy decided to skip the party. I guess we were supposed to be agonizing along with her—and maybe, in that Bush/Quayle era, scoffing that she'd made the wrong decision. But I found myself feeling what a friend of Murphy's finally vocalized: The child wouldn't even know she wasn't there.

So much of what passes for guilt in us working mothers is really denial. We tell ourselves that little Ethan or Olivia will be traumatized if we miss their first steps, but it's really the adults who feel cheated of the opportunity to fuss and kvell. So much of this so-called guilt is longing on the part of us moms for some romanticized notion of motherhood, replete with mom-assisted paint-by-numbers and endless rounds of ring-around-the-rosy. It is much less about what goes on daily with a flesh-and-blood child. Call me cynical, but I'm not sure that Charley noticed or cared that the person putting a Band-Aid on his playground boo-boos was Hazel, not me.

The truth is, even if I hadn't been working, I wouldn't have been a very good Band-Aid-sticker-on-er or swing pusher or puzzle helper, although I've done plenty of those things, and more, in the evenings and on the weekends. But to make that my life's work for however many years? I don't think anybody would have benefited. Other women seem to do it, it's true. I veer between thinking that (*a*) they're simply better human beings than I am, and (*b*) they're lying about how much they like it. In fact, like my friend with the antidepressants, most of these women seem to enjoy not the activity of being with their kids but the martyrdom of it, the look-what-I'm-doing-for-my-kid-and-how-unselfish-I-am halo staying home gives them.

About half of the mothers of kids in Charley's class are working at least part-time. There's Maria, who designs handbags; Lauren, who works in advertising; Paulette, who writes children's books. The mother of Charley's friend Nick is an independent management consultant. And for the most part—and I gather this is unusual in the fiercely competitive world of New York private schools—there's little conflict between the employed mothers and the ones who stay home. The school generally schedules symposia and curriculum meetings and presentations for 8:30 A.M., after drop-off, or sometimes in the evenings. The sign-up sheet for the Christmas fair—held, thankfully, on the weekend—is about 50-50, working and not. There's rarely a must-attend event that happens at 11 A.M.

Still, there is some tension bubbling under the surface. One morning one of the stay-at-home mothers referred to herself, quite pointedly, as a "full-time mom." Those three words made my blood boil. I've been a mother every second of every day for the past ten and a half years, whether I'm researching an article or pushing a swing. Would anyone dare to suggest that a woman who worked in a factory, or as a cop or a firefighter—a woman who worked at least partly so that her children could have food and shoes and the occasional trip to Toys "R" Us—was any less a mother than my school acquaintance, who'd had the privilege to opt out of the workforce?

Motherhood is a state of being, I felt like telling her. *It's not a job description.*

A couple of years ago, I had two jobs. On Monday, Tuesday, and Wednesday, I got up, got dressed in an office-appropriate outfit, and went to the offices of a popular women's magazine where I was a contributing editor. On Thursdays and Fridays I put on my bathrobe and went to my home office and worked on my book, which was published the following year. Ironically, Charley preferred the days I went to the magazine, because on those days I'd take him to school and even if I wasn't available to pick him up at 3:20, I was usually home—and available to him—by dinnertime. On school holidays he'd come to work with me; he loved the soggy pancakes in the company cafeteria and the high-speed Internet hookup on my computer.

The other days should have been more Charley-friendly, since I was only going downstairs. But my son told me, more than once, that he disliked my work-at-home-days because I seemed farther away. He was clearly talking metaphorically: writing a book, we both soon discovered, required a concentration and focus that even putting out a magazine did not. Besides, because my constitution is such that I can only write in the early morning, on Thursdays and Fridays I'd arrange for Leo or Hazel to take Charley to school so I could get straight to work before I'd had a chance to fully wake up and talk myself out of it.

We missed something on those days, no doubt about it. The morning rituals, the breakfast, the getting dressed, the trip to school (never mind that that now ends with "See ya, Mom" instead of a preschooler's hug and kiss), represent some of the closest times I've had with Charley, the times our bond is the strongest. It has been on those trips to school that he's told me about his problems with T, the boy with whom he has his first love/hate relationship. It was on one of those trips that he confessed to me his love for Y, about whom I promised I won't say any more. It's on those morning trips that we invented our own word math problems (Charley may be the only child in history who ever asked his mother to lay off the bedtime stories in favor of made-up thought puzzlers) and debated the relative definitions of two of our favorite words, "whatcha-macallit" and "thingamajig." My sister Liza, a stay-at-home mother to her now-grown children, always told me that her best moments with her kids came in the car on the hour-long ride to school. There's something about being in an enclosed space together, especially in the half-awake morning, that loosens inhibitions and makes conversation flow.

So if I could change anything, it would be to take back those mornings I missed. But I'm afraid I don't admit that very often. In fact, it shames me now to remember how perversely I behaved when an acquaintance told me her husband takes care of their school-age daughter in the morning. "I just can't deal with that stuff," she said. I nodded knowingly—I DO know—but inside, I was turning from an understanding Dr. Jekyll to a venomous Mr. Hyde. "What kind of mother must *she* be?" I muttered. Apparently, the need to feel superior is innate, at least in me, and strong.

On the other hand, the one thing that's not in short supply in our household is conversation. Charley knows, sometimes in detail, exactly what I'm doing when I'm not taking him to school or picking him up. When I went on business trips—or when, after my book was published, I went on a small publicity tour—we talked several times a day. I've explained multiplication, arranged playdates, and discussed the latest developments with Y from across the country. And Charley, unlike most kids his age, actually asks questions about what I do: "Did a lot of people come to your reading?" And the perennial "I hope you read the parts of the book that are about me."

I also tell Charley about the people I work with and, occasionally, a (sometimes bowdlerized) version of conflicts in the office. He likes to hear about that stuff, it seems, and he likes to relate his own experiences to mine. He also likes to talk about his father's work. I've overheard him bragging about us (I admit we both have cool jobs) and I'm flattered, but mostly I'm glad he has an example—two examples, actually—of what it's like to take your work seriously, of how to interact with others in a professional way, and of the value of doing a job and doing it well.

My work is another bond between us, in fact. One fall his second-grade teacher told me that for all his excellence in reading comprehension, he hated to write and would find just about any excuse to avoid constructing the two-paragraph essays that were required almost daily. I couldn't help but laugh. I wanted to say, "Yeah, well, when he starts eating everything in the house and threatens to smoke cigarettes to help his concentration, I'll really be convinced he's a writer." But instead, I just listened.

The next night, I decided to tell Charley about my day.

"I had a hard time writing today," I said. "No matter how much time I spent at the computer, I couldn't seem to think of anything to say. It was soooooo frustrating. You know what I mean?"

"Same, Mom," he said. "That happens to me all the time."

From there ensued one of the most helpful conversations about procrastination either of us might ever hope to have.

All this said, the truth is I sometimes think about scaling back my work schedule in a couple of years, partly because, yes, Virginia, I'm getting older and more tired, but also because the older Charley gets, the more—not less—he needs me. You know that expression: Little children, little problems; big children, bigger problems? Well, I don't know about problems, per se, but I certainly believe that adolescence poses bigger issues than just about any other time in life. I love Charley's school, and his friends and their parents and the wonderful Hazel, who is morphing into more of a housekeeper than a babysitter these days anyway. But I want to be the one to answer the bigger questions about why there's a homeless man sleeping on our corner, or why, all of a sudden, he can't seem to get Y on the phone.

I fully expect Charley to start talking to me less, not more, as his hormones take over. I know that many days he'll probably come home from school and shut himself up in his room. But I also know that sometimes you need someone to be there when you slam that door. I want to be the one he rails against. In other words, the less he thinks he needs me, the more I plan to be there.

● ● ●

I haven't regretted my choices in the past ten years. They've been right for all of us. Because I work, Charley has a sense that there's a whole world outside of our little family. He knows that women exist on this earth for reasons beyond driving car pools, cooking dinner, and setting Game Boy rules. And maybe, just maybe, this is a message he'll carry with him throughout his life. Maybe, just maybe, when the time comes for him to choose a life partner, he'll gravitate to one who knows a little bit about the professional world, as well as the personal one. Or maybe not, and that will be another lesson motherhood teaches me: how to let go.

The other night Charley was working on a report for school, a kind of family tree of names and dates and marriages and accomplishments. After a couple of minutes, he looked up at me, stumped. "What was Nana's job?" he asked, pencil poised over the section marked "grandmother."

"Hmm," I replied. "Well, actually, Nana never really had a job other than taking care of Pop-pop, your aunt and uncles, and me."

Charley paused for a minute, and then, in that world-weary way that ten-year-olds have perfected, nodded knowingly. "Oh, right, Mom," he said. "There once was a time when women didn't work, wasn't there? Is that what they call the Dark Ages?"

That's when I heard the familiar voice in my head. "Bingo," it said.

Feminism Meets the Free Market

● ● ● *Jane Smiley*

For people who have read her novels, Jane Smiley needs no introduction. She won the Pulitzer Prize in 1992 for *A Thousand Acres;* the 1997 movie version starred Jessica Lange, Jason Robards, and Michelle Pfeiffer. Her most recent books are *Good Faith, A Year at the Races,* and *Thirteen Ways of Looking at the Novel.* She is a member of the American Academy of Arts and Letters. Jane lives in California with her teenage son and many animals. Her two daughters are grown.

For many of us whose children are still young, the challenge of whether to work or not, or how much to work, is framed by our desires: Where do we most want to be? How can we be in two places? Work pulls us in with its rewards of financial compensation, self-esteem, and intellectual and social stimulation. Home beckons to us with the joys of our children and freedom and creating a warm and inviting refuge. Jane describes a different world, uncharted territory for women graduating from college in the early 1970s, without mentors, role models, or the concept of a glass ceiling. Where are those women now? What do their experiences mean for younger mothers today?

often think my micro-generation of feminists, born, say, between 1947 and 1952, were given a precious gift by our older sisters in the Friedan/ Steinem/Millett generation: the gift of a certain obliviousness, a certain unquestioning belief not only in our own abilities but also in their usefulness.

I was in college, at Vassar, between 1967 and 1971, and in graduate school at the University of Iowa between 1972 and 1978. My friends and I were fortunate enough not to have to address the question of whether we could take up a vocation, as women of older generations had been forced to, but only the question of what it would be. The world seemed to lie before us, no less so and perhaps more so than it did before our brothers and boyfriends, because they were subject to the military draft and we were not.

Our choices seemed to be purely personal ones. Where did our talents lie? What were our most likely achievements? We received another boon, too, in that not much was expected of us, at least not by our parents or boyfriends or peers. Because really, no one knew what to expect of girls anymore.

We were in many ways regular girls, chosen by the mechanism of the SAT to go to elite colleges, where we then selected literary endeavors the way other students chose pre-med. The singular, driving sense of uniqueness and alienation that had been formative in the lives of earlier women writers, that had given them not only vision but motivation, was not required of us. At our colleges, we were encouraged to read the "masters" with confidence and skepticism, to feel no hesitation about inserting ourselves into a literary tradition that we knew was overwhelmingly male but perhaps, we thought, merely a result of the happenstance of history.

Compared with women as few as five to seven years older, we almost easily went on to become doctors, journalists, art history professors, curators, lawyers, actors (Meryl Streep was in my class), editors, entrepreneurs, and so forth. So, perhaps, it is fair to ask our group to serve as an index of the relative success or failure of feminism. It is our group who started out with the least friction, and who perhaps by now should have gone the furthest in the quest to balance meaningful work and raising children.

A full generation has gone by since my friends and I set out in the 1970s. Most of us have daughters of our own. Some of us are ready to be grandmothers and CEOs.

Have we done what we intended?

Where have we gotten and why?

Malinda* was one of the first three women admitted to the University of Iowa law school. She graduated third in the class. Antagonism from the male students was routine. Her boyfriend once overheard several students in the men's gym attacking Malinda by name for "taking a spot in the law school that a man should have had." But she was there, and she was a success. After passing the bar, Malinda took a job at the FDA. She has two sons. Now she works from home.

My friend Mary was at the Iowa Writers' Workshop with me. She had a top fellowship and a good publication before graduation (rare then). Her heart was in publishing though, not in writing. After graduation, she took a job as an editorial assistant in New York. By her mid-forties she was publisher and editor in chief at Viking. She has three children. Now she works from home.

Barbara got her doctorate in English with a specialty in drama, was regularly promoted, and is now an associate provost in charge of faculty development at a large university. She doesn't consider the more prestigious positions she is frequently asked to apply for. When her husband, who is eight years older, retires in a few years, the chances are she will work from home without having become the provost or the president of any university at all. She has two sons.

My friend Susan became a successful literary agent. She has two birth children and two children adopted from Vietnam and Colombia. She also has custody of two of her siblings, who require complete care. She works from her office part of the week, from her home part of the week.

Molly, who learned Mandarin Chinese in college, put together her

*Some of the names in this essay have been changed.

own consulting firm in the late 1970s and was one of the first Americans to visit China and set up contracts between American firms and Chinese suppliers. She has three children, and she works from home.

I work from home, too. When I was forty-six and a distinguished professor, a winner of the Pulitzer Prize, and a successful author, I quit university life. I have three children.

Our case histories are more telling than they appear on the surface. What they tell is how feminism and America slammed together and changed each other. Choices that seem personal and feel personal are expressions of sociology and culture as much as of psychology and individual history.

One of the things that is important to understanding our collective experience of balancing work and family life is that home wasn't the problem that brought us home.

Home was the refuge when the workplace drove us out.

My daughter, who is twenty-six, wishes American feminism had produced a society like Norway or Sweden, where child rearing and family life are considered the business of the entire country. Where there is no premium placed on traditional "family values." Where good prenatal care, breast-feeding, excellent day care, good medical care, anti-child-abuse laws and programs, and proper educational facilities are considered the rights of all rather than the privilege of a few. If that is our standard of success, then American feminism has failed indeed, because it has failed to promote the common good of women and children.

All over the United States, services that help families are randomly distributed. When I lived in Ames, Iowa, for example, work was ten minutes from home, which was five minutes from the day care, which was across the street from the grocery store, which was five minutes from the school, which was two minutes from home. This is the cardinal rule for "having it all"—have it all inside a very small perimeter, so that you can get to any problem ASAP. I had excellent, affordable day care and a medical clinic and hospital moments from my house (which was large and not expensive). Local child care benefited from the fact that Iowa State had a home economics department where students could major in early-childhood education. Often those graduates went to work in local centers, which were overseen by the community as well as the state. A child stuck at home with Mom was at a disadvantage: few children to play with and not much to do compared with well-planned and superbly supervised activities that were far too fun and messy for my house, at least, such as the paint table, the sand table, the water table, the extensive and up-to-date playground equipment. Ames was day-care heaven.

Maybe that was not the reason the choice between children and work never seemed as stark to us as it does to women now. After all, my friends in New York, Washington, and the Far East did not live in day-care heaven and had to do the best they could with the resources at hand. I trace our fairly laissez-faire attitude primarily to how we ourselves were raised. Malinda was the eldest of eight kids. I had a working mother and lots of cousins. Susan was one of five, Molly one of four. The World War II generation that raised us did not nurture us as much as they trained us—to mind our manners, to keep our opinions to ourselves (I never said the word *no* to any adult), to show respect to parents and teachers ("ma'am" and "sir"), and to be useful (Malinda and her sisters cooked the family dinner every night). Otherwise, we did pretty much what we wanted, out and about in the neighborhood.

As mothers we maintained that what worked for our parents would work for us. Keep our children safe, give them something to do, leave them alone, and achievement would follow. We have, in fact, reared fabulous kids, girls and boys who have turned out lively, intelligent, responsible, sociable, fun, and even well-mannered, more or less without Mozart in the womb, special black-and-white infant mobiles, or prestigious schooling.

Malinda's story turned out to be the most interesting and, I think, the most revealing. When she went to work as a lawyer for the Food and Drug Administration in the late 1970s, her job was to get botulism-tainted canned goods off supermarket shelves. Mushroom soup was the biggest danger; the heat that wrecks the quality of the soup is not much higher than heat that destroys the botulin bacteria. Malinda never lost her enthusiasm. If she saved one kid from blindness or death, that was a good year's work for her.

When Ronald Reagan was elected, though, deregulation meant that Malinda's own agency and her commitment to consumer protection came under attack. Her work environment became more or less a war zone for almost twenty years. The last straw (more like being hit with a two-by-four) was the "Gingrich Revolution" of 1994. The Republicans made it their primary goal to obstruct not only regulation itself but also the daily workings of the Clinton executive branch. Republican members of Congress used soft money to hire people, usually young people at low wages, to harass people like Malinda. She was required to report on her time and activities during the course of a working day, and threatened with a congressional subpoena if she didn't keep a daily log of meetings, and supply notes of those meetings, and account for periods when she was, perhaps, parked in the wrong parking place. The Republican goal was enforced time-wasting. If businesses didn't like regulations, certain members of Congress would see that there was no time and no personnel to enforce them. After years of this, Malinda quit the government and went to work for a pharmaceutical company that was trying to get approvals for drugs that Malinda considered promising. Her idealism was buffeted but still intact.

Mary was ambitious, too. When she went to work in publishing, she wanted to be Max Perkins, the famous literary editor who cultivated F. Scott Fitzgerald. Great writers were her idols. Knopf, her publishing house, was full of respected, fatherly editors who had been molding American literature for forty years. Most mornings Mary got there earlier than anyone else and rode the elevator with Alfred Knopf himself.

Publishing soon changed, too. Smaller houses were taken over by larger houses, which were taken over by nonpublishing conglomerates whose executives couldn't understand why publishing has such a low profit margin. Reforms were instituted to bring publishing in line with, say, the manufacture of refrigerators or the production of motion pictures. The sorts of literary properties Mary was interested in had no status in these terms. Publishing became a matter of sneaking the quality in as a Cinderella-like stepsister to cookbooks, blockbusters, and self-help books. That was one difficulty.

The other difficulty was that even as Mary made her reputation and rose from position to position (by switching companies, not, as in the old days, through internal promotion), her companies would be taken over. Sometimes everyone who had hired her would be gone in a matter of months, sometimes her job description would explode, sometimes the mission of her publishing house would transform, and often her staff would be trimmed. She was on an endless roller coaster of corporate change with an ever-greater focus on profitability.

Even so, there were women all around her. In publishing, as in few other fields, women did get into positions of power, partly because men in general were no longer reading as much, while women readers were still looking for good books. Eventually, Mary got her dream job as publisher at a prestigious literary house, with hands-on power and editorial input into the publishing of good literary properties. She meshed nicely with her bosses (who were based in England). It seemed that she had survived the publishing earthquake. Then her company got taken over one last time, her job description was rewritten, and she looked around the industry at her possibilities for promotion or similar jobs. The similar jobs had vanished. Promotions were into positions that had nothing to do with publishing and everything to do with corporate power jockeying. Women were in those jobs, it was true. But they were not jobs that Mary had ever foreseen herself doing. So she astounded her friends by quitting, going home to Brooklyn, and cooking for six months.

My friend Molly is the one who had to make the classic choice. When she was traveling back and forth to China, she fell in love with an investment banker who also spoke Chinese. Their careers did not jibe easily, and she ended up abandoning hers and following his. They lived in the Far East, in luxurious circumstances, for almost twenty years, then he cashed out, they retired to Marin County, and he took up yoga. His career has probably been more lucrative than Malinda's, Mary's, Susan's, Barbara's, and mine put together. It is also true that Molly worked hard and lived in many more exciting and exotic places than the five of us did. Now she is looking for a job. She told me she might qualify to work in the financial-aid office of her local college. Her résumé, after all, is almost twenty-five years old.

When I look back, I think that Molly was the most enterprising of us to begin with. She saw an opportunity unfolding and seized it. Many times she found herself walking down the street in Beijing, the only westerner she could see anywhere. But even then Molly was someone who operated by serendipity rather than intention. She, too, seems to have had the sort of life she wanted, and to feel no regrets that somehow she has ended up "traditional."

In the meantime, Malinda, who had switched from government to the private sector, discovered that the executives of the company that she thought would develop beneficial drugs were instead engaged in accounting fraud. After she spent some time trying to save the work that had been done getting the drugs approved, she and the company parted ways.

The lesson here is that it was not Sweden where we ended up living in our feminist generation, but conservative America. Issues of the common good are considered suspect and sometimes even "un-American." When we started out—when Malinda, in particular, started out—she could easily have stated her goal as the C. S. Mott Foundation does: "A just, equitable, and sustainable society."

The fight for civil rights, feminism, and environmental preservation might have led the way to such a society, showing every American that equal rights in a democracy, collective concern for children, and willingness to protect the shared biosphere are good for every citizen. That goal, as self-evidently good as it seems to many Americans, has not proved popular with others. It turned out that if we feminists were going to succeed (gain power, gain influence, change the world, get famous, achieve economic security—I doubt that our ideas of success were very sophisticated when we started out), it had to be according to the individualistic American model. Success became defined by surviving change and adversity, being adaptable and tough, and understanding and possibly making use of the perquisites of power.

Those of us in government and business had our ideals challenged most directly and roughly and were presented with the starkest choices. Our work lives played themselves out in free-market terms, not in common-good terms. We "made it" one at a time rather than as a group. It is not feminists, in this sense, who should take the blame for not getting ahead. It is progressives in general who should feel humiliated that we allowed the debate to shift away from the goal of a decent, humane society where both genders, all classes, and all races have a sense of partnership in the larger whole. We allowed both government and business to be taken over by greed, selfishness, tribalism (promoting one's own group at the expense of others), hypermasculine exaltation of winning at all costs, ignorance, and simplistic thinking. As our nation has gotten more complex and more diverse, the Left abdicated its responsibility to make that complexity more understandable and less frightening, and other, more brutal ideas prevailed.

My second daughter, who is twenty-one, holds the baby boom generation responsible for "wrecking the world," by failing to restrain corporate greed and power and indulging in American triumphalism evidenced in the idea that invading any country we want to is right and good. She isn't wrong. As a mother and a citizen, I regret the results of the last twenty-five years. I think the world we live in worsened when it could have improved. Feminism brought more women into the workplace, but it did not make the majority of children's lives better. Environmentalism failed to forestall global warming because it failed to prevail against the oil companies and the auto companies who found it more profitable to ignore common sense and mine low mileage for high profits, and against the exaltation of consumerism, which has accelerated the disintegration of the natural world. The unregulated free market has promoted cheating, theft, and corrosive competitiveness and rendered everyone's lives more insecure.

For a novelist, though, individualism is second nature. All novels are about an individual learning something, succeeding at something, gaining something, or losing something. In spite of my ideals, as a novelist I have found the changes of the last twenty-five years perversely stimulating. Do I wish all common goods had come to pass and that Ralph Nader were president? I don't know. Novelists are naturally out of sync, ironists and skeptics. The threat to art comes from power itself, no matter the ideology of the ruling party. Our politics and culture provide me with endless material.

A novelist benefits from an ongoing sense of being an outsider. Her job is to observe. An observer needs some detachment. From my home, I observe. I read, I watch, I gossip, I gather material. I go to places and check them out. I listen to the opinions of others and try out opinions of my own. I cultivate theories. The time and space in which to do this is both a necessity and a luxury, since distraction slows progress. What I am doing at home is marinating, ruminating, idling. I used to do this maybe three or four hours a day. Now I do it seven or eight hours a day. I used to come out with a book every couple of years. Lately I've been coming out with a book every year. I used to have one or two ideas in my head. Now I have five.

The lives of my friends attest to the relative achievements and failures of feminism. If feminism's first way is to change society and the second way is to change oneself, feminism in my generation has not succeeded at showing women a definitive way to do either one. Just as we have not made our society humane and decent, we have not created a new American woman who routinely succeeds in accordance with the male model and competes with men on an equal basis. In fact, younger feminists have rejected that ideal.

There is, of course, a third way. My friend Susan has made the best of the changes in the publishing world and has earned plenty of money. She is powerful in the lives of the writers she represents. When she sets out to place a book, she usually succeeds because she is smart and aggressive and she knows publishing. She lives in a large house that she has expensively remodeled. What Susan has done with her house and her garden is emblematic of her whole life—her work life, her family life, and her moral life. She has made a safe and beautiful space and brought the unlucky, the unwell, and the uncared-for into it. When she set out, in her late forties, to adopt her two youngest children, she made good on her vow to take children that other couples might not want. These two children, now seven and two, are thriving. Susan's entire family is more actively charitable than any other I know. And they aren't short on parties or vacations, either.

Barbara has chosen another form of the third way. Ambition and a willingness to pitch in have earned her a powerful and well-paid position at a large university that is esteemed in some fields but more often a stepping-stone for administrators to better-known and wealthier campuses. Universities actively seek out qualified women and attempt to lure them away, diversity being not only desirable but also expensive for the institution and lucrative for the female job-seeker. Barbara has turned aside tempting offers. She adheres to the Smiley geography rule for having it all and has cultivated her family life at the expense of what could have been her ambitions. The third way says, though, that positively influencing the students and faculty of Iowa State University is as useful as positively influencing the students and faculty of Harvard University.

Feminism produced all six of us. We are all feminists. We have husbands and partners and are to some degree more dedicated to our vocations than the men are. Mary used to say, "I have a career; he has a job." The difference, as I look back on our schooling, is that the boys were looking for a good way to earn a living. The girls were looking for a way to live.

What do our children think of it all? My twenty-five-year-old daughter is the oldest of our fourteen offspring. She intends to have our sort of family (wife with career, husband with job, children), only more technically perfect than I was capable of (compared with herself, she considers me something of a bumbler). My twenty-one-year-old daughter has the same aspirations except that she imagines her family life will include frequent world travel. Both of them prefer potential husbands who are likely candidates for staying at home with the children, and both have perfect confidence in their ability to earn a living.

Susan's two daughters, too, are preparing for careers, husbands, children, and extra dependents. Mary's daughter is training to be a painter or photographer. Complaints about the example we have set are few and far between. They don't imagine themselves staying home with the children; nor do they think of us the way Mary sometimes characterizes her mother: an intelligent and creative woman whose ambitions were repeatedly frustrated by caretaking duties at home. Do our daughters have complaints about their childhoods? Indeed they do. But their complaints do not lead them to make their own lives on a different model. As for the boys, the older ones haven't committed themselves to any sort of girl, and the younger ones seem to take things as they come.

We can't talk about feminism without recognizing that many of our notions about women when we were in college were ignorant and naïve. I doubt that any of the six of us had a true picture of the lives of women of color, or of lesbians, or of women who work at the most basic jobs and barely earn a living. Nor did we understand our connections to those lives. I am positive that none of us knew that for many of the world's women, being bought and sold, either as wives or as sex slaves, remains a real danger. If we gave a thought to chadors, burkas, and all they represent, I would be amazed. We might have had a notion of clitorectomies, because Alice Walker wrote about them, but they seemed very far away. We were twenty. Like all twenty-year-olds, we were self-centered. We hardly knew what was up with the boys we dated, and they didn't know much more.

Possibly the clearest thought we had was the thought of our vocations. George Eliot was more real to me than most of my relatives. As I said, we got lucky. Women (and men) who came before us left the door unlocked and ajar. We pushed it open and walked through. Our daughters are more aware. If they expect us to have done more, and expect more of themselves, we are lucky again—a sign that we've made progress (and given ourselves some younger allies).

But we also cannot talk about feminism without talking about deeper personal questions than ambition: What sort of life is a good one? What is worth aspiring to? What do we make of what we learn over the years? How do we fit into the ideals professed by our society? What sort of example do we want to set for other women? When faced with a difficult choice, what are the terms of our decision?

There are always several "goods" an individual can choose—the public good, the good of one's immediate circle, the good of one other person, the good of oneself. Without being selfish, an individual may choose moral virtue over benefiting others, or the pursuit of a spiritual path over the exercise of worldly talents. A sense of vocation, especially when it is deeply felt, makes such choices easier.

My guess is that the choices Malinda and Mary faced after twenty years of unfettered free-market turmoil in business and government offended their original conception of their vocations, while the choices I face in my work bolster mine. My plan was always to be as free as possible, to say what I wanted to say, only striving for more eloquence. Their plan was to be effective, and their effectiveness came to an end.

Susan's vocation, I think, was always to be a matriarch, in work and life, and she has succeeded. Barbara's vocation, I think, was to do something useful and interesting. None of us began with an explicitly political vocation, but look at Hillary Clinton, another of our micro-generation. No, she didn't revamp health care in America, but she did a good job mothering Chelsea, stood up to the vast right-wing conspiracy, put up with Bill, and may yet get to be president. For our micro-generation, our job was not to write the book or make the plan as it was for Steinem, Friedan, Millett, but to serve as examples, positive and negative, of how ideals and plans are realized in the real world. The good sign is that our daughters have not repudiated our lives but have decided to do us one better.

Happy

Anne Marie Feld

Anne Marie Feld is a journalist and grant writer. She lives in San Francisco.

On the afternoon my mother died, she left work early. Her day as a computer programmer at Chase Manhattan Bank skidded to an abrupt stop courtesy of a systemwide computer failure. All employees got the afternoon off. It was late December. My sixteenth birthday. Gray, snowless, cold enough to make the lawn crunch underfoot, but close enough to Christmas to make a few uncrowded hours seem like a gift. Or, in my mother's case, a curse. Rather than enjoying some last-minute shopping or hitting the couch, she methodically cleared her desk, drove the Honda home, let the dog out, fired up a pot of Turkish coffee, and hung herself in our garage.

Twenty years later, my father insists that she wouldn't have died that day if the systems hadn't gone down. He might be right. Work gave my mother a structure that sealed the madness inside, if only for small chunks of time. Idleness brought trouble.

My memories of my mother all have her working at something: cooking one of the four homemade dinners we rotated with take-out pizzas, McDonald's, and Chinese food; staying up all night peeling wallpaper off the walls when she decided to redecorate; poring over obscenely fat textbooks to get her master's degree. In home movies, my sister and I, long-limbed and small-bodied, dance and do gymnastics in the foreground. My mother lurks in the background, head cut off, washing dishes or zooming diagonally through the frame on her way somewhere else. Though my mother worked full-time, my sister and I never lifted a finger in the house on Center Drive. It was spotless, free of the piles of clutter and frozen tides of dust that mark my own house.

My mother's madness seeped in so quietly that my father, an optimist to the end, was able to ignore it, believing that it would get better on its own. In our house questions about what we did and how we felt went unasked. Or if asked, unanswered. My sister and I ate alone in our bedrooms by the flickering light of black-and-white televisions. I wasn't told about my mother's two earlier attempts at suicide and would never have guessed. Suicidal people raved and ranted. Madwomen were locked into attics, where they could be heard moaning or rattling chains. Occasionally, they set fire to country estates. Or so it seemed in movies and novels, my only real points of reference. They certainly weren't picking up fudge-striped cookies at the supermarket or dropping the kids off at the community pool on their way into the office. From fielding calls on the yellow rotary dial phone in the kitchen, I knew that my mother saw a therapist, a woman named Barbara, whom she tried to pass off as a friend. I knew better. My mother didn't have friends.

When I was fourteen, my mother started sleeping on the living room floor and wearing a dark gray ski hat with three white stripes. She seemed to drink nothing but gritty coffee and red wine poured from gallon bottles stored under the kitchen sink. She would send me into the pizzeria to pick up our pie, because the guys spinning crusts were talking behind her back. As I limped along in my teenage bubble, very little of this registered as alarming. This was how all families were. As my mother's madness amplified, she came to believe that our house was bugged and her boss was trying to hurt her. But as long as there was a computer program to write or a carpet to vacuum, she could be counted on to do it, and do it beautifully.

Until my early thirties, I thought that my mother was trapped in perpetual motion by work and circumstances. She was born in Sweden at the close of World War II. When she was seven, her mother abandoned the family, leaving my mother to cook and clean for her father and brother. A lover of all things ordered, she studied mathematics and did well in school. On her twenty-first birthday, she was sitting alone in a disco in Stockholm when my father, a Hungarian refugee working as a dishwasher at a nearby restaurant, asked her to dance. He kept asking until she relented, to, as she put it, "make him go away." A year later, they were married and living in a high-rise studio in New York City. On Sundays they walked down to Angelo's Pizzeria, ordered two slices, and split a Coke to save money. They resolved to wait three or four years before having children, to give my father a chance to get a foothold in the job market and allow my mother some time to figure out her next move. Three months after their city hall wedding, I was conceived.

In the early years of her marriage, my mother stayed home, earning money in ways that seem impossibly old-fashioned now—knitting doll clothing for a specialty retailer and taking in sewing. Neither of my parents felt there was anyone they could trust to look after me. When I was three and in preschool, my mother, mathematics degree in hand, found the best job she could, working the candy counter of Alexander's department store. A year later, in 1971, my sister was born, and my mother was back at home, raising the children she trusted to no one else. I have few memories from that time. One is of my father sitting at his giant teak desk, textbooks open, Hi-Liter in hand. I can see his back, clad in a goldenrod sweater, hunched over as he read. He had already gone to technical school and gotten a job in that shiny new field, computers. Now he was studying for his MBA. My mother told him, "Just study. I'll do everything, the housework, the cooking, the kids." He did. They got ahead.

By the time I was ten, my mother was the one earning her master's degree while working full-time. In 1977 we moved to a nice Long Island suburb, into the yellow-and-white split-level house on Center Drive, with a cascading goldfish pond and crab apple trees in the backyard. Thirty years later, I'm awed by a mother who kept house and raised two children while working five days a week. Who could completely sublimate herself, uncomplainingly, throughout her twenties and her thirties, for the good of her family. It was an incredible act of self-sacrifice. I believe it killed her.

In her insistence upon getting things done, on living an ordered life, my mother managed to miss out on the nourishing aspects of family life and life in general—laughing at silly things, lying spooned on the couch with your beloveds, sharing good food, the tactile delight of giggling children crawling all over you. Without this, family life is an endless series of menial tasks: counters and noses to wipe, dishes and bodies to wash, whites and colors to fold, again and again in soul-sucking succession.

On the morning of the day my mother died, I made my way out the door to catch the 7:10 bus to school. My mother and twelve-year-old sister were just waking up in their sleeping spot on the gray carpet in the living room. They sang "Happy Birthday" to me, my mother's beautiful, low voice frosted with my sister's tinny soprano. Eight hours later I stepped off the Bluebird bus, looking forward to a languid afternoon of *One Life to Live* and *All My Children*. My mother's car was in the driveway. I dropped my knapsack on the window seat, stroked the dog's dusty ears, and called "Mommy?"

Her purse sat on the table. I checked all the rooms, then opened the door to the garage. Twin frosted panes from the garage door let in enough light for me to make out the dormant lawn mower and rusty-chained bicycles. My eyes landed on her body, hung motionless and high from a rope tied to a bicycle hook in the ceiling. She was dressed for work, in gray wool slacks and a white button-down shirt, crosshatched with red and blue stitching. I stopped breathing. My heart started to bang, feeling somehow too swollen for my chest. I sprinted up the steps three at a time and out of the house, terrified that whoever did this to my mother was going to get me too.

I sat outside on the cold concrete stoop and looked up the street for a long time. House after split-level house stretched along the curved road with one thing in common: No one was home. All of the parents in my neighborhood worked, and since I had taken the early bus home from school, the kids were still gone as well. I sat hunched over my legs, arms circling my shins, heart slowing, beginning to know that no other person had done anything to my mother. I stood up, slowly opened the screen door, went back into the house, and dialed 911.

The aftershocks kept coming. Watching my twelve-year-old sister trudge up the lawn, excited and flushed from seeing the police cars. Lying to her about the "accident" my mother had had. Talking to the police around the Scandinavian-design dining table we never used. Calling my father, getting him out of a meeting to tell him. Watching the police photographer head grimly down the garage steps. Seeing the garage open and frowning men roll a black body bag out on a stretcher. Later, in the car, after we picked my sister up from the friend's house I'd sent her to until my father could get home, my father said tightly, "It's just the three of us now." I looked out the window at the dark road spinning by and said nothing.

Together, we sloshed through a sea of awkwardness. The wife of a friend of my father's bought me a dress to wear to the funeral, a maroon velvet Gunny Sax monstrosity with puffed sleeves and lace trimming. The funeral itself was mostly filled with teens, but awkward discomfort brimmed in even the adults' eyes. Regular funerals are hard enough; the funeral of a suicide tests even the most socially skilled. When all the robotic "Thank you for comings" had been finished, my sister tried to open the casket when no one was looking. My father stopped her just as she was about to lift the lid. "I just wanted to see her," she explained, fighting tears.

"I'm sorry, my Sweet Sixteen is canceled," I said over and over into the phone. As I made call after call, my best friend sat with me on the pale blue bedspread my mother had sewn on her ancient Singer. My hands were numb by the time I was done, and cold sweat ran down my wrist, wetting my sleeve. I didn't cry. For the first time in my life, a large formal party had been planned at a local catering hall. Favors—clear Lucite boxes filled with Hershey's Kisses, decorated with pink and silver hearts—sat in a bag in the garage, waiting. On the day the party was to be held, I stood in Loehmann's. My mother's party dress, a gray wool sheath with long sleeves, lay on the counter. The clerk told my father that the garment couldn't be returned. My father looked at the clerk and said very quietly, "But she died." They took the dress back.

I spent the next fifteen years running from the first thought I had after finding her body: Whoever did this to her would do the same to me. I would not let family or work drag me down. The easiest solution was to stay an adolescent. This was not a problem in high school, as I was, in fact, an adolescent. In college, I stayed far away from the computer and math buildings on campus and majored in literature. How I was going to apply a lit degree to the real world, given that teaching terrified me, never occurred to me. And the subject didn't come up on the strained visits home to visit my father. On Christmas day, a new family tradition evolved. We'd go to dinner at Benihana, not because it was the only place that was open, but because the silence stung less when we sat like a row of pearls in front of a Japanese man who shouted "HiYa!" as bits of shrimp, beef, and vegetables flew from his knife.

After college, I steeped myself in a place as far from Long Island as I could manage: San Francisco. Every night I'd put on a short black dress, tights, and platform boots and belly up to small, scarred stages, gazing at would-be Kurt Cobains, or boys in porkpie hats whaling Louie Armstrong covers, or nodding to the beat as shaved-bald deejays spun in corners of warehouses while hundreds of people raved, shaking water bottles over their heads until the sun shot weak rays through dirty skylights. Rent was $365. Work seemed optional. I walked out on my job at a local TV station, started working on low-budget documentaries and scribbling song lyrics in black-and-white composition books, picking out three-chord melodies on my guitar.

Writing was like a stray cat that followed me around, gliding between my ankles. A friend randomly asked me to edit his book. Yelling that fact to a stranger in front of a blaring speaker at a rave one night brought magazine assignments. No pay, but restaurant reviews meant free food, and writing about clubs gave me an excuse to go out more. I loved it. After ten years of fumbling, I'd found what I wanted to do. I took a job as an editorial assistant at a small city paper, becoming assistant editor, associate editor, and managing editor in the space of a year. Soon, money flowed in the streets below our downtown offices. Websites with millions in venture capital muscled the ravers and artists out of warehouse spaces. Editorial salaries tripled. I jumped jobs three times in two years. At the peak, my new boss met me outside of my soon-to-be-former workplace like an illicit lover, with a contract, a bottle of Moët, a DVD player, and a signing bonus big enough to buy a car for the long drives through the sun-browned hills to Silicon Valley. It was a great job, writing movie reviews and interviews, the culmination of everything I thought I wanted.

On assignment at the Telluride Film Festival, in line waiting to review a movie called *Better Than Sex,* I chatted with a tall, dark-haired man next to me, who happened to live in San Francisco as well. Back home, Dave and I started seeing movies together, always picking films with *Sex* in the title. A few months after we'd run out of movies about fornication, he finally kissed me, with sincerity that hurt my heart, under a lamppost outside his front door. I was wearing knee-high black leather boots. He was wearing sheepskin slippers, the same slippers he's wearing now as I write this, though they've been replaced once and are now held together by electrical tape. I say this not to prompt him to buy new slippers (Christmas is coming, and his mother will do that), but because it's a certain kind of man who wears slippers before the age of thirty, definitely not the kind of man I had much experience with.

He phoned every day. He listened. He smiled a lot. He told me I was beautiful. He made up rap songs about our love. He wanted to talk about everything, from politics to my period. He wanted children. He was, as my best friend's father said, "a good citizen."

A week after that first kiss, waking up in his soft blue sheets for the first time, I accepted his offer to lend me a pair of white chenille guest slippers from Ikea. I teased him mercilessly, but I never felt more looked after than at that moment. I knew with perfect clarity that I loved him, and that nothing else mattered. We found a house together, a 1920s cottage on a street of Spanish Mediterranean houses in every color of the rainbow. There was a litter of half-dead juniper trees in the front yard. The steps were crooked. But inside, the hardwood floors glowed, the French windows overlooked a hillside, the breakfast room peeked into a garden. We split the down payment fifty-fifty and started packing.

Driving alone through a torrential downpour to the title signing for our house, I lost it. In ten years in San Francisco, I had had ten apartments, thirteen jobs, and at least as many boyfriends. I didn't do stable. I convinced myself that Dave, who made more money than I did, who was known to say things like "It's against my principles" and mean it, was obviously a con man planning an elaborate sting to separate me from my down payment. The year that we'd spent together was the setup for the graft. Now I was going to be out twenty-five thousand dollars and a boyfriend. It was a hop, skip, and jump from there to standing at the side of the road, homeless and utterly alone, the victim of aiming too high.

My hands were shaking when I pulled up outside the title company. But Dave was standing there, under an umbrella, waiting to walk me from the curb to the building, smiling. I laughed; everything was fine. We moved into our little tan house on my thirty-fourth birthday. A year after that, just back from our honeymoon, he carried me up those wonky steps and across the threshold before collapsing from exertion on the blue sofa in our office, the only room we had fully furnished. Eight months after that, sitting together in the garish pink-tiled bathroom that we had meant to renovate before getting pregnant, a plastic stick with a pink line told us that our remodeling was going to have to wait.

I never planned to be a stay-at-home mom. I certainly didn't like the label, which sounded like I'd be joining a group of women grounded for bad behavior. I'd had a job for the last twenty years. Not working didn't seem like an option.

"I just don't know what kind of mother I'll be, whether I'll want to work at home or in an office," I lamely told my boss six months into my pregnancy, my belly already forming a wedge between me and the fake-wood conference-room table.

"We'll make it work," he assured me, promising the holy trinity for working moms: Work at home, set your own hours, go part-time if you like.

On my first visit, the ob-gyn calculated the baby's due date: my birthday. I was terrified that my day of personal infamy would be shared by the next generation of my family. Friends spun it beautifully: "It'll be healing. It'll give you back that day." I rolled my eyes.

The contractions didn't hit hard until Christmas night, four days after my thirty-sixth birthday. Ten copies of my natural-birth plan remained in my small green suitcase as I labored. Fifty-six hours after the first tremors hit my abdomen, three hours after the epidural wore off, I pushed Pascale into the world. I wasn't thinking about my mother. Or about my sister, who stayed at the head of the bed, tirelessly cheering me on when I thought that my body would rip in two. Or about Dave, who watched tearfully as our daughter poured out of me. I thought nothing, and just lay there, shocked by pain and exhaustion. But when they returned her raw, chickenlike body to me after bathing her, my first thought was that she looked like my mother.

During the flood of tears—the baby's, mine, and Dave's—that flowed during my first six weeks postpartum, I wrote nothing but logs: "Left breast, 2:15–2:37 am, poop/wet," in ink that my milk made run. I didn't think about going back to work. I was so attached to Pascale that I would literally hold her on my lap when I used the toilet. I slept when she slept, curled around her body like a shell in the dark cave of our bedroom. I didn't shower for days at a time. Dave spooned food into my mouth, so that I could breast-feed her while we ate, or brought me warm slices of sourdough toast wet with butter, so I didn't have to leave her side while she slept. Dave and I sang her songs and stared into her blue eyes as they drank in the world. We trundled her into the Baby Björn and showed her beautiful, curious face off to everyone we knew and everyone else. We combed her ginger-colored hair into themed styles—twenties shopkeeper, Bob's Big Boy, Donald Trump. We took hundreds of photographs.

Co-workers visited every few weeks, bringing boxes of curry and tuna melts, always asking when I was coming back. May, I'd say, when my family leave is up. Before long, April rolled around, and my boss left a message, wondering when I'd return. I screened the call, holding Pascale in the groove on my hip, staring at the phone.

I couldn't, for one second, fathom going back to work.

It wasn't an intellectual decision. I didn't think about financial dependence, or losing prime years of my career, or what it would feel like to be home day after day. I just wanted to be next to her far more than I wanted anything else.

When Dave was just my boyfriend, we'd lie in bed in my little studio apartment that overlooked a gray slice of the Pacific Ocean and dream our future. We spoke about both working part-time when we had kids, so that we could co-parent and still pursue careers we loved. Sitting around our dining room table three years later, taking a hard look at our finances, we never even mentioned the dream of equally shared parenting. Dave was going to have to be the breadwinner, or we'd have to move. If we scaled back our spending, we could just about afford for me to stay home.

Crossing the Bay Bridge on a brilliant blue-sky day, I called my boss and told him that I wasn't coming back.

"I understand," he said graciously. "Family first."

I flipped my cell phone closed and felt shock seep in. For months afterward, when I woke in the night, my restless mind always returned to this: How could he let me go without so much as an argument? Eleven months later, I still feel like my job broke up with me.

When that dumped feeling returns, a look from Pascale often burns it right off. I didn't understand, though other mothers had tried to tell me, how much space mother love takes up. How it makes my heart feel too big and clumsy to fit in my chest, and brings pools of happy tears in the corners of my eyes. How bringing her into the bath with me, watching her toothless smile as her toes hit the water, feels baptismal. Eavesdropping on Dave with Pascale when he doesn't know I'm listening, coaching her to say "Dada," singing made-up songs about putting on shoes, fills me in a way that work never did. As I stuff rice cereal and strained carrots into her bowed mouth, or race around the room maniacally pushing her Teletubbies lawn mower to get her to crack a smile, I revel in the slow pace of our life, the not-doingness of it all.

I don't grind my own baby porridge or worry about where Pascale will go to preschool. Try as I might to keep the house clean, I still pick wet dust bunnies off her tongue at least twice a week. I'm not hauling her to Gymboree or Music Together. The one time we did mom-and-me yoga, Pascale cried for an hour and a half straight, even when I balanced on one leg and rocked her in my arms during tree pose. I do sometimes storm out of my house in a scraggly ponytail and sweet-potato-stained yoga pants to plead with the workmen hammering nonstop on neighboring houses to take a break until Pascale is done with her nap. And I succeed often enough to keep doing it.

Last week, after six lonely days of flu-imposed exile, I wandered with Pascale into the neighborhood playground. Fifteen nannies gave me a cool once-over and quickly looked back at their charges. A lone other mom and daughter ambled over, placed a doll in the infant swing next to Pascale, and pushed and chatted for a few moments. I smiled so hard my face hurt, feeling like a desperately horny guy on a Saturday night. I had to stop myself from following when they left for a diaper change.

When another nanny entered the playground, her compatriots shouted greetings and flocked around her, talking and laughing. I just watched, pushing Pascale on her swing absently. "What am I doing with my life?" I wondered, as I pried her fingers from the chains. She screamed like a wounded cub, and kept it up as I buckled her into the car seat and all through what was supposed to be her afternoon nap, all through what was supposed to be my writing time. All of this played out against the sound of trees being fed into a chipper outside her window. This time the workers didn't stop when I asked.

A day like that gives me a tincture of the Molotov cocktail of isolation and frustration that was my mother's life. It's enough to make me follow Dave around the house with an angry crease between my eyebrows, listing things we have to get done. I thank my lucky stars that he loves me enough to sit me down in the white chair in our study, the only room that's off limits to Pascale, and say kindly: "Anne, you're scaring me."

When that happens, I try to remember the second realization I had after I found my mother's body. That what she did, she did to herself. Accomplishments don't mean happiness, and they're a fatal substitute for relationships.

I picture my family's home movies, my mother's figure a blur across the screen. I try to imagine myself as the mom in the home video, laughing, throwing my arms around Pascale's fat little body. Walking her up to the dog park, seeing her arms and legs flap in the backpack when she spies the dogs and hawks that are movie stars to her eyes. I imagine the flickering shapes of our future, the dance routines and pedicures and piano lessons and first tastes of sashimi and museums and swimming in every ocean on the planet. I see us smiling together.

It's too soon to project how work will fit into the rest of my life. But I won't miss Pascale's life, or mine, in the race to get things done. This, I hope, will keep me sane. Better than sane. Happy.

I Never Dreamed I'd Have So Many Children

Lila Leff

Ah, the days before children. When we plotted confidently how our partner would shoulder half the child-care burden, how we would simply find a good nanny and walk out the front door to work. Or how we would blissfully stay home and teach our spawn to speak French by age three without ever hearing the *Barney* theme song. Reading the essays of the two pre-mom contributors in this collection is a flashback to a simpler yet just-as-complicated time, when our worries about becoming mothers were all hypothetical.

Lila Leff is originally from Long Island but has made Chicago her home for more than a decade. She and I met on a summer day in 1987 when she gave me a ride from New York to our summer jobs teaching teenagers at Longacre Farm, a camp in Pennsylvania run by friends we had in common. Lila went on to become an actress and playwright and to start the Umoja Student Development Corporation, a not-for-profit youth organization based in Chicago. She never romanticized marriage, and openly harassed me and other friends who did get married (she had some good points), meanwhile entertaining us by dating some of the least suitable men on the planet. But she never ridiculed us for having children or for working hard at jobs we loved. The sacredness of work and children, she clearly understood.

never dreamed I would have so many children. It wasn't in my plans, and it seemed not to be in the stars. At least not in my plans for the stars. I was destined to be a famous actress and playwright. By the time I was ten years old, my destiny was extremely obvious to everyone. And only partially because I announced it repeatedly to anyone who would listen.

I grew up on Long Island and realized right away that I was not like the other girls. Girls in my grammar school were really into things like what color tassels were on the velour throw pillows on their beds, and playing hairdresser, and stealing their moms' nail polish to give themselves a forbidden pedicure and then seeing how many days they could go without taking their socks off in front of a family member.

I, on the other hand, was an idea girl. I wanted to have more profound, life-changing ideas than anyone else, anywhere. And then beat people over the head with them. I was the girl whose curls tended to flatten on one side from too much smushing and who never stopped talking long enough to look vague, mysterious, and/or slightly inaccessible. I felt sure that I was, in fact, from the planet Zlor. I believed in a dark, basementlike part of me that the fur-coat-and-nose-job girls who seemed not to have a care in the world were the feminine ideal. The cutest, most popular boys fell all over them; the same boys looked at me with a mixture of boredom and fear. One thing was for sure: I was destined for a very different life, in a place where people talked about meaningful, important things and experienced bone-crushing, breath-squashing kinds of love.

In college, still trapped on Long Island, it seemed to me that the same girls who had cared so deeply about throw pillows in grammar school now talked endlessly about getting married and having kids. The regular girls had grown into regular women. My polarized ideas around girl-dom/girlhood/girlosity had only increased in the jump from high school to college. I came to think of babies and marriage as Long Island things.

Possessions that weren't really you, yet somehow defined you. How that translated into womanhood was extremely clear. "Regular" women got married and had children, and women like me didn't. I had grown into a woman who was extremely proud, defensive, and ashamed of what felt like a genetic predisposition to always be *other.*

Complicating my outlook was the plot of my mother's life, imprinted on my brain. My father wanted a stay-home-mom kind of gal, and so Mom was, until my brother turned twelve and I turned ten. One day in 1977 she decided that she was overweight and understimulated. In a matter of weeks she joined Overeaters Anonymous and went back to finish college. In what seemed like minutes she became someone else. And the message to us children was clear: We were not enough to hold her interest. This is how we saw it because everything was about us and always had been.

It is important to know that early in their courtship, my mother pursued my father, and I don't mean in the casual, wiggle-a-little-when-you-walk-by kind of way. At the onset of what was a purely platonic friendship, she threw herself a surprise party and prepped several male friends to corner my dad and talk about how great she was. She installed a separate phone line in her home and gave the number only to him, so in case he called, there would be no danger of a busy signal. And the kicker: When her best friend invited her to Europe for two weeks, expenses paid, she said no. Because it would have meant missing the chance to be at a wedding where my father would be and where she was sure that, once and for all, she could get him to fall for her. He did fall for her. She has never been to Europe.

While my father's falling for her means the world to her to this day, as my mother discovered when I was ten, that didn't mean it was *all there was.* My father, a criminal lawyer, was as used to unmitigated doting from my mother as we were. He saw my mother's defection in legal terms. He marched around the house for the better part of a year muttering, "She broke the contract. You know, a verbal agreement is binding. She said she'd raise her children. Can't even keep a contract. What kind of a woman abandons her family?" This was his approach with the invisible jury who marched beside him as he processed my mother's transition.

I tried to handle the situation in what I felt was a more emotionally mature and practical way. First, I mobilized outside resources. Specifically, when my mother started her social-work internship and constantly left us with TV dinners in the freezer and a note propped up on the counter, I began regularly calling the Runaway Hotline. My intention was to report her. "My mother has run away," I told the first volunteer counselor I spoke to. I did not receive adequate sympathy and so changed my tune rather quickly. "I might have to run away because my mother hates her children and only cares about her clients and their children," I told the next five counselors. This was more effective.

Bob Howell was my favorite volunteer counselor. He had a velvet voice that sounded as if it came with a beard and thick eyebrows. He worked on Tuesdays and Thursdays when my mom had her late nights, so I always requested him when I called. He made uh-huh noises way in the back of his throat, which made me feel deeply listened to and completely heard. The last night I spoke to Bob Howell he asked me to think about something. "Don't moms get to have a life too? Right? Your mom already sacrificed to get you guys through the early years. Doesn't she get to find her own way now that you can find your own way?"

"No," I told Bob Howell. "She broke the contract. What kind of a woman breaks the contract?"

I didn't call him anymore.

But I did understand. My mom wasn't a mom anymore. She had a new job now where she got to be a person. And so I moved on. I started calling her by her first name. I also decided that when it was my turn, I would go to Europe. I wouldn't give up half my life as a sacrifice. Staying home with kids was a shallow promise you made because you thought hooking the guy was worth more than having a self. I didn't want any part of it.

The fall following college graduation, I drove to Chicago, a city I'd never seen, to become a famous playwright. I had hardly even visited places outside of New York and, like all good New Yorkers, didn't know exactly where the rest of the country was located once you got west of the George Washington Bridge. But I'd heard Chicago had good theater and good Thai food, so I figured the rest would fall into place. I moved into an apartment above a dance club, which seemed really cool until I realized that a strong bass beat, if loud enough, could actually lift my head off the pillow. I sat beside Lake Michigan furiously scribbling lines of dialogue, waiting to be discovered and turned into a famous playwright. After two weeks it became clear that no one was noticing me, so I decided to get a "real" job.

In college, when it came time to narrow my focus, I picked all available liberal-studies areas and glommed them together into an English, theater, and psychology major. Somehow, with these qualifications, I was hired to staff a safe house for women in prostitution. I listened and cared, learned how to play a mean game of spades, and drove away a pimp trying to bust into the safe house. My life was about to begin at any moment.

The first of my high school friends got married. I was independent and unfettered. One Saturday night, instead of going on a blind date, I stayed home and cleaned my very own bathroom in my very own apartment and read *The Brothers Karamazov.* I cried because I was so happy to finally be allowed to be as weird as I had always been.

My next job was working in "prevention" with low-income/homeless adolescents on the North Side. For me it was instant love: the kind of knee-buckling, primitive love I hear mothers talk about when they bond with their newborns. My first summer in Chicago, I worked with ten kids ranging in age from eleven through eighteen. We spent two days a week figuring out how to write a play that captured adolescence in a violent neighborhood. We went through improv, scene after scene. I sat back on my heels, roaring with laughter at a first-date improv, lost in tears at the far-too-real theatrical construction of a funeral of a peer killed by gun violence. Every night for a week I paced back and forth until 4 A.M., figuring out how to script the kids' words without losing their truth, trying to dream up ways to challenge my kids to greatness. Our mantra was "I am for myself and I am for all of us." We said it every day at the beginning of rehearsal and at the end. It was corny and it was absolutely true.

At the end of the summer, with tears pouring down my face, I watched them perform for their families. Whatever happens to them, I thought, they are mine now and I am theirs. We have helped to raise one another. Tina is now a grammar school teacher. Sokari was murdered two days before he was to start college. My precious Corey has done time for every crime you can think of, and last I heard, Jazz had graduated from college and was applying to medical school. This kind of love is the stuff of parenting. It is not necessarily about having raised a child from start to finish but about having interceded with faith that is pure, far-reaching, and all-consuming. I had found the best of both worlds. I got to have kids and I got to have purpose. These were not mutually exclusive concepts. I was onto something important.

I don't remember when I stopped saying I was going to get head shots taken soon or that I was about to start writing my next play. Only that the other details of my life grew smaller and the world I shared with the kids grew larger until suddenly they were my entire world. My life ran on its own self-firing pistons.

Around that time, the first of my closest friends, weirdos like me, started to have children. On Thanksgiving my Uncle Bob asked, with love, "When are you going to get married and have some kids? You'd be a great mother."

"I'm busy now," I told him.

And I was busy. Though not too busy to notice the occasional pang, sometimes turning into a steady pain that grabbed hold of me and clung for days. First, one of my oldest friends from grammar school had a kid. She had always been even more antimotherhood. Now suddenly she was consumed by a newborn. She kept working, because she had to, but she told me that every moment away from her daughter's babyhood was like acid eating away at her stomach. I had nowhere to file this information.

My closest friend in Chicago had her first child, an accidental pregnancy. I was with her and her husband when it was time to bring the baby home from the hospital. Collectively, the three of us had spent perhaps five minutes of our entire lives with babies. We couldn't figure out how to dress her. It took all three of us to stick the little hat on her bald head. "We're gonna break her," my friend said over and over while her husband and I told her to shut up. "I know we're going to break her."

Within a month, her husband got a good job in Alabama and she was forced to uproot her life and move to a place where people talked too slowly and were constantly polite. Suddenly, without having planned to be, she was a white stay-at-home mom married to a black man in the heart of the South. "How do you feel?" I would ask her at the end of each day when we checked in. Her answers were always the same: "Miserable, tortured. I am way too cynical and hostile for these people." But she saved the baby updates for last. "She is the best thing that ever hap-

pened to me," she always said. I didn't know how these things fit together. The pang I felt wasn't envy exactly. It was more about feeling left
behind, like there was something that I wasn't able to grasp, to which my
closest friends had access. But I was busy and I was moving forward. The
pangs were sharp but always short-lived.

I never had a plan, not the way some people have a plan, with flow
charts and graph paper, or at least a small list with a calendar attached.
Finding my children was like a spiritual journey. I tuned in to the qui-
etest, sanest, wisest part of myself. I asked it to love my kids, and as a result, it needed to love me too. I studied what wasn't fair in the world of
under-resourced, undereducated kids in our country, and I worked hard
to make it fairer. The next thing I knew, I had started Umoja Student Development Corporation.

Umoja means "unity" in Kiswahili. Umoja is about loving kids properly who have been given so little it's hard to believe they were raised in
the same country as white kids from Long Island. When I started the organization there was just me, based in a high school where less than 10
percent of the graduates went on to college. Don't even start me on the
kids who didn't graduate. Now 70 percent of graduates go to college;
fewer and fewer drop out every year. There are eleven staff, including
two kids from Umoja's early days, and we are in a second high school
and preparing to add two more.

Working in an African American community forced me to review my
otherness again, in a way that was reminiscent of my girlhood struggles.
This time I chose differently. I struggled to find my identity in an honest
way that wasn't simply oppositional, the way defining my "girldom" had
been. I wanted to be someone who listened, acted, and reacted as genuinely as I could possibly manage, as myself, finding similarities and hon-
oring differences. Whatever the hell that means. I think it means that I
never pretended I wasn't a white, Jewish girl from New York who cared
deeply. I tried never to say stupid, naïve things like "I'm color-blind." I
never believed anything but that the kids and I belonged to one another.

Finding my kids was like at last arriving on the right planet, my long-
lost Zlor. I was surer of my connection and commitment to them than I
had ever been of anything. I didn't know what it was like to look at some
toothless bald little person and want to slay dragons while simultaneously shifting all of my career goals, like some of my new-mom friends

did. But I knew, intimately, the deep parenting love that carries you through long nights and too much work, that makes you selfless and sacrificing, that is spiritual in nature, even if you are not.

While balance never seemed possible for me, that first decade in Chicago gave me more life than I ever could have hoped for. In addition to the kids, I made the richest and most wonderful network of friends and kept my old friends from home, the other "*others.*" I laughed a ton, never slept or exercised enough, had chubby thighs, read voraciously, and went on crazy adventures to places like Greece and Prague. And I fell in love quite a bit. I was really good at falling in love—especially with men who were not smart enough, not kind enough, not funny enough, or all three. It was an added bonus if they had a drug problem and were chronically underemployed.

The more time and distance I gained from the conclusions I'd drawn growing up, the more years I spent learning to be authentic with the kids, the happier I became, and the clearer it was that ideas from the past—no longer so easy to name—were still holding me hostage. I didn't know how to picture loving a man who loved me or having a family or figuring out how to figure out if I wanted to love a man or have a family. So I decided to do the things a girl does when she turns thirty and realizes she feels more adolescent than she did at twelve: I started therapy and decided to never again date a man until I figured out what it was I could expect from myself, for myself, when I got into a relationship.

And while I was at it, I figured I would try to find out what the expression "relationship nonnegotiables" was supposed to mean. Since I'd always been a precocious learner when I applied myself, I assumed that the whole process would probably take six months at the most. Two years later, awash in tears and accompanying spit bubbles, I turned to my therapist and said, "I've been too afraid to let the right kind of man love me," while she nodded furiously.

I said this as though it was a brand-new concept. She smiled gently, probably thinking, *Yes, you stupid numb nut, I've been saying that for two years.* Instead she said, "You're ready to be afraid, but to let the right someone love you anyway."

I blew my nose and said, "I want that to be true."

Then, in fairly short order, several things happened. The first was that I went to Mexico with my friend Janet and somehow, on the last day of our vacation, through every fault of our own, we ended up on a sailing adventure called the Booze Cruise. We were nearly old enough to be every other passenger's mother. A bunch of twenty-somethings were doing shots and dancing to reggae. Janet promptly joined them. I felt like being reflective about the whole vacation and so sat on the quiet side of the boat sipping Caribbean punch and watching the sunset.

At one point Janet called me over to meet the people she was hanging out with. They were closer to our age, a group of guys from Seattle. One of them, James, was so breathtakingly handsome and coiffed that I was automatically suspicious. I have never trusted men who view hair-care products as allies. He had an entourage of two girls; alarmingly, one was named Tiffi and the other Tiffany. They laughed at everything he said, even when it wasn't remotely humorous. I started to feel that particular brand of alienation I call Long Island Lost and wandered back to the quiet side of the boat.

After a little while James came over, free of all Tiffi/Tiffanys, and sat next to me. "I'm sorry to bother you," he said. "But I'm always drawn to the mysterious-looking woman who seems to be thinking about important things."

I nearly wet myself. Had he been hired by my mother or my therapist to remove the shrapnel left behind by a Long Island adolescence?

The rest of the night passed in a blur. The Tiffs asked him to join them at another bar, and he declined. The two of us walked through the streets of Cabo San Lucas until daylight came and I had to rush to the airport to catch my flight. We held hands and kissed a little bit and he told me that he was a third-grade teacher in Seattle. He assured me that the hair-care product was a gift. We told each other our little-kid secrets, in whispers. Before we kissed good-bye, he said that if I lived in Seattle, I would be his girlfriend and he would cook me dinners, take me camping, and fuss over me when I had a cold. I said that if I lived in Seattle, I would let him.

He was the marker of change. Not the turning point—that had been the long, torturous prerequisite and mine to have alone. But he marked the moment I realized I was ready to be loved by the right kind of guy.

I met John, the man I married last November, shortly afterward. I fell into love as though I'd been born to it. When I told him that I had always worried that men found me too intense and scary, kind of intimidating, he looked genuinely perplexed. "I can't imagine anyone finding you scary," he told me. He has lived by those words. I have felt so safe with him that I don't need to be scary. He is my match—in humor, intelligence, and compassion. I have never admired another man more or dreamed of loving one more deeply.

Yet the idea of having children that actually come out of my body scared me to tears, for any number of reasons. For one, it seemed like the choice was to either have and love a single child or to keep loving all of my children. I mean, really, how could there possibly be room for both? When Uncle Bob asked if John and I would be having children soon, before it was too late, I told him, "I already have children."

John is adopted and has always wondered what it would be like to create a biological relative, to get to know someone who shared his blood. But he has also said that he would love to adopt, to foster, or to let our life together lead us where it may.

And then our life led us to another sweaty, crowded high school auditorium for what was my seventh Umoja/Manley High School graduation.

I don't remember much about my own graduation from high school. My best friend and I car-pooled, and I borrowed my mother's bright blue plastic sandals that cut into my heels. That's it. Yet I remember every one of my kids' graduations, detail by detail, from the beginning song to the final march out with balloons popping and families screaming and me rubbing the heel of my fist aggressively around my eyes. I can clearly picture Jerome's enormous feet in their orange crocodile shoes poking out from under his graduation gown as he accepted his diploma and concluded six years of high school; the youngest of five brothers, he was the first to become a high school graduate. Or Andre, who repeated sixth grade three times and couldn't read when he entered high school. He has a pronounced limp from a birth defect, and it took him a long time to cross the stage when I called his name to receive a college scholarship for Tuskegee University, where he had been accepted for the fall.

They come back to visit me on their breaks from college. They sit in my purple cubicle of an office on the wobbly guest chair with their newly sprouted facial hair, and I tell them the story of their graduation. I remind them about the shoes and the smile on their faces when they walked across the stage. I am the keeper of that memory, and it is an honor.

At last year's graduation, the mother of one of my favorite girls grabbed me around the waist and practically picked me up. "We did it!" she screamed, then threw me into a crowd of extended family and said, "This is Octavia's other mama." And even though I am underpaid, way way way overworked, my thighs are still chubby, and I am always tired, that moment, like so many of my moments, makes my life absolutely worth it.

One day recently, as I was leaving work, one of the teachers flagged me down. He and his partner had just adopted a baby girl from Guatemala, and she was asleep with her arms wrapped around his neck. "Don't you want one of these?" he whispered, so as not to wake her.

"But what would I do with my other seven hundred dependents?" I asked him.

When he said, "You get to have both," he locked his eyes on mine and somehow, for no known reason, a mail slot appeared and the letter of possibility was delivered. This time it did not take two years of therapy and a trunkful of tears.

I drove home to tell John that I had been afraid of having children without knowing it. I told him that I wanted to try, if he was still willing. And that maybe we were too old to have our own, maybe it wouldn't work. But that somehow, I was ready to be afraid and to do it anyway, just like I did when I fell in love with him.

I also told him that I could not become completely responsible for our household. I could not and would not do all of the cooking and cleaning and child care.

"Do you do all of the cooking and cleaning now?" he asked, somewhat rhetorically, because in fact, I did slightly less than none of it.

"Not so much," I admitted. "But that's what people say all the time. That it's a certain way before kids and then, suddenly, the woman gets stuck with everything."

"We are not people, we are us," John said. "And we'll find our own weird blend of balance and psychosis, just like we already do, okay?"

"Yes," I told him. "Yes, we will."

I called my mother later and asked her if she saw her time as a stay-at-home mom as wasted, as the lost years. I had always wanted to ask her that.

"No," she said with complete certainty. "I see it as one of the greatest chapters of my life. But all chapters lead to the next chapter, and there is nothing worse than hanging around in a chapter after it has already ended."

That made sense because that is how my life has always felt. Like the next chapter is always arriving and taking me with it.

There is no magical end to my story. I am thirty-seven and I fell in love and got married and I hope that I will have a child. I picture her as a little girl, with John's blue eyes and my weird hair. I will bring her to meetings and events and she will be bounced around on the lap of lots of social workers, teachers, and kids. I imagine that John and I will patch together a compromise life. Maybe we will each work at home two days a week. Maybe on the fifth day we will figure out some kind of child care that other people have figured out before us.

I don't know how the plans that John and I make will unfold. I do know that there are many possible lives and we won't get to have them all at once. But maybe, if we're very lucky, we can have one after the other after the other. For all I know, I will choose to stay home with my baby for a couple of years, working part-time as a consultant, helping other people help my kids, instead of doing it all myself. I am confident now that having my own child will not make me love my other children any less. As it turns out, there is a lot more room in my heart for the bone-crushing, breath-squashing kinds of love I always imagined.

On Being a Radical Feminist Stay-at-Home Mom

Inda Schaenen

Why do women who enjoy paid work give it up to become stay-at-home moms? What is it like to devote most of your waking hours to your children for fifteen years? When I learned there was a woman who had written an entire book explaining to parents how to get their kids in bed every night by seven, I thought I might be onto some answers.

Inda Schaenen is the author of a parenting guide called *The 7 O'Clock Bedtime* and the novel *Things Are Really Crazy Right Now.* She is a writer and part-time teacher with Springboard to Learning, an enrichment program in the St. Louis public-school system. She lives with her husband and three children in St. Louis, Missouri.

Every wise woman builds her house;
the foolish plucks it down with her own hands.
—Proverbs 14:1–2

Y ou must be a Great Mother," people say to me.

These are people who know my children: teachers, other parents, our friends and extended family. In a sense they are evaluating the job I have been doing for the past fifteen years. This work, as the column of zeros on my Social Security form attests, is strictly voluntary. Profound personal gratification aside, I consider this work my long-term contribution to the body politic. And so I generally accept the praise I receive from the community as a pat-on-the-back bonus, akin to a monogrammed paperweight.

Still, the label troubles me. It implies that the way I am raising my kids is so extraordinary that other mothers can only stand back and admire my performance. In fact, the skills I bring to raising my children are simply the skills most women and men bring to the paid work they do if they do their work mindfully, attentively, ethically, responsively, imaginatively, playfully, purposefully, and seriously. In no field, including motherhood, do these skills necessarily come naturally. Not everyone can apply his or her talents to the rearing of children, or take pleasure in doing so.

So my first point is this: In an ideal world I would not be a Great Mother. I would be an average mother.

My second point is more prickly: If you are not the kind of woman who always tries to bring your best adult self to the raising of your children (modeling desirable behavior, admitting mistakes, taking responsibility for your actions, supporting your children through both hard and easy times), then you have no business taking full-time care of your children.

And the world has no business pressuring you to do so.

This is no less true for women than for men, but for women it is more painful to accept. Why? Men are given cultural permission to opt out of fatherhood. Disinterest or ineptitude seem universally acceptable excuses for men to bow out of day-to-day child-rearing tasks. Men and women alike pronounce rousing huzzahs for any father who manages to tie shoelaces in the morning rush, or remembers for once that little Alex is allergic to soy sauce. What a Great Dad!

For all mothers the standards are considerably higher. We actually have to remember what our children need all the time. With a kiss and a cup of coffee, fathers leave town for a week. Mothers don't check out for an *afternoon* without leaving behind a veritable dossier of preferences, pickup times, reliable neighbors, playdates, and doctors' numbers. This inequity means that all day and every day, working mothers wrangle with two opposing sets of needs: the needs of our jobs and the needs of our children. We wrangle daily. We wrangle hourly. And still, our efforts to integrate mothering and working for pay are vexed and bedeviled.

How could they not be? It is impossible to bring your best self to two separate full-time jobs simultaneously. Raising young children is a full-time job. This has got to be the most milked and least comprehended refrain of all time. Why should *anyone* be expected to perform two full-time jobs well?

There's nothing wrong with women who only feel alive while arguing cases in a courtroom. Or with those who spend the best part of their energy flying large aircraft at tremendous speeds. Such professionals can be perfectly capable and affectionate part-time caregivers. It is possible to love your children without taking twenty-four-hour custodial care of them.

At the other extreme, why should children be trapped with at-home mothers who are merely and meanly parroting the hardwired responses they heard from their own mothers, or with those who load private garbage from their own tragedies (the abuses, the divorces, the betrayals) on their children? Such women are perfectly inadequate full-time care-givers. It is possible to take care of children around the clock and not love them very much at all.

It should be a twenty-first-century truism that not every woman is destined to be her own children's primary caregiver. It should be a twenty-first-century truism that not every woman needs to be a mother.

● ● ●

Fifteen years ago when my daughter was born I knew that I needed to be a round-the-clock mother. I had visceral convictions, some founded on solid theory, others on idiosyncratic developmental quackery, about what was right for her and what was wrong for her. I nursed her on demand. I bathed with her every night for years. I carried her on my body in slings and backpacks. I looked her in the eye and felt really comfortable only when we were together. I attended to my daughter's needs, observed her developments, and nurtured her essential nature.

I experienced motherhood as total immersion. I viewed everything—everything!—as if through a refracting prism trained on my daughter and two sons, who were born three and six years later and received the same kind of care. The books we read, the clothes they wore, the schedule we kept or did not keep, the toys they played with, the playdates we arranged, the food we ate, the music we listened to—everything in my daily life streamed into the care of my children. My husband was completely present in the care of these infants and small children, but essentially his role was to back me up.

It's way too early to know if the job we're doing with them will result in kind, thoughtful, playful, responsible, morally centered adults who figure out how to put their gifts to use in the world. This is my goal. Most of the time they are on the mark. Plenty of times they are not. So I remain vigilant, the guardian of their best selves. This is what it means to me to be a parent, to be the lover and custodian of children whom I have brought into the world.

For me, love nourished an ability to care for my children day and night. Pure physical and emotional affection softened reason. Reason tempered indulgence. My husband jumped in when I was spent. To be the best parent I could be, I cultivated an intimacy with my children—perhaps I still do—that other mothers might find suffocating. But knowing my children the way I do, I am less plagued by doubt than I might be had I not immersed myself totally in my children's lives from their very first breaths.

Being this kind of mother would have been impossible had I been working full-time.

I think this wholehearted, all-encompassing commitment to my children bugs some women. Perhaps they suspect I must secretly consider myself a morally superior mother. All I can say is: I am the mother I am because of the person I am. The choices I've made emerge from a complex emotional, psychological, and intellectual brew. They spring from my weaknesses and my strengths. They spring from the vexations, bedevilments, and quivering uncertainties I experienced long before having children.

As a teenager and very young woman I was brainily gung ho about saving the world. By the summer of 1980 it was all arranged: I would begin in Togo. Unfortunately, just before flying to Africa I suffered a crisis of direction and proved unable to leave my room, let alone fly to another continent and dig wells. It turned out that I had a great deal of unfinished business from childhood blocking my way. (Boring seventies stuff: bitterly divorced parents, buried feelings, and a bad habit of turning good healthy fury into impotent tears.)

By the time I graduated from college I was over the crisis. I knew myself to be a decent writer, although I did not sense how my ability to write would figure in an adult life. Temporarily insulated from economic distress by the remains of a modest college trust fund, I had only to stay alive. I spent my early twenties knocking about, working dumb jobs and writing stories and novels that now sit in file cabinets. At twenty-five, living with a man I'll call M., I got a job as a staff writer for a New Jersey weekly. I was given a town and daily lunch-hour lessons in journalism from three fellow reporters. The good people of Peapack/Gladstone may recall the way I covered the Great Police Department Crisis of 1987, when during a public meeting the mayor scandalously called the townsfolk jackasses. I loved this work and proved capable.

After a year or so, M. and I got married and moved to Baltimore. During this time, I contracted hepatitis A and in a jaundiced heap came crashing down like Goliath. Recovering months later, weak and skinny, I sat across a diner table with M. to plot on graph paper how we might fit three children into the next ten years. Of course it now seems obvious that as near death as I was, fretting at all times that my liver would conk out for good, simply talking about having babies made me feel more alive than dead. ("See? I must be okay because I'm planning to have three, count 'em, three kids.") Without a solid career plan, I knew only that I wanted children.

Our first attempts resulted in two miscarriages within a year. Naturally, I needed something to blame. Those shitty raw oysters in Oaxaca. The pesticides on my food. The neighborhood cats who used my garden as a litter box. The three-hundred-foot broadcasting antenna that loomed over our row house expressly to shoot electromagnetic waves into my ovaries.

Everything in the whole world was to blame, and I was mortally afraid. I was afraid of a hepatitis relapse. I was afraid of not being able to have a baby. Superstitiously I worried that when M. and I had chosen to terminate a pregnancy some years before, we cast away our right to reproduce.

Mostly I was afraid of dying, of dying of liver failure before ever really getting to live. When I was most scared I would shake uncontrollably from head to toe. I was afraid that I wasn't a late bloomer as I'd always believed but in fact a person who would never bloom at all.

In 1989 I got pregnant again, this time by accident. M. and I had sworn off trying. Honestly, I cannot recall anything about how or when our daughter was conceived. By then I was a reporter at a Baltimore weekly. My editor was a single mother with two school-age children with whom she checked in by phone every day at three-thirty. How did her life hang together? Like an anxious third-year medical student around a seasoned surgeon, I observed this woman work through her days. I eavesdropped on her telephone conversations; I kept track of how and when she put either kids or job first.

Another reporter was also pregnant, and for the next eight months she and I compared notes across the newsroom. Because my friend covered medicine and science, she knew plenty of fun facts: the cesarean rates at the various hospitals, which OBs favored forceps, what the latest studies revealed about vaccinating. Then suddenly she was gone, delivered of a baby girl. Eight weeks later, loaded with impressions and water weight and tipping the scales at 204 pounds, I was gone too. Off the working-day map into terra incognita.

After six months I went back and shared a reporter's job with my friend. For a year I produced two or three stories a week. She produced three or four. My husband studied at home as I worked part-time around our daughter's nap schedule. The morning nap was for interviewing and researching, the afternoon nap for writing. I filed my stories from home and went into the newsroom once a week for an editorial meeting. For us it worked. I was a full-time mother and a part-time reporter.

So, at twenty-nine I was neither a particularly young mother nor a full-fledged career gal trying to decide whether or not to abandon a decade's worth of accomplishments. I did not know then that I would come to be a Great Mother. I truly did just stumble into jobs—writing and mothering—that I proved able to do. Once a mother, I put all larval worldly accomplishments on hold and entered the state of immersion I described earlier. And when we moved from Baltimore to St. Louis I quit entirely my part-time work of becoming a famous writer and world saver.

If only balancing motherhood and work were an uncomplicated matter of choosing what's right for ourselves, of saying something like, "You know, I just don't feel like I'm me without my work. I live for law (or for medicine, for books, for basic scientific research, for schoolchildren). There's just no way I can stay home full-time." Or the opposite: "Given who I am, I just couldn't feel right about having a child without making a full-time commitment to that baby from the second it's born."

If only, way back in our young lives, we could know what kinds of mothers we'd turn out to be. If we knew we'd be patient at forty and awful at twenty. Or never, ever, be good at it or even like it. Then our choices along the way would be far easier.

Of course we are given only clues and hints about our future selves. And even these hints may be misguided. My mother tells me I never played with dolls; she worried about my apparent lack of maternal in-stinct. Our competence and incompetence may take us by surprise.

I hear women say, "There's just no way I can stay home full-time." They have their babies and go right back to work. Then they begin to feel torn to shreds, stressed out, furious, and guilty. Other women say, "As their mother, I am the only person who can raise these children the way they need to be raised." They quit their jobs and stay home. Then they begin to feel torn to shreds, stressed out, furious, and frustrated. The only difference is that the working mothers are torn to shreds by guilt while the at-homes feel torn to shreds by frustration.

Meanwhile, we're not merely choosing what's right for ourselves. We're supposed to be choosing what's right for our children, each of whom has certain nonnegotiable needs. Some of them need a lot. Some need relatively little. No prenatal sorting formula matches the warp-speed career mother with the fat, jolly baby who sleeps through the night. Or the cheerfully altruistic mother with the colicky infant who needs to be held constantly. Tough luck. We are individually responsible for meeting our babies' needs, no matter what those needs are. Perhaps for the first time in our whole lives, we are not entitled to anything, at least in our children's early years.

Now throw in all the other people—the inhabitants of the village it famously takes to raise this child. Maybe Daddy's jealous of the love he once monopolized. Maybe Grandma has decided to probe our insecurities with feigned inquiries as to baby's weight gain and sleep habits. Maybe the whole kit and caboodle of friends, co-workers, and extended family feel that the time is right to weigh in with simpering suggestions. Even before we begin to make those "to work or not to work" choices, the village is chiming in. Like a judgmental Greek chorus, the villagers sound their opining cries. "Nurse him!" "Let him cry it out!" "Put a hat on her!" "Give her some solid food, she's hungry for God's sake!"

"Dear village," we pray. "Shut the fuck up!" But we pray in silence, for new mothers tend not to talk back to the village. We're too tired.

Transformative, enlightening, and exhausting, caring for newborns is a limited engagement, over and done with in a matter of months. But fatigue nips at our integrity. Some of us stop putting the baby's needs first and begin to cut corners on care. Say, for example, I don't want to wait until after nap time to go to the grocery store. Instead of laying Baby down after lunch, I let her fall asleep in her stroller, push her through the chilly aisles, and park her in the kitchen back home while I put food away and start dinner. There's no difference between a jostled nap on the go and a quiet sleep in a crib, is there? Now I can make it out for a seven o'clock movie, which is what I really wanted all along.

At times, every mother convinces herself that something she does is all right if it makes Mommy feel better. We have all suffered the ill effects of this justification because, like most slogans, it stomps over all individual exceptions. Sure, sometimes Mommy's need to see a movie is more important than Baby's rest. But sometimes Baby's need for a long, uninterrupted nap is more important than Mommy's need for cultural stimulation. The art of parenting lies in knowing when and how to meet varying sets of needs, including your own.

I know my kids need to get enough sleep every night, but what with homework, sports, and time to play video games (after all the hard work at school they deserve a little downtime), I just can't bring myself to make them go to bed early.

Who has time to make breakfast in the morning? I'm lucky if I get them to choke down a granola bar. It's just easier not to fight everything every step of the way. Gotta pick your battles, right?

I've heard these excuses equally from working and at-home mothers. Not wanting to appear judgmental, I used to slither out of replying to these confessions. Now I don't slither. I shrug and say something like, "Well, we all do what we need to do, I guess."

That is what I say, but this is what I really think: "Why are you looking for ways to get out of doing your job responsibly? If this is honestly how you feel, what are you doing raising children?" When I slack off, I hold myself accountable; I'm not going to excuse another mother for mistakes I chastise myself for.

We will always disagree on the right amount of television our kids watch, or what kind of slang is appropriate, or whether it's polite to wear a hat to the dinner table, or whether a working mother is on the whole better or worse for children. These are matters of personal choice and opinion. It's the individual integrity underlying all of these choices that defines us as parents and people. When we feel our behavior is wrong and continue anyway, we cannot laugh off our mistakes and expect others to think we're "just doing the best we can."

Early into motherhood, the working mother comes face-to-face with the question of her work, that thorny rose. What, then, must she do, the smart, ambitious, loving mother of a new baby? The way I see it, she must do two things. First she must honestly assess herself. Second, taking into account her skills, inclinations, economic resources, and personal gifts, she needs to decide whether she wants to be the full-time or part-time caregiver of her own children.

Here is how these two options play out in our country today:

Option one: She withdraws temporarily from full-time employment. She declares child rearing to be her full-time unpaid work, and relegates her profession to part-time status, increasing her hours in the world as her children mature. For obvious reasons, the babysitting required for part-time care does not need to meet the same standards as full-time child-care arrangements.

Option two: She goes back to work and places her child in a good day-care program, with a trained nanny or skilled babysitter, or with another family member (Daddy, Grandma, Auntie Eve, My Other Mommy), who agrees to act as the full-time parent. Declaring her work for pay to be her full-time job, she outsources her other full-time job, the raising of her child during the preschool years. The collaborative child-rearing team puts the child's needs first at all times.

In both these cases the child will be fine, in theory. In practice, as we all know, option one's kinks are obvious. Only the economically secure can consider it, and mothers need to *want* to stay home in order to do the job well.

Option two's flaws are more complicated. With respect to valuing, training, certifying, and remunerating child-care workers, our nation is backward to the point of being socially irresponsible. Finding skilled, legal, reliable, professional child care for the first five years of a child's life is a crapshoot: a matter of serendipity, word of mouth, availability, economic class, and immigration policy.

The mother who selects option two in the United States of America is often foiled. Which means her child is foiled. Which is absolutely unfair. An option that is only theoretically possible is not a true option. To make option two viable and optimal requires the massive collaboration of us all—parents, elected officials, government regulators, business leaders, journalists, and educators.

But how? How can we back up the female lawyers, doctors, astrophysicists, firefighters, diplomats, and accountants? Not to mention the cooks, janitors, construction workers, secretaries, and hamburger flippers?

Questions beget questions. How can we get rid of yearlong waits for choice day-care facilities? How can we make sure no babies are strapped into car seats in front of television sets at substandard day-care centers because mothers simply must return to work? Is it possible to staff twenty-four-hour-care centers to help women who work night shifts as nurses, bus drivers, and bakers?

Women with children must not wind up guilt-ridden and angry because they want to or need to hold paying jobs. If day care ever achieved a universally high standard, mothers could make choices free and clear of the fear, suspicion, and self-doubt that drives wedges between working and at-home mothers. If every woman had the option of high-quality day care, the guilt and frustration of choosing to work or not to work would be the stuff of personal soul-searching rather than the fuel of public outrage and woman-to-woman discord. Our private angst could remain private.

We need a federal educational commission with a mandate to develop standards, systems, and facilities for the care of young children. This commission would also recruit, train, license, and subsidize the men and women with a gift for child rearing. These child-care facilities could be small and community-based, similar to local fire and police stations, and the care they offer could be available to children of working and nonworking mothers alike. In exchange for their professional dedication to children, the employees would receive competitive full-time salaries, health benefits, and the social recognition and respect earned by doing a job necessary for the highest functioning of our national community.

I am not the first person to say this. Generations of skilled and visionary economists and educators have long argued that we need to rechannel our vast human and economic resources into building a sustainable child-care system. But not enough people see the connection between the long-term health of our society and the needs of women and children.

My kids are older now. Their need for me continues to evolve, as does the way they need their father. Heaven forbid we ever find ourselves a patricentric nuclear family, but the balance of power has evened out between M. and me with respect to our children. I still seem to be the one who keeps track of socks, fingernails, and where we keep the colored pencils. But M.'s inherent independence and adventurousness seem to be granting him greater appeal and increased authority. Like her father, our daughter loves to paddle icy river rapids in a kayak. I will always prefer a nice hot bath. In the day-to-day time they spend together, our sons watch their father closely. How does he cope with frustration? How does he make peace with the compromises adulthood demands? How does he express the joy he feels in their presence? How often does he shave?

As M. ascends, I recede.

After more than fifteen years, the part of me that from time to time howled in anguish from neglect and suspense—the person who is capable of contributing more than three marvelous citizens to the world—is out of the house. I'm teaching. I'm writing. I'm back in school. At forty-four, I figure I've got thirty-five years of active participation in life before the time comes to hang out on a beach, read, and nap all day.

All of these developments my daughter files away for future reference. She has her eye on me, and we talk openly about the trade-offs a woman makes when she decides to have children. I've told her that she cannot have everything all at once, and that she will have to own up to the consequences of the choices she makes. I also tell her that not every woman has to—or gets to—become a mother.

That said, I hope I'm setting an example my daughter can be proud of. With all due respect to Langston Hughes, I also hope that not all deferred dreams dry, fester, stink, or sag.

I intend mine to bloom.

Being There

Reshma Memon Yaqub

Reshma Memon Yaqub's story highlights the immense importance of reliable child care in the lives of working moms today. In the debates over one-on-one home care versus group day care, what gets lost is how critical any form of good child care is to every working mother. You can't work without it. And as Reshma's story shows, it's worth planning for, although not every woman starts doing so years before having kids, as Reshma did. Her story also demonstrates the hopes and dreams held out to younger working moms today—without much guidance or support on how to successfully combine work and family.

Born in 1972, Reshma lives in Maryland with her husband, Amer Yaqub, and their two sons, Zain and Zachariah. A freelance writer and contributing editor for *Parents* magazine, she was a National Magazine Award finalist in 2002. Her work appears regularly in a wide range of publications including *Parents, The Washington Post Magazine, Reader's Digest, Glamour, Good Housekeeping,* and *Rolling Stone.*

When I was five, my parents stuck my new baby brother's crib in my bedroom. When he screamed in the night, I was supposed to tiptoe into my parents' room and quietly wake up my mom without disturbing my dad. Then my mom would feed him and I would crawl back into my bed until it was time to get up for school.

Even at five, I understood and resented the reason for these nighttime theatrics. My father's sleep was not to be disturbed because he had to go to work in the morning. He couldn't afford to be tired. My mom apparently could, because all she did was take care of three kids (one an infant) all day long. Not a "real" job.

"But I go to school!" I wailed to my mom after a night of broken sleep, trying to elevate myself above her housewife status, closer to my dad's working rank. "Isn't school important? Don't I need my sleep for that?" My mom just smiled that slightly sympathetic, close-lipped smile that you give to self-important five-year-olds, the same one I now give my four-year-old son when he demands to know the reasoning behind whatever injustice has been committed against him.

A few years ago, I asked my parents about this long-ago nighttime setup. They looked at me quizzically. My mom simply shook her head and told me I was imagining things. Never happened, she says. Must have been a dream.

A dream? I know it was real. I remember my brother's empty-bellied shrieks jolting me awake, the pain of crawling out from under my warm covers, the bright light of the hallway, and the darkness in their bedroom. I remember how resentful I was, how angry. How smoothly and silently my mom leapt up from her bed, as if she hadn't been sleeping at all but merely waiting for me. Nearly thirty years later, I recognize that same code-orange sleep/alert state in my own mother-self.

The fact that my parents don't remember this episode means it probably wasn't a long-term arrangement. Maybe it only happened that one night, or for a few weeks until my brother slept more predictably. But it was long enough for me to vow that I would never be a mommy whose sleep didn't matter. That I would be somebody with a real job, who merited eight hours of sleep, no matter who was howling in the night.

Both my parents wanted me to work. Expected me to, in fact. The only reason my mom didn't work was that she couldn't on a technicality. My dad was a diplomat, a Pakistani working for the World Bank in Washington, D.C. Though my parents had lived in America since before my brothers and I were born, my mom's spousal visa status prohibited her from working for money.

It practically oozed from my mother's skin, how much she wanted to work. She was never the domestic type. Like me after her, she never cozied up to the stove or the mop. She threw ugly looks at the dishes that insisted on piling up around the sink, mocking her with their ketchup stains. But still, she did her home thing and she did her mom thing, and she did it well. She simply, if somewhat reluctantly, accepted her fate, as women of her generation were bred to do. She was always there, always in the background, almost like wallpaper, which, to a kid, is just about the highest compliment you can give a mom.

My father clearly respected her. He taught us by example to appreciate her, sincerely and out loud, for every meal she put in front of us. And while he may have made the money, she was in charge of it. She made it her job to save and stretch and mold it.

Still, both my parents would gaze admiringly at the women around us who put on business suits and marched into elevators alongside my father. "Be one of them," my mom would often tell me. "You'll be happier. You'll be more respected."

But there was always a caveat.

"Don't be one of them for so long that you forget to have children," my dad would say. "The ones who don't have kids, they look sad. They feel empty. Besides, a marriage without children can falter; kids are the glue that keep you together."

So from the beginning I knew I was supposed to be both worker and breeder. In that order. Or maybe at the same time. Or one, then the other, then back to the first. We never got to that part of the discussion. Nobody ever explained how I was supposed to be in two places at one time, or at least with my brain in one place and my heart in another. No one ever told me whose hand my kid would be holding while I went up that elevator alone.

Fast-forward a decade. I am about to graduate from an Ivy League college, with a $100,000 education that my parents have willingly paid for, with the explicit understanding that I will work after graduation. My brothers and I don't have to pay our parents back for the years of tuition, but we do have to establish careers so that we can support ourselves and pay for our own eventual kids' eventual schooling.

I am newly married to a boy I have loved since I was twelve. While I am in college at the University of Pennsylvania, he is getting his M.B.A. at Columbia University in New York. We are living apart, so I am exhausted from our every-weekend travels, and from cramming four years of schooling into three, so that I can graduate early and be with him. I am so burned out that I decide, in my last semester, that I am not going to work after graduation.

Not. Going. To. Work.

I don't merely decide this. I proclaim it in my bimonthly editorial column in *The Daily Pennsylvanian.* In this column, which runs with my picture above it, I rail against the limited choices that society has thrust upon women over time, the carefully labeled boxes we are put in, the tight corners we are backed into. Isn't the fact that women of my generation are expected to work for money, I write, just as bad as the expectation that our mothers should not? Wasn't the feminist movement supposed to create choices for us, and not just replace one obligation with another? I declare in my column that I, for one, am proudly choosing to be a housewife. So there. With a body-length sigh of relief, I skip out on the entire job-recruiting process that seems to be consuming my fellow graduates.

My parents are not impressed. But Amer, my husband, doesn't care if I work or not. His new job as a marketing assistant for the Quaker Oats Company pays enough for us to live in a two-bedroom apartment in a swanky downtown Chicago high-rise. Living there amid my new Royal Doulton "Old Country Roses" bone china and Thomasville furniture and half-unpacked boxes and with my long-awaited husband, I know I have made the right decision. I dutifully rise each morning to squeeze

Amer fresh orange juice before he walks the seven minutes to his office, which we can see from our bedroom window. After he leaves, I crawl back into bed and stare at his building and try to figure out how to spend my day in a city where I know no one and have nothing to do.

After three weeks I stop getting up to squeeze the juice. I sweetly suggest that he can damn well pour his own from a carton. The exhaustion from eighteen straight years of school is starting to wear off. The exhaustion of being a bored housewife is starting to set in.

One day I wake up and decide that I was mistaken. I do want to work. I suddenly and very badly want to be a marketing assistant for the Quaker Oats Company. It looks fun. It's a short commute. My husband seems to like it. Luckily, the company has an active recruiting program for undergraduates, a step under the one that M.B.A.s like my husband are hired into.

Never mind that I know nothing about marketing. That I majored in political science. (I had desperately wanted to major in my religion, but my parents had nixed that, because they said I'd never get a well-paying job with that degree.) I just know that Quaker Oats is the right place for me. I will wear a business suit and be one of those happy women riding the elevator alongside my husband.

Thanks partially to my husband, and partially to the fact that mine was one of a few colleges where Quaker Oats recruited undergrads, I land an interview. Debbie, the HR woman, agrees to let me come in for a second round with the University of Pennsylvania applicants. The other nine applicants are college seniors tackling the standard recruiting process. Two, maybe three, maybe none, of us will get offers, Debbie informs us, smiling the smile of somebody who already has a job.

Inexplicably, I long for this job, perhaps as badly as I longed for my husband when I was twelve and he was sixteen and didn't notice that his little sister's friend had a crush on him. I now have that same lust for the Quaker Oats Company. I read up on it. I pray for it. I shop for it. I do mock interviews with my slightly bemused but supportive husband. And indeed, it looks like I have a chance.

On the morning of the second interview, I arrive early and hang out in a conference room with all the other Penn applicants, who have also arrived early. One of the college seniors, a woman, stares at me, and not in a friendly way. Just as Debbie walks in and seats us at the conference table, this woman says loudly enough for the group to hear, "Aren't you the girl who wrote in the school newspaper that you don't want to work?"

In slow motion Debbie turns to me, her eyebrows arching, her lower lip wedged between her teeth, her smile growing faker by the second. I sputter a hasty explanation of feminism and choices and backpedal as fast as I can. Debbie smiles at me abstractly. The traitor smiles too, knowing there is now one less person in her way. I want to hold her neck down on the conference table with one hand while I yank her hair with the other.

That soulless Wharton bitch gets my job offer.

Defeated, I seethe in my apartment for a few days, trying to figure out how to pick up the pieces of my shattered life and nonexistent ruined career. One morning I decide to try an exercise from the self-help books that have been my lifelong companions. Sitting on the floor of my bedroom, in plain view of the despicably ugly Quaker Oats Building, I make a long list of all the qualities I want in a job. Then I try to figure out what jobs have those qualities.

Following an hour of analysis, I determine that I am temperamentally suited for two possible careers. I could be a college admissions officer. Or I could be a journalist. I pick up the phone book and start calling colleges in Chicago and find out that it takes at least five years to become the person who reads applicants' essays and decides if they get in or not. That fact, along with the convenient reality that three newspapers and a wire service lie within walking distance of my apartment, leads to my ultimate decision.

I will be a writer.

And of course, eventually, a mother.

After five years of assorted writing jobs at the *Chicago Tribune, The Philadelphia Inquirer,* and the *St. Louis Post-Dispatch,* six years of marriage, a big move back to our hometown outside D.C., and a decade of sound sleep, I realize I had better start thinking about phase two: children. I don't want to morph into that sad, elevator-riding, ovary-shriveling woman. Though I am not quite yet ready to breed, I start mentally moving into mommy mode.

Soon, torn between two job offers from competing business magazines, I opt for the one that will let me work full-time from my home in-

stead of at the magazine's New York office. I turn down the local magazine, even though at twenty-five, I would have had fun being around
other young journalistic minds all day instead of alone, in my basement,
with my computer. But I make this choice for the sake of my unborn, un-
conceived children. Someday, I tell myself, when my kids are here, I will
want a job that lets me work from home. I will want a nanny watching
my kids right under my nose. I will want to avoid a two-hour round-trip
commute, which would mean an extra two hours that my kids are in
child care every day. So I grab this gig and hang on to it for dear life, the
first of many critical decisions I will now make based on . . . child care.

For the next few years I work diligently and sleep soundly. Mine is a
pretty easy writing job, requiring only about thirty hours a week.

Meanwhile, my nearby parents and in-laws grow increasingly desperate for their first grandchild. The pressure all centers on me, as if my husband is extraneous fluff. They beg, plead, bribe. They swear on their
unborn grandchild's life that they will take care of him so I can work, so
I can vacation, so I can live a life unencumbered by children.

So I can sleep.

At twenty-eight, after nine years of marriage, I finally spawn. Motherhood comes at this exact moment in no small part because of child
care. The grandmas are available, willing, and—as they repeatedly and
plaintively point out—still healthy enough for the job. Now I am the
mother of a boy. I have six weeks maternity leave, plus two weeks vacation, from my job.

Like many new mothers I have no idea how the whole work-mommy
thing is going to play out. I wing it, hoping for the best. I plan to keep my
home-based writing job. I know this baby isn't going anywhere. Through
some alchemy, the job and baby are supposed to merge seamlessly. The
grandmas are the key. To that end, our three families decide to move to
the same development, to houses within walking distance from one another. So now I've taken a job based on child care, and bought a bigger
house in a development that I cannot afford, based on child care. All for
a boy in size 1 diapers, and whatever siblings he may someday have.

Though I have read all the requisite books and magazines, and taken
the hospital's newborn-care class, I am brutally shocked by how hard
this baby thing is. None of my friends have babies. I don't realize what I
have gotten myself into until the baby is crying in the night, snatching me

from REM, and dumping me into flashbacks. Only this time, after I throw off the covers and my eyes adjust to the light, there is nobody for me to go wake up. My mommy is not in the next room. Somehow, I'm the mommy, the one who's supposed to make the noise stop.

After his two weeks of vacation are up, my husband learns to sleep through the crying. It is not until much later that I realize he's not actually sleeping through it. He's just lying there, trying to go back to sleep, confident that I can handle it. After all, he has to get up for work the next morning. He can't afford to be tired. Since I am on maternity leave, "not working" the next day, I can nap with the baby, right? Unbeknownst to me—because we had never discussed it and assumed, like people in love do, that we wanted all the same things—he thought he had married a woman like his mom. A domestic goddess in all the happiest ways. A woman who wouldn't mind getting up with the baby while her husband sleeps. Who would consider it her primary role, if not her privilege.

I have no idea how this man I have loved for sixteen years can be so mistaken about me. I have grown up just like him, with all the rights and privileges of any boy. But now, largely because I am nursing and have to feed the baby anyway, I don't fight the arrangement. I take to sleeping in the baby's room until Zain sleeps through the night. It is too hard to come back to my bed after each feeding and listen to Amer snoring, and not punch him awake, and not pull his hair.

The whole mommy thing is so hard, so consuming, so sleepless, that the days I work feel like vacation days. Strangely, after the initial rush, the grandparents don't seem all that eager to take over my mommy job. They wanted the grandkid; they just don't want my child-care schedule. Perhaps, like me, they were unprepared for the responsibility. They didn't realize how much I had been counting on them, how much I had actually believed that they would care for my baby so I could work.

Neither of the grandmothers have ever been employees, so they don't take my being an employee very seriously, particularly since I work from home, with no visible boss, no visible clients. So eventually, they get a little lax about their hours. One suddenly has a lunch she needs to go to. The other has a dentist appointment, or the plumber is coming. Surely I can reschedule my conference call, can't I?

I can't exactly force the grandmas to work for me. They have their own lives, their own commitments. And their incentive is flagging.

They've already bagged the grandchild. My mother-in-law has even been lucky enough to score a second, right on Zain's heels, thanks to my husband's brother and his wife.

When my mother-in-law and my mother each announce that they'll soon be out of the country for a month (they have often visited relatives abroad for this long and, unbeknownst to me, had plans to continue doing so), I realize I need another plan. After an almost unbearable number of false starts, I finally find Sally, an amazing nanny, to come to my house from 8 A.M. to 2 P.M. That means I work a full-time job in six hours. Then I work a mommy shift for another six. Then my husband asks for dinner and I sweetly suggest that he can damn well make it himself.

Two years pass. I know I want a second kid, and I know I want Sally to be this second kid's nanny. She plans to retire when her youngest child graduates from high school, so I have to get pregnant in time to have my second child turn two (old enough for preschool) by the time Sally retires. If I were a Home Mom, my second kid could have come three or four or five years after the first. But because I'm an Office Mom too, and Sally holds my place half the day, I have to consider her schedule as well as my own desires. My nanny clock ticks louder than my biological clock. So I get pregnant a full year before I would have had I been a Home Mom.

Now I have gotten a job, moved, and conceived two children based on . . . child care.

I struggle with the guilt of being away from my children for up to half their weekday waking hours. But I don't feel guilty enough to stop doing it. I believe with equal conviction that the undivided, loving child care I've found for my kids is as good as the care I give them. Better in fact, because it means that when I am with them I'm not tired and cranky from having been with them all day.

Feeling smug in that knowledge does little to stave off the guilt, though. Especially on days when Zain says, "I don't want to go with Sally. Why can't I stay with you, Mommy?" I rush him out the door with a cheery smile and a promise to play Candy Land that afternoon. I can't tell him the truth: "Nothing scares me as much as the idea of being away from you all day, every day—except the idea of being with you all day, every day." Yes, my children need me, and I need them. But I need me too.

In the end, I wonder, will my sons look back at the way I raised them, and believe I was always there for them, the way I remember my mother? Probably not. I'm not always there.

Will Zain and Zach make some bad choices in life and blame them on my part-time absence? Could happen. Still, I trust that when I am there (which is most of the time), I am really there. And when I'm not, the ripped wallpaper caused by my absences is painted over in bright colors—Daddy, Nana, Ummi, Sally.

I'm constantly relieved that I have a terrific nanny and two loving grandmas to back up my part-time work schedule. I don't know how other working moms do it. I couldn't walk out that door every morning knowing that my kids would be a hundred times better off if I turned back around and stayed. Working motherhood combined with shitty day care constitutes its own circle of hell. Have kids, the world tells you. Go forth and breed. But when it comes down to backing up moms and kids, our society sucks.

Upon Zach's arrival, Amer and I adopted a divide-and-conquer strategy for the nights and mornings. Amer gets up with four-year-old Zain, and I get up with baby Zach. After a few months, we all slept through the night, but when there's a bottom that needs to be unstinked or a bad dream that needs to be scared away, I revel in the fact that it's not just my problem. Sometimes when Amer crawls back into bed at 3 A.M., I make gleeful snoring noises.

Still, because Zach is the littler one, I'm the parent who loses the most sleep. But I no longer feel like punching Amer and pulling his hair when I come back to bed. Because after Zach's birth, I made a decision that for once is based not on child care but on Mommy care. After any particularly sleepless night, I drop the kids off at their daily dropping-off points and, instead of going to my desk, I go to my bed. I draw the drapes, let my eyes adjust to the sudden darkness, pull up the covers, and sleep the sleep of the old days. It may mean a day of lost wages, but it also means a day of finding myself. Because whether or not I get paid for the twelve to sixteen hours a day that I work—at my desk, in the backyard, in the kitchen—I am somebody with a real job, who merits eight hours of sleep, no matter who is howling in the night.

Russian Dolls

Veronica Chambers

When I was twenty-two and the Teen Features editor at *Seventeen* magazine, one day I opened a small white envelope addressed to me in loopy teenage-girl script. Four sheets of poetry written in ballpoint pen fell out onto my desk. The poems were not quite professional enough for *Seventeen* to print, but each one contained a stark image or eloquent phrase that caught my attention; this young writer was obviously talented, in addition to being passionate and persistent. I wrote her, explaining the poems' flaws but also encouraging her. She wrote back almost every week with more poems. I began to fall in love with this young teenager from Brooklyn who signed each poem with pride, Veronica Victoria Chambers.

Soon afterward, she did get her work published, writing for *Seventeen, The New York Times, O: The Oprah Magazine, Newsweek,* and many other magazines, and going on to write several books, including *The Joy of Doing Things Badly: A Girl's Guide to Love, Life and Foolish Bravery; Having It All? Black Women and Success; Miss Black America;* and many children's books. She lives in Los Angeles with her husband, Jason. They have no kids yet, but that doesn't mean she doesn't have quite a lot to say about motherhood. One day she hopes to write *The Joy of Mothering Badly: A New Mom's Guide to Doing Everything Wrong but Enjoying Motherhood Anyway.*

When I imagine becoming a mother, the picture that floats into view is one of those painted Russian dolls with five smaller dolls hidden one inside the other. On the surface, yes, of course, I want to be a mother. But when I start to untwist the dolls, what's revealed is that there are many "mothers to be" inside me. The doll who wants to raise children but is wary about pregnancy itself. The doll who knows that the miracle of childbirth is an amazing thing. The doll who really just wants to adopt. And the doll who would be happy diverting her time and resources into being a truly great aunt to the nieces and nephews she loves and adores.

I am thirty-three years old. I've been married, happily, for two years. My husband and I want to have kids. We also want to have time to be married first. My husband proposed after eight months of dating. It wasn't exactly a shotgun wedding, but before we start a family I'd like to know Jason for longer than I've known my dry cleaner in Brooklyn. I'm a writer with a novel and several nonfiction books under my belt. Jason is a freelance journalist who writes about architecture and travel. We love what we do, and what we want to do more than anything is to have a stint abroad before we create a family.

I have gotten adept at fielding the question nearly everyone asks: When are you going to have kids? I have listened, more times than I've cared to, to people telling me about my chance of having healthy children decreasing dramatically after thirty-five. Tick tock, tick tock. Just the other day a close friend said, "Your timetable sounds good, as long as birth defects don't scare you." Which I thought was cruel. Despite the fact that I have discussed these pregnancy statistics again and again with every ob-gyn I've ever had, there are still days when I picture myself waiting to have a baby at thirty-seven or thirty-eight or thirty-nine and having a baby who is dramatically, drastically disabled. Wouldn't it be my fault, ultimately? Especially since my husband just turned thirty. If he were the woman, the timetable we've concocted would be just fine.

When I doubt my choice to wait, I tell myself that if something goes wrong and we have a baby with a birth defect, it will be God giving me what I deserve for being a selfish, heartless bitch. Even though I'm not a mother yet, I'm well schooled in the womanly arts of guilt and self-flagellation.

Perhaps I am thinking of Russian dolls because I've recently been watching an old BBC miniseries starring Alec Guinness called *Tinker, Tailor, Soldier, Spy.* Guinness's character, John le Carré's Smiley, is trying to find out who among his lifelong colleagues in the British Secret Service is actually a Russian spy. I cannot tell you who it turns out to be because the series is roughly eighteen thousand hours long. It hails from an era in England long before there was Wagamana for lunch and Madonna and Gwyneth Paltrow starring in West End shows, from that dark period in the early 1970s after the Beatles, when Mike Myers was a kid playing hockey in Canada, dreaming about making a movie like *Austin Powers.* A period in England when there was absolutely nothing to do but watch television. I cannot tell you who the mole is in Alec Guinness's operation, but I can tell you that among my posse of friends—working mothers, stay-at-home mothers—I am most certainly the spy.

I happen to have a lot of older friends who already have children. For years, literally, I have questioned them relentlessly: How did they meet their husbands? How long after marriage did they have kids? How many kids did they plan to have? Who provided child care? Who decided how long they'd stay at home? And on and on. I've asked so many questions that by the time I turned thirty, I'd written a book about women, work, family, and balance called *Having It All?* The question mark being my acknowledgment that at the end of all these questions are more questions because as any mom knows, balance is an elusive and ever-changing fantasy.

When I met the man who became my husband, we began to talk about what our family might look like long before we actually became engaged. I told him that I did not want to be a mother until my late thirties. I had, in fact, felt like the mother in my family since I was a little girl. Ever since I can remember, my little brother was my responsibility. When he dropped out of school, began dealing drugs, and eventually landed in jail, it was I who spent days tracking him down, buying him dinner, hiring a lawyer, and visiting him in prison. My mother never went to the prison. Not once.

Who doesn't feel overwhelmed by her family? The people in my life, who for a very long time thought my complaints about my childhood were just therapy speak, truly understood when my mother toasted me at my wedding. She said, "There would be nights when Veronica would call me crying and ask for advice and I thought, 'Why is she calling me? She's much more capable of being the mother than I am.' In many ways, I think in a past life, she must have been my mother and I must have been the daughter because that's how I think of her now. Veronica is my mother."

From her, this was high praise. To me, her words ignored the fact that despite whoever I was in a previous life, I needed a mother in this one. My twenties had been a blur of family obligation and caretaking. I knew that if I became a mother too soon, I would resent it. I needed at least one decade of my life when I wasn't paying other people's bills, shopping for their groceries, driving all night to tend to their emergencies.

I also told Jason, way back when we were courting, that I had seen too many friends go through infertility treatments and that I wasn't interested. All of my years as a spy in the country of motherhood have given me something close to a plan. Ever since I was a child, I have wanted to adopt. My mother was a *60 Minutes* fanatic, and I must have been watching with her when I saw a segment about the long list of couples who wanted to adopt white babies and the equally long one of real black babies no one wanted to adopt. I was around seven years old, and from that day on, I started referring to my dolls as my "'dopted babies." Certainly, during my own tumultuous childhood when I bounced from household to household, this passion for wanting and feeling wanted grew. On more than one occasion, my own "straight-shooting" mother (her words, not mine) told me that "if abortion had been legal, you would not be here today." Other times, when I cringed at her screaming, she would say, "If I wanted to kill you, I would've drowned you when you were a baby, when it would've been much easier."

Under the best circumstances, I want to have one baby and adopt one baby. If biology doesn't cooperate, I'd be happy adopting both babies. Jason agrees. He, too, for different reasons, is a passionate advocate for adoption. And while I know that motherhood, of all things, does not hold to plans, I find comfort in ours.

We have so many friends in the midst of early parenthood that Jason and I have talked about natural versus epidural births, nannies versus day care, public versus private school. The tension among women on these issues can be so great that sometimes each word out of my mouth feels like either an indictment (if my choice differs from that of a mommy friend) or nonsensical babble (if my mommy friend thinks that I'm clueless because I'm not there yet). So as I stand here with my nose pressed up against the glass of Mommyville, in a strange way, Jason—not another woman—has become the confidant for my dreams of motherhood. He does not judge me, he does not take sides, he does not shut me down. And because the children I am imagining will also be his, he's invested in my dreams. Which I guess is the way it should be.

A few months after we were married, I got a teaching position at Bowdoin College in Maine. Jason was still working as an Internet editor in New York. I had never visited Maine before the college invited me to be a writer in residence. Jason flew up on weekends. I missed him during the week, but I was grateful to have that time, so fresh off our summer wedding, to think about married life and let the magnitude of the changes sink in. We rented a lovely riverfront house off-season. The front was all glass. To my surprise, I loved everything about Maine.

What I loved most was that the lobster was cheap. So cheap, each week we bought two giant lobsters with the deposit returns from our recycling. So there we were, on an idyllic Sunday afternoon, watching the river and eating lobster. It was one of those perfect days when you want nothing more than to be still. Jason poured me a glass of wine and asked a question. "So if I made enough money that you could stay home, would you?"

I was instantly intrigued, especially because Jason does not make enough money for me to stay at home. Had he been offered another job? Won the lottery?

No, Jason said. The question was hypothetical.

So I asked him, "Stay home and write?"

He said, "No, stay home and take care of the house and the kids one day."

"No writing at all?"

"No," he said.

We went back and forth for what seemed like ages. If I were home, then I'd want to write. Jason explained that I'd have no time to write, just to tend to the house, care for the kids, and throw lovely dinner parties for our friends. I asked if I could volunteer at a local school, study French, learn to play the piano.

"No, no, no," Jason said. "You're very busy at home."

I finally said, "No, thank you. If you had enough money and I couldn't write, then I wouldn't want to stay at home."

"Now ask me," Jason said.

So I did.

We talked a lot about Jason staying home with our future kids, and we're still talking. He says he would love to do it. It's helpful to know that Jason has the patience of Job and a great sense of humor. Just yesterday, we were at the premiere for the DreamWorks animated film *Shark Tale.* As we were riding in the elevator to the parking lot, a woman asked her toddler what her favorite part of the movie was. The little girl, whose head was crowned with curls, whispered, "The part when the two fishes kissed." Jason laughed out loud. I know that laugh. It's the same laugh that flies out when he's reading a Martin Amis novel or watching his favorite TV show or telling a really good joke. Jason is utterly and infinitely fascinated by children. He also has the great gift of not taking things personally. If a child says, "I hate you," Jason laughs that same belly laugh. "Ha," he says, at the very thing that would reduce me to tears.

As for me, I love the idea of Jason staying at home. If I could continue to make the bigger income, I'd be all for it. However, there are big what-ifs in our equation. I'm a writer, not a lawyer or a doctor or an investment banker, and my income fluctuates wildly.

There is also the fact that as a writer, while I occasionally work in an office, most of the time I work from home. I know from experience that the more time I spend at home, the more housework I do. Even now, without kids, if I have five days at home to "write," I will spend two of those days cooking and cleaning and candlestick making. Jason comes home and says, "Why did you clean? You're supposed to be writing." But I can't help myself. Which means if Jason is a stay-at-home dad and I'm a stay-at-home writer and the house isn't clean and the pantry isn't filled, I'm going to catch an attitude. I don't know how I'll resist the call of little children wanting me to read a story or go out and play hide-and-seek. There's nothing a writer loves more than a good distraction—or two or three. If I'm home and not writing, then I'll be mad at myself. And more likely than not, I'll take it out on Jason. It would be wrong. But I could see it happening.

So here we are: My husband might one day be the stay-at-home dad to my working mother. I love my work, I make good money, and Jason would be, I believe, a great stay-at-home parent. But spy that I am, I know there aren't many women out there whose husbands stay home—I've investigated thoroughly. We know friends of friends whose husbands have been laid off and are at home, and those are ugly situations to witness. The men still don't do their fair share of parenting, and they resent their wives' full-time jobs with full-sized paychecks. I don't worry about that for me and Jason so much.

But I do worry about my own ability to let go of, well, everything. I already spend a good amount of time researching summer camps and music programs for my nephews. I also spend way too much time shopping for cute clothes for all the kids in my life. If you add to the equation homework, testing, and after-school activities, I'm pretty sure that I'll have an opinion on everything. Moreover, I suffer greatly from the disease of not just wanting things done but wanting them done my way and on my timetable. I will be upset if my husband blows off playdates. I will be furious if he misses deadlines, parent-teacher conferences, snack obligations. I will question his ability to manage anything at all if he forgets to fill a prescription or doesn't schedule an important doctor's appointment. It's not a pretty truth about myself, and Lord knows I'm working on it in our marriage now. But I can see that having kids and having my husband in charge will exacerbate what are my already admittedly unrealistic standards.

My twelve-year-old nephew is living with us this summer. He and I have been pals since he was three years old. This is the first time he's visited us for the whole summer. Unfortunately, I'm working on a television show, which is really a grind. Yes, you get a hiatus when you wrap. But during the actual season, you eat two and sometimes three meals a day on the set. At least two days of the week are twelve hours long; during the season, there are no sick days or vacation days. Save it for hiatus. I tell myself that someday this could be good. Three whole months home with my kid would be better than what any nine-to-five offers. But the nine months of working on the show are absolutely brutal. So Jason, who has the more flexible work schedule, changed his hours so he can be home with Jesse at four every afternoon.

The two of them have bonded in ways I can only begin to imagine. I feel like the dad who goes back to work three days after the baby is born and watches from the perimeter as his wife and newborn develop an intense, impenetrable closeness. This could be because at the heart of things, my husband is really a twelve-year-old boy. Jason and Jesse go to the farmer's market together and make pizzas from scratch. They play Monopoly with all the trash talking of a corner basketball game. They go and see the latest Harry Potter movie. Without me.

I know enough about motherhood to know that along with the joy, there is darkness, too, a darkness I did not dare write about before. I am reckless and relentless as I spy on the stay-at-home and working mothers, playing both sides of the cloak-and-dagger game. When I'm with a friend who is a stay-at-home mom, I agree with everything she says. Yes, of course, public school is abominable and private school isn't much better, so of course she needs to be home after school, to check homework and drill on French verbs for Friday's test. Yes, of course, she needs to chauffeur her kids to all their sports activities, because, as she explains with a conspiratorial grin, "if you're not in the car pool, you have no idea what's really going on with these kids." Yes, I say, you are absolutely right.

Then I'm out with a friend who is a working mom and I agree, of course, she's absolutely right, the stay-at-home mom at her school who yelled at her for not remembering to send her daughter's snack to the end-of-the-year party is not just a bitch but a super bee-yatch, who is bored and sexually unfulfilled and turning all her dominatrix tendencies onto her poor children, who will probably drop out of school and start selling drugs in about fifth grade.

Really, though, that's just the tip of the iceberg. At times my double-agent work snowballs until I no longer know my own addled mind. With one friend, I say, yes, she's absolutely right, the drugs are there for a reason and any woman who passes on the epidural is a damn fool. The next day I have tea with another friend who has just come from a meeting with a midwife. At this particularly midwifery institution, you give birth in not just in any old birthing pool but in a giant hot tub with music, cold drinks, and snacks.

"It's like a spa," my natural-birth friend whispers to me. "You would really like it."

I nod, genuinely enthused. "A spa sounds good."

I want to be able to say that all the judgment and aggression and competitiveness I witness among working and stay-at-home mothers surprises me and absolutely must change. But that wouldn't be honest. I've been party to this one-upping and henpecking and know-it-all-ness my entire life. It's as if becoming a mother puts us back into a sorority or junior high school, into some petri dish of experience where what other females think and say and feel and do counts more than anything.

The one thing my stay-at-home and working-mom friends share in the country of motherhood is a superiority gene, some may call it a gift of vision, that convinces them that women who don't have children are, despite their educations and accomplishments, dumb as doorknobs. I've sat through many a heated conversation about the merits of staying home with kids versus continuing to work, sports versus languages, sleep-away camp versus day camp, during which I have been silly enough to offer an opinion only to be shut down more condescendingly and viciously by wise Goddess Mothers than I have ever been shut down by any man.

"What do *you* know?" Goddess Mother number one asks me. "You don't have children."

And I admit that I don't.

"Then you have *no* idea," Goddess Mother number two will chime in.

At this point I will say something about being an oldest child who practically raised my brother, about being an oldest grandchild, about having nieces and nephews, until the Goddess Mothers start to cackle. "Nieces and nephews?" they say, in the tone one might use to mock a small child.

When I try to explain that I am very involved in my nephews' lives, in particular, doing school applications, summer-camp applications, back-to-school shopping, funding 529s for their college education, the Goddess Mothers laugh. "That's sweet," they say. "But you still have no idea."

What amazes me most is that these are the same women who will talk about how disconnected from the world they feel. In the very next breath, they'll say, "Sometimes I go whole days without talking to another adult." Or "I used to read the paper in bed at 11 P.M., but I just gave up. I hate the fact that I feel so stupid because I'm not up with current events." The Goddess Mothers know what it's like to be put down, and yet in their own spheres of power and influence, they are absolute in their cruelty. I know it's a symptom of their powerlessness. I know it's because they get far too little credit for all of the amazing things they do. But I wish they wouldn't take it out on me.

A few weeks ago, we were out with old friends of my husband's, a young couple who came to dinner with their new baby and raucous tales of giving birth. They wanted to share the gory details with us and they were trying to be helpful.

The husband said, "When they shoved that epidural needle into your spine, I almost passed out!"

He and his wife collapsed into giggles.

My own face was ashen, which for a black woman is rare. "They shove the needle into your spine?" I asked.

Yes, the wife said, right at the base of your spine. Then the husband said, "Yeah, what I was worried about was what if you jerked back and the needle slipped? You could have been paralyzed permanently."

And I'm thinking about my other friend, the one who has had multiple epidurals and never once mentioned the little bit about the spine, and the word I'm thinking is *bitch*.

And I'm also thinking about whether Jason, in addition to staying home with our kids, could be the one to bear them as well.

I remember as a child hearing my mother and her friends say over and over again, "It's like childbirth—you forget the pain." They always said it in an utterly honest and genuine way. Over time, I came to see this as one of the few gospel truths about womanhood. You never hear women say that anymore. I am all for a more sophisticated understanding of our mental and physical states, but if I read one more article about vaginal tears in natural childbirth, horrendous recoveries from C-sections, the suicidal undertones of postpartum depression, and the lingering mystery of SIDS, I am going to buy myself an old-fashioned chastity belt and tell my husband, "Too bad, so sad, this shop is closed for business."

I understand that knowledge is power and women share these stories to feel connected. But I am beginning to think that there's a part of this journey to motherhood that I want to make alone, without the weight and worry of so many other women's experiences. How will spying on other mothers help me when I don't know where my own journey will take me? I don't know yet if I can conceive. I don't know yet if I will adopt one child or two. I don't know yet if I will have a long labor or short labor or what will go wrong. But I watch the mommy wars and I can only imagine the worst because it's the worst that leaps out at me in the stories I hear and the books I read.

The other day I watched a friend's three-year-old punch her in the face. Children can be mean. They can be dangerous. They can destroy bodies and careers and marriages. They can be awful in ways that I do not have the creativity to imagine.

I don't think adopting a baby would make life easier. Several of my really good friends tell horror stories about adopted siblings who, despite being brought into loving homes, seemed genetically programmed for self-destruction. These stories—of drug abuse, violence, suicide—scare me too. But as one mommy friend once said about me, I have the gene of being able to love passionately children who are not related to me. I've never had particular fantasies or passions about wanting a child who came from me. The in vitro clinics are packed with women who feel strongly about having biological children. If I'm not one of those women, shouldn't I go with my strengths and adopt?

This summer, as I logged long hours writing a television sitcom at an office and on a ten-city cross-country tour to promote my novel, I was jealous of the closeness between my husband and his nephew. A few weeks into living with us, my nephew said at dinner one night, "Jason makes such great food."

I said, "I can cook too."

My nephew looked at me and said, "I have no idea if you can cook. I haven't even seen you pour a bowl of cereal this summer."

So despite the fact that it meant giving up my 6 A.M. workouts (good mommy training, I tell myself), I began to make breakfast for Jesse. I kicked Jason out of the kitchen at night and began to cook dinner. One night as Jesse asked for seconds (I'd made pork chops with apple-cider gravy and egg noodles), "So, you still don't think I can cook?" I asked him.

"No," he said, "you can cook. And your food tastes better. I think you use more butter and salt."

Which is absolutely true. Truth be told, if I had to lace his food with opiates, I would do it if it would convince Jesse that I am as good a cook/surrogate parent as Jason. I'm not even a mother yet, and I'm already willing to go to the mat to be the favorite. I know what a powerful sunbeam a child's affection is. I melt to pieces when my niece says, "I miss you," or when she announces with pride, "You know why my aunt bought me this dress? Because she loves me *thiiiiiiiiis* much." The other day, I just fell apart when a girlfriend called to say her five-year-old daughter begged her to call me for a playdate. When my nephew is happy, when he's just read me a book report or taught me a new dance or whipped my butt in Monopoly, it's like we're two figurines in a snow globe where the sky is magical and it is snowing but we are warm and safe. Jason likes to joke that our children will love him more. Deep down, I think he's probably right. Jason, like so many guys, has an easy confidence. He expects to be loved, because he is a great guy. I am like so many women: I don't expect to be loved. I think that love is something I have to work hard for, and earn again and again, day in and day out.

A good friend of mine was married for ten years before she had a baby. When she did, she said, "That whole time, it was like my husband and I were just dating. The baby made us a family." At the time, it sounded like something new mothers say. But after having my nephew for the summer, I know, just a little bit, how she felt. Jason and I alone are a couple. He's my family. But it's a very small family. Jason, my nephew, and I were a team: a self-contained unit that could also split into different units and configurations. Having the three of us together was a glimpse into how a child multiplies the possibilities and experiences of life.

Sometimes Jason and I talk about not having children at all. Honestly, I can't see that happening. My spying is filled with many more moments of lust than of loathing. The way a newborn perks up at the sound of her mother's voice, or a toddler collapses in his mother's arms after a bad spill makes me feel envious. At some point, I'm going to hop on that table or into that birthing pool. Or go through the joys and rigors of adoption: the lawyers, the exhilaration, the waiting, and the feeling of stepping, forever and inadequately, into the birth parents' shoes.

These days, I feel as if the decision to try to become pregnant is not unlike deciding to climb onto the hot seat in one of those dunking booths they have at county fairs and school fund-raisers. Jason and I will make the decision to become parents together. But I'll be the one who climbs into that dunking booth, puts my best game face on, and says, "Sock it to me." Despite what I've learned (and not learned) from my working and not-working mommy friends, what makes me brave enough to take on the entire enterprise is that when I fall, biologically and psychologically, into the depths of motherhood, Jason will be standing there next to me. I can picture him tossing a few high ones at me, but I know he will also be waiting with a towel and a blow-dryer, watching me get soaked, helping me to float on the waves of his laughter. I can't wait to see which Russian doll bobs to the water's surface.

Peace and Carrots

Carolyn Hax

Carolyn Hax writes a hugely popular advice column for *The Washington Post*, "Tell Me About It," which appears through syndication in more than two hundred newspapers. She has also written a book about love titled *Tell Me About It: Lying, Sulking, Getting Fat . . . and 56 Other Things* Not *to Do While Looking for Love.* She was named one of *Time* magazine's "America's Best" in September 2001 and *Editor & Publisher*'s Special Feature of the Year in 2002. She lives in Connecticut with her husband and three kids.

am thirty-seven. I have three boys under nineteen months old. I write a nationally syndicated advice column. Here's how I threw myself into the middle of the working-versus-stay-at-home-mom fight, publicly, before I even had kids (heh):

July 4, 1999

Carolyn:

I am 29 and have been dating a 33-year-old man for almost a year. We have had some pretty serious disagreements about family values.

His mother stayed home. Boyfriend is also fortunate enough to be able to support a family on his salary alone. Therefore, he feels very strongly that when his (future) wife has kids, she should stay home to raise them (at least when they are very young). He maintains that a child raised by a working mother suffers from the lack of care and nurturing.

That is fine if a mom wants to stay home, but I may not. And how nurturing is a stir-crazy mom?

My mother not only worked but also went to grad school, and was still there for us. I don't have any serial killer tendencies yet. I also enjoy my independence and career—I never thought I would be asked to give up everything. That is completely unnecessary!

I think a child benefits from the quality of time with Mom, not just the quantity. I have tried to explain this, but he doesn't seem to want to hear. I wish he would just accept my choice and support me. He doesn't understand that the decision to work is one the mother needs to make on her own.

—My Decision

Oh, great, drag me into this.

You may not be a serial killer, but your signature scares the hell out of me. Yoo-hoo, ever heard of "fathers"? This isn't "my" decision, it's yours and his. And if you truly view child-rearing in terms of what is and isn't "necessary," then please don't breed.

Don't get me wrong—it's not like I'm dying to side with your boyfriend. He would have wifey stay home by fiat, so the notion of shared decision-making eludes him, too. And where's his offer to stay home? It's still women's work?

I'm grown, I'm female, I'm married, I work; to say I've given this issue some thought is a grotesque understatement. To arrange my own priorities, I ranked all the basic baby-rearing scenarios (at least till school age) by desirability:

1. *Stay-home parent or parent who works part-time (tie);*
2. *Parent who works at home;*
3. *Happy working parents who make the kids their priority;*
4. *Stressed-out working parents who alleviate their guilt with trendy moronisms like "quality time";*
5. *Orphanage;*
172. *Negligent, abusive or otherwise toxic parent, working or non-.*

Why does home win? For one thing, as my sister so memorably put it, for nannies it's still just a job. Having, say, Grandma baby-sit negates that particular day-care drawback, but it still leaves the other: all those lost hours between parent and kid.

The verdict on day care is complicated (and still being written), but studies indicate that the quality of care—physical, intellectual, emotional—is the prevailing factor in a child's development, not mom vs. paid care.

But it doesn't take a study to point out that the parent who chooses home and does it right will tell that child, "You come first." In return, the parent gains the intimate knowledge of a child's day-to-day life that, sorry, just isn't available on the three-hour-a-day plan.

In fact, I have yet to meet the working parents who'd refuse the one-salary option to gain that slow, sweet, unstructured time with their little monsters. That's "quality time"—not the weekend ball-

game in some MasterCard ad. So enough of this 40-hours-of-day-care-is-just-as-good, please.

If I ruled the Earth, it would be tempting to hold everyone to my standard (and distribute the cash to support it), but in the end, the work question is just too personal. I know I'm not up to the 40-hours-plus-parenthood task, but it would be a neat bit of ideologic denial to then declare that no one is. As you said, your mom did just fine; plenty of working parents do, if they care enough to. Likewise, a lot of hyper-protective stay-at-home parents may as well pack up their botched little science experiments and ship them off to therapy.

That's why my rule-the-Earth standard has only one nonnegotiable condition—the kid comes first—and a set of questions:

Can you afford to reduce or drop one salary?

Is one parent in a better position to do so?

Does that parent want to?

If not, why are you having kids?

If you can't take the pay cut, do you have the dedication to be good working parents?

Whatever you decide, are you both committed to your decision? To each other?

Would you want to be your kid?

I'd make that last one a "no" in your case. Unless you both muster respect for each other's views and flexibility to accommodate them, you'll be a tense, unpleasant, incompatible pair.

And, frankly, I wouldn't want a mom who describes staying home with me as "giving up everything."

Five years and three kids later. Possible reasons I no longer care about the working-versus-stay-at-home-mom fight (in no particular order):

I have three children under nineteen months. I don't have time to care.

I am happy.

I am old enough now to have known enough people making enough bizarre arrangements work (and making textbook arrangements fail) to persuade me that anyone who thinks she can judge what's best for other people's kids is either arrogant, psychic, or high.

My own choice defies classification. I work full-time, from home, with hours so flexible that I can work entirely during the hours my children are asleep, if I choose to. I don't choose to. My husband, Kenny, is a stay-at-home dad except for a twelve-week part-time coaching stint in the fall. In a few weeks, when his season starts and I run out of maternity leave, our eighteen-month-old twins will start three days a week of day care and spend the other four with me and/or Kenny. The four-month-old will remain home full-time, so we've hired a part-time nanny for any hours that Kenny's work overlaps with mine. I'm sure we're doing something terrible, but when Kenny and I tried to figure out what it was, we got confused, then Toddler One bit Toddler Two and the screaming woke up the baby and we forgot what we were confused about.

Caring about the way other women choose between their careers and motherhood strikes me as strangely myopic. Sexist, even. Where's the dog in this catfight? Don't men's choices count as much?

And what about a woman's choice of man? Suddenly, that guy whose career success you found so attractive ("husband material," I think you called him) becomes the guy who's never home to help with the kids. Imagine.

The happiest parents I know are the ones who are part of an attentive and like-minded team. The unhappiest are the ones who had children only to find every gap in their relationships exposed. If anything, the home-versus-career choice is just the afterthought to the ten-pound baby of choices—with whom you'll be raising your kids.

In the few years before I became a mother, I went through hell. I got divorced, watched my mother die slowly of a gruesome disease, moved three times—or was it four?—and spent a goodly amount of time alone in a sparsely furnished rented home processing the idea that my life wasn't going to resemble anything I'd ever imagined, particularly that, as a newly single thirty-four-year-old, I might never be a mother myself.

I can't say I'd jump at an opportunity to relive that stage of my life. Even more horrifying, though, would be the idea of never having gone through it. What a delusion-buster. There are things that matter in life and things that don't, and the gulf between the two is never wider, clearer, or more significant than when it feels like everything that matters to you is going to shit.

Fortunately the gulf doesn't completely close or cloud over when the bad time passes. Social absolutes, quests for perfection, visions of how your life is supposed to be, and any other smug certainties remain safely and, I hope, permanently on the things-that-don't-matter side. What matters still matters. Love, compassion, humor, tolerance, integrity, flexibility, and enough guts to accept that life is flawed, that *your* life is more so, and that you're just a flaw with a job. Assuming you have a job.

Oh, and effort matters, too. Effort is huge.

I hear people agonizing or passionately debating about the ways they "should" raise kids, and I feel bad for them. My new certainty is that any arrangement can work as long as a parent is selfless (and then lucky) enough to make it work. Which means my list of smug little questions has been packed away but for this one: *Would you want to be your kid?*

Own up. Then make peace with your choices from there.

Unprotected

Natalie Smith Parra

Mother, grandmother, and writer, Natalie Smith Parra is an editor of *Justice: Denied* magazine and a writer in residence for InsideOut, an organization that teaches creative writing to incarcerated youth in Los Angeles. Her writing has appeared in *Creative Nonfiction* and *Calyx.* She lives in Santa Monica, California. Her story silences the erudite debate over the superiority of at-home versus working motherhood; truly bad mothering exists in a hellish and all-too-real category of its own.

was a seed blown in the wind. I grew roots where I landed, worked long hours to keep my kids fed and clothed and the rent paid. I was nineteen when Jonathon was born, twenty-one when Sara came along. The children's father, busy training for life as a minor thug, gave us little help. Jonathon and Sara learned to pull folded clothes out of baskets of clean laundry while I got ready to go to my underpaid jobs at print shops scattered throughout Los Angeles. The kids learned to finish their cold cereal and carry the bowls to the sink, they learned to hug me good-bye with their skinny arms, and later to have their homework finished before I arrived at their after-school program at six o'clock to take them home to one of our cheap stucco apartments.

I was a working mother.

My jobs never came with medical insurance. I remember sitting at the welfare office in a blue plastic chair alongside rows of tired women while my kids poured quarters into vending machines. I waited for hours to see a caseworker and then shrank in my chair as she told me I needed to see the district attorney regarding the whereabouts of *your lowlife husband*. I didn't understand why a lowlife husband negated my kids' need to see a dentist, but I understood that this woman in her three-piece suit and clicky heels was telling us that we had nothing coming.

A lifetime later, when I was thirty-two, I remarried. Paul was a political activist from a big East Los Angeles family, a solid guy with principles, a good father, one who would stick around. When our daughter, Sasha, was three she watched *The Wizard of Oz* for the first time. Each night she would wait for Paul to come home from his shift as a paramedic pulling people from the wreckage of cars on Los Angeles freeways. When he walked through the front door she would run to him, carrying a scraggly black Halloween wig. "Daddy, put it on," she'd say. And he would.

"Now, chase me, Daddy, and scream, 'I'm going to get you, my little pretty!'"

Paul would chase her through the house cackling, with that tangled black mess flying behind him and Sasha running and screaming and laughing. He did this every evening for months until Sasha tired of the game.

I had left the less-than-lucrative printing trade years before and dragged myself through a state university. I now had a job teaching English and Spanish in a big urban high school. But I found my mission advocating for the rights of my immigrant students and their parents, much as I wished someone had done for me in those frightening and lonely days as a single parent. About the time Sasha turned four, on the Fourth of July, a racist anti-immigrant group held a demonstration outside the Westwood Federal Building. They demanded deportation of all Mexican immigrants and waved placards with ugly messages like MEXICANS: THUGS, BUGS AND DRUGS; one pictured a battered corpse under angry block letters spelling out KILLED BY ILLEGAL ALIENS.

Another teacher, some parents, and my teaching assistant organized vanloads of students to attend the counterdemonstration. News reporters interviewed me in Spanish and English, and that night when we gathered at my house to watch the news and eat spaghetti, I saw a woman at the height of her power. Wearing denim shorts and a white T-shirt, my legs tanned by the summer sun, I stood facing the camera and spoke about justice for my students, for the millions of immigrants doing the shit work in Los Angeles. We all have moments in our life when we are at our most beautiful, and that day speaking into those microphones surrounded by my students was one of mine.

I had no idea what was growing inside me.

Doctors showed me a shiny sheet of X-ray paper with a cancerous lesion the size of a quarter on my left lung. They told me I would be dead in months. I was thirty-eight. Sasha was four.

My diagnosis hurled me backward into a world as dangerous as fire, more insecure than anything I could have imagined a decade and a half earlier as a young single working mother. Fear gnawed at me until at times I felt an aching emptiness in my belly. The only way to fill it was with Ativan or Valium. It was an existential crisis, and it was something else: the nakedness and vulnerability I had felt as a young mother, a cold, hungry fear I thought I'd forgotten. I was not part of the world, I was its victim, this time because of a fast-growing tumor, pasty and gray, that by the time of my operation had fiercely adhered to my aorta. My working-mother status became suddenly, irrevocably irrelevant.

I knew Sasha wouldn't remember me if I died; in a few years I wouldn't exist for her. She wouldn't know how it felt when I pressed my lips to her silky dark hair and breathed her little-girl smell of sweat and baby shampoo. She wouldn't remember what a happy child she was, the joy I felt at six o'clock on Sunday mornings opening my eyes to her propped up on one fat elbow, smiling wide-eyed, inches from my face. The time she dressed our dog up in a green skirt and tank top and we paraded through our East Hollywood neighborhood. She would be too young to remember our trip to Big Sur, how we sat on Pfeiffer Beach as the sun set over the Pacific, yellow and pink and pale green all swirling together in the sky like wet mother-of-pearl. For her, watching that sunset with my arms wrapped around her to keep her warm would disappear as a memory and remain only as a faded photograph. The thought of myself as nothing more than a void in her life pushed me into action.

My husband had a job with benefits, so for the first time in my adult life I was free to not return to work after my diagnosis. In between chemotherapy and radiation treatments, I taught Sasha to read and applauded when she stood on the bed and gave a dramatic reading of *Corduroy*. I hired a piano teacher and sat on the sofa, my eyes glowing with tears as she played "Violets Are Blue," stretching her chubby fingers to reach the keys and singing in her off-key baby voice. Ironically, cancer freed me to parent Sasha in a way I never could have imagined doing with Jon and Sara.

One night after my diagnosis my husband's mother and sister came over to cook for me. They made a thick chicken stew and homemade tortillas with fresh salsa. Jonathon, Sara, and Paul drifted away from the table, and I sat with Sasha's grandmother and aunt. A shroud of loneliness blanketed me as evening pulled in the light. I thought of my little girl and what would become of her.

"Will you watch out for Sasha if I die?" I asked. "If Paul remarries, will you make sure his new wife treats Sasha well?" I couldn't keep the pleading out of my voice.

Paul's sister Gloria recoiled. She tossed her head and pushed back her chair from the table. "My brother wouldn't act like that," she said, affronted. But my mother-in-law knew exactly what I meant.

"I'll be watching every minute," Dora said in the usual mix of Spanish and English that we use to communicate. "That's what happened to me when my mother died. My stepmother sent me to an orphanage." She shot Gloria a look. I could count on Dora to protect Sasha when I was no longer there.

The doctor's stainless-steel scalpel saved my life. But months later, I was still running. A tension headache could bring on great heaving sobs; I was so sure that my cancer had recurred and was in my brain. I ran as you do in a nightmare, afraid I wasn't running fast enough, afraid to look back over my shoulder.

At some point I did look back. I realized that the cancer stalking me was losing ground. The first anniversary came and went. Most patients with my diagnosis die in a year. The second anniversary passed. Sasha turned six. I didn't think about cancer for half a day, then a whole day. Sometimes several days would pass without my obsessive ruminations on my own death. When Sasha turned ten, I thought only of my cancer when I went for a checkup.

"You're cured," said the doctor who had told me there was no cure. I left behind a lung and a vocal cord, but I was able to protect my daughter from having to pull her clean clothes out of laundry baskets alone for the rest of her life.

I realized that although I'd protected Sasha from a mom dying of cancer, I couldn't protect her from the world.

Sheri* was Sasha's first real best friend. They met at school, and I was thrilled when they became close. Having been so close to dying, I realized that you can never have enough friends, enough people in your life, enough memories.

The first week the girls met, Sasha invited Sheri to sleep over for the weekend. Sheri began to prefer our house to her own. Sometimes she came after school and stayed for days. Every afternoon the girls seemed to discover a new coincidence that proved destiny had brought them together. Sheri was born six days before Sasha. They both weighed sixty-five pounds, and both their initials were S.P. The kids at school called Sheri Shrimp and Sasha Sushi; together they were Shrimp and Sushi.

*Some of the names in this essay have been changed.

They planned to make a web page with that title. They buried their secrets on blue lined paper under a hydrangea bush in my front yard.

There had been times as a stressed-out single mom, as a married mom dying of cancer, that I thought I was a bad mother. Then I met Alex.

Sheri's mother was beautiful. Her full name was Alessandra, and she had black hair and skin as white and smooth as moonstone. She sat at my kitchen table talking breathlessly about her new job, one night per week, as a waitress at For Play Gentlemen's Club. At age thirty-eight, Alex saw this job as a good first step to a career as a stripper. I imagined I knew what Alex hoped for. I remembered my own pathetic hope that each crappy job would free me from those lean years of single motherhood. Alex's dark eyes sparkled when she was excited, and her Greek accent wrapped itself more thickly around English words. "All the girls, you know? The stripteasers? They all drive BMWs and Mercedeses." Her hands flew while she spoke. Gaudy rings with octagonal blue and orange stones caught the light from the kitchen window. Outside was the hydrangea bush where Sasha and Sheri had buried their little-girl secrets.

One Saturday night I took Sasha and Sheri to see *A Midsummer Night's Dream* at an outdoor theater. The air was finally cooling after another stifling summer day, an ocean breeze wafting the scent of sunbaked grass and pepper trees, sweet and spicy through the canyon. After the show, some girls teased Sheri about her pierced nose, pointing and laughing.

"I feel sorry for Sheri," Sasha said after her first visit to their apartment. "She doesn't even have any toys, just a little table next to the futon where she keeps a few things, makeup and hair stuff. Her mother isn't that nice to her either. Some soda spilled on the seat of the van, and her mom yelled and yelled and called Sheri fucking stupid."

"Sheri must have been embarrassed," I said.

"She was," Sasha said, her dark eyes flashing anger. "But it's Alex who should be embarrassed."

"Stress," I said, remembering flare-ups of temper from years past that I was not too proud of either. "A single mother trying to survive in a foreign country. It's just stress. Anyone in that position would be stressed."

Jonathon was two and Sara only a few months old the year I worked at Pronto Printing in Hawthorne, a small, run-down suburb of Los Angeles, south of the airport. The tiny shop was sandwiched between a thrift store and a Laundromat. I worked the counter, taking orders for business cards, letterhead stationery, and cheap wedding invitations while my younger sister Stephanie and the owner's stepson Phillip worked the presses in back. Phillip was training Stephanie. He set up the machines, aligned the plates, and inked the rollers. She fed the paper. But mostly they joked around and smoked weed in the alley outside, then soaked rags in cleaning fluid and set them on fire, howling with laughter each time a flaming rag flew across the workroom like a small doomed comet. I listened to them and cringed, waiting for Phillip's dad to get back from a business call and fire all of us.

One summer afternoon, quitting time at Pronto Printing, I tidied up my drafting table, put away the tapes for making perfect corners and decorative borders, lined up my pencils with their pale blue nonreproducible lead and Rapidograph pens, straightened the rolls of masking tape, and wiped down the board with a damp rag. I had bought my rusted Ford Falcon from a junkyard near the L.A. harbor for two hundred dollars. The door creaked as I pulled it open and threw my bag on the backseat. I turned the key, turned it again, and let my head sink to the steering wheel. "Fuck," I said. Stephanie got in and sat shotgun. "Don't flood it," she said. "Wait a minute and then try it again."

"Goddammit," I muttered. I had twenty minutes to make it to the babysitter's before she charged me extra. I had nothing extra to give her. Phillip finally talked his dad into loaning him the delivery truck. The three of us screeched up in front of the babysitter's two-story tract house with a few minutes to spare. Stephanie and I jumped out, and Phillip roared away in the truck. We knocked on the babysitter's door.

"Back here!" Miriam called, and I followed the sound of her voice to the den next to the kitchen. Jonathon, my two-year-old, was in the backyard kicking a ball with other toddlers. When he saw me he ran into the house and wrapped his chubby arms around my knees. Before I had a chance to bend down and hug him I noticed my infant, Sara, on the kitchen floor, propped up against a dirty pillow with a receiving blanket tied around her to hold the bottle in her mouth. The nipple had slipped out, and Sara was struggling to find it, twisting her tiny face as far as she could, turning red with exertion. I looked at my daughter propped on Miriam's worn linoleum floor and felt like someone had socked me in the stomach, a hopelessness that seemed insurmountable.

"Why do you have the bottle tied to my baby?" I asked.

Miriam came into the kitchen pulling on a pair of latex gloves. "I can't sit here while she eats every time. She's slow."

"I thought that's what I paid you to do!" I said, outraged now, holding my baby, bouncing her against my chest, my lips pressed against her warm head.

"When you've raised as many kids as I have, then you can tell me how to do it," Miriam said and laughed.

I threw the diaper bag over my arm and stomped out, Sara over my shoulder and Jonathon's sticky hand in mine. "Fuck you," I mumbled so Miriam would hear but the kids wouldn't.

We hitchhiked home. I sat on the curb cradling both kids on my lap while Stephanie stood in the street raising her thumb and cussing at each car that passed us by. By the time I got home I was hungry and exhausted. The kids were whining. I had only the energy to heat up soup and wash a load of clothes before I fell asleep. I woke up the next morning frantic and called my boss to ask for a few days off, unpaid of course, to get my car towed and fixed and to find a new babysitter to watch my children while I worked.

Alex complained about her roommate. Worms crawled in the rice, she said, and the house was filled with cockroaches and moths that flew mindlessly toward the bare ceiling lightbulbs. Alex and Sheri paid five hundred dollars a month to live in a corner of the living room. She was desperate to move, but she couldn't rent her own apartment, because she had no Social Security number, no credit history.

I remember that after my operation, when, for the first time since my diagnosis I was free of cancer, I became suddenly depressed. Tears would leak from my eyes for no reason, and I slept a lot. "I don't know what's wrong," I told my husband one afternoon. "This is the time I should be less depressed, not more."

"I know what's wrong," Paul said. "When you had cancer, you had something to fight. You've always needed a good fight."

Alex and Sheri became my cause. I could help Alex control her temper, help them to find a decent place to live, provide them with a little more stability, the way I wish someone had helped me when I was struggling.

I talked to Simin, a friend from college. She had an extra room in a large apartment. At first she was nervous about Sheri, not sure she wanted to live with a child. But Simin was an immigrant herself, having fled from Iran, leaving her political books buried in a field after the 1979 Islamic revolution. She'd had no relatives to fall back on and knew what it meant to depend on small kindnesses. She agreed to have Alex and Sheri move in.

Only a few days later she confronted me about Alex. Alex yelled in the mornings. Sheri didn't go to school much because Alex liked to sleep late. Behind the closed bedroom door, it sounded like Alex was hitting Sheri. We agreed that I would talk to her.

Alex and I spoke in her red van one day in the alley behind my house. I watched a scruffy-looking crackhead enter a hole in a chain-link fence, then minutes later reappear. Alex talked fast and claimed she was much better than she used to be. She told me of the years after she had moved from Greece to London, how the rain and the clouds depressed her, how she took Sheri to the markets to sell the jewelry she had made, how one day a woman cheated her of a couple of pounds. She was sure Sheri knew about it but hadn't told her while it was happening. "I hit her all the way home," Alex admitted. "Then I locked her out of the apartment. She slept the whole night on the filthy hallway carpet with just a little cushion from the sofa. In the morning her eyes were just two slits in the middle of red mounds of skin from crying so hard. She said, 'Mommy, if you don't hug me, I want to die.' "

I hid my disgust. It was hard to do.

I tried to believe Alex was getting better. She admitted her wrongs, a sign that she was willing to change, right? But I wondered: Could someone abuse less and less until one day they just stopped altogether, like quitting coffee or cigarettes? In my mind hitting your child would be something you would have to renounce all at once.

Even during my insecure and stress-filled days as a single mother, I had never hit my kids. My father had hit us with belts, and as a child I had vowed that I would never hurt a powerless person.

I was, however, accused once of child abuse, nearly two decades ago. Jon and Sara were six and four. I had worked my way up the printing hierarchy and was a production coordinator in a low-slung factory building in North Hollywood. The company was called H & H Printing; the workers pronounced it "H und H," like Germans. H & H did much of the printing for the Southern California Republican Party. The other workers and I ate lunch perched on wooden pallets of shrink-wrapped flyers that extolled the virtues of a second presidential term for Ronald Reagan. We joked about burning our own anti-Reagan message onto the plates before they went to press. I suppose I was the face of Reagan's welfare mother. I hated Reagan as much as I hated Harry, the rotund, red-faced owner of H und H.

I lived in fear of Harry's temper and resorted to feeding Jon and Sara liquor-store breakfasts of small donuts in cellophane and cartons of chocolate milk to avoid being late to work. I lived with the guilt about my terrible mothering. Late one night, as if in an act of divine retribution, a hard knock on the front door jarred me from my task of folding little T-shirts and rolling tiny socks into pairs.

I opened the door to an officer from the Los Angeles County Sheriff's Department and a woman in a flowery dress and strappy sandals standing in the yellow porch light. The officer showed me his badge, while the woman explained that she was from Child Protective Services and wanted to see Sara.

"Sara?" I asked. "Why?"

"We have a report," the woman said, "that your daughter is covered with cuts and bruises."

I stood aside while they pushed through the door into my tiny house with its brown carpets and Formica-topped kitchen table, the TV blaring. I remember thinking they were too big for my house. Their presence sucked the air out of the rooms. And out of me. I don't remember ever being as scared in my life as I was that night.

I led them into the bedroom, giving silent thanks that I'd picked the toys up earlier and that the kids, asleep on their Snoopy sheets, were bathed. I pulled back Sara's comforter to reveal her sleeping in a pajama top and underpants. A few buttons had come undone, exposing her pale belly. I felt like throwing myself down on top of her to protect her.

The CPS woman pulled the comforter back farther so she could see my girl's skinny legs.

"Band-Aids," I said, suddenly realizing where the story about cuts and bruises had come from. "She was covered with Band-Aids, not cuts and bruises. She likes Band-Aids."

Would the fact that I hadn't stopped her from plastering herself with Band-Aids indicate bad mothering? Maybe I had been lazy, watching from the front porch as Sara paraded up and down the sidewalk with her imaginary battle wounds. But did that indicate negligence? Could I lose my child because she covered herself with a package of Band-Aids?

The officer laughed. The social worker was less impressed.

"I won't do anything right now," she said. "But I'll go to their school tomorrow and investigate."

I didn't sleep until the early hours of the morning, dozing off just before the alarm rang. I dressed and fed Jon and Sara and hurried to work at H & H. I waited for another late-night knock. It never came.

Thanksgiving is a big affair at my mother-in-law's house in East Los Angeles. Our huge Latino family gathers there to eat and dance, and the house is fragrant with the smell of roasting turkeys and giant pots of tamales. From the wrap-around porch, you can see the buildings of downtown Los Angeles outlined in green and red lights, long, neon-colored rectangles.

My sister-in-law Gloria and I sat outside with our feet up, stuffed from too much food. Gloria told me about a high school friend of hers who had been sent to a foster home. The foster father got her pregnant, and then the family kicked her out. She was living an impoverished life with the baby, a girl, two years old now. I had just seen a *Frontline* documentary about a girl who was taken from her young mother and put in the care of a foster mother who duct-taped her to a high chair and taped her mouth shut. The child died. Our supposed protectors can't do their job any better than the abusive parents they take children from. From the window, I drank in the sound of loud salsa music and my kids inside dancing, screaming, laughing.

I wasn't sure I wanted Sasha to be friends with Sheri. I hate the way this sounds, but I wanted Alex and Sheri to disappear. During the next several days, I searched the Internet for parenting support groups and anger-management classes and found little that someone without financial means could afford. I e-mailed Parents Anonymous and they sent me a thick brown envelope, which I passed on to Alex.

Alex found out she was pregnant. She wanted more kids, she said, but now was not the time. She arranged an abortion and asked me to go with her. I picked her up in front of Simin's apartment. After Alex climbed into the passenger seat, Sheri leaned her head in my car window. "I hope you don't die," she said to her mother.

Outside the clinic sat one lone right-to-lifer at a table displaying maudlin horrors, including a jar in which a flesh-colored mass sprouting tiny hands floated in formaldehyde. The woman's wrinkly, too-tanned skin looked like the overcooked top of a muffin that you could stick your finger through. She wore tight green polyester pants. Her blond hair was burned brassy by the sun. "Don't go in there!" she screeched as we walked by. I flipped her off. I had always wanted to do that. It didn't make me feel better.

The waiting room was decorated in a southwestern motif, pale green and tangerine, with pencil drawings of Native American women on the walls. Alex approached the receptionist, who sat behind a frosted glass window.

"I hope God doesn't punish me," Alex said to me.

I leaned across the low white table and said, "If you're worried about God punishing you, you should stop hitting Sheri."

"I know," she answered.

But maybe she was just scared. Maybe agreeing was her penance before her god, to save her from death during the abortion.

A few days later Alex dropped Sheri at my house. Sheri stared after her mother as she walked away. "It would be better if she would get in a car accident and die," she said.

I laughed. A short, nervous, stupid laugh.

Sheri looked at me. "Well, she beats me up," she said.

I asked for details.

"Last week, remember when you were going to pick me up, then she called you and said I couldn't go?" She pinned me with her impossibly blue eyes.

"I remember that," I said.

"She got mad because I didn't understand my math homework and hit me hard on the back of the head with my math book."

I winced.

Then Sheri recounted the story of being left in the hallway all night. She emphasized her fear, how long the night seemed, not the red skin of her eyes in the morning. She told of clenched fists and broken glass, covering bruises with makeup, slaps to her head, Alex dragging her along the floor by her hair.

"I don't know what to do," I said. "I'll do something. Give me time to think about what to do."

What I did was organize a New Year's trip to San Francisco for Sasha, Sheri, and me. We stayed at the Sheehan, an old hotel that had been converted from a YWCA, decorated for Christmas now with garlands of pine, red velvet bows, and shiny gold bulbs all strung along clean walls the color of custard. We saw *The Nutcracker* at the opera house and rode the cable cars. The girls begged to go on the Powell line over and over, thrilled by the way the tinny car clung to the steep hills. One sunny day between storms a friend drove us to Point Reyes National Seashore. The girls rolled down the windows and sang along with Sheryl Crow about a left-behind friend, Marie. We hiked down a steep trail to Mc-Clure's Beach and looked up to see a majestic Tule elk with antlers watching us from a hillside, backlit by the sun.

On the afternoon of New Year's Eve, we ducked into the Goodwill on Haight Street. Inside, the air smelled like my grandmother's closet, face powder and dampness and years. I followed the girls through rows of old clothing that threatened to submerge them: floral-print housedresses, sweaters, men's shirts, and cheap suit coats. Piles of children's pajamas and overalls, the fabric worn thin and shiny from too many washings, reminded me of Jonathon and Sara's piles of clean laundry that I would hold to my nose in the quiet of the apartment as they slept. I thought about the passing of years, grateful that Jonathon and Sara were safe, Sara at UC Berkeley and Jonathon a recent college graduate too, married, with a young daughter.

I wondered about all the children who had worn these T-shirts and tiny pants. Were they all fine too? Had cancer caught some of them unprotected? Had the parents who were supposed to guarantee their safety abdicated their roles? Or were the children running in the park and making holes in the next size of sweatpants?

Sasha's voice caught me by surprise. "Shoes!" She grabbed Sheri's arm, and they pushed their way through the aisles of musty castoffs. The girls threw off their sneakers and left them in a careless pile on the floor. Sasha reached out to stroke a pair of lavender sling-backs, the leather worn off the toes; Sheri fingered the fringe of a pair of dirty white cow-boy boots. Occasionally they emitted greedy little gasps.

Then Sheri let out a breathy, excited squeal. "Look!" She pushed her purple-socked feet into black patent-leather tap shoes. They were perfect except for the missing ribbon tie. We bought them, and Sheri clicked down the aisle in her three-dollar tap shoes, arms out, liquid hips. We spent New Year's Eve at the gaudily decorated hotel. Sasha and Sheri, each wearing one tap shoe, danced in the lobby.

Our last evening I took the girls to see the movie *Real Women Have Curves*. The main character makes an agonizing choice to leave her mother in order to pursue her own dreams. Afterward, sitting on the edge of a fountain outside the theater, Sheri asked me, "So what will happen to the mother?"

Rain followed us back to Los Angeles, the kind of huge, pelting rain-drops that come after a long dry period. We had had an idyllic week in San Francisco, but I hadn't done anything about Alex.

Sasha begged me to let her go to a movie with Sheri and Alex. I spent the evening reading with a queasy feeling and periodically worrying about the way Alex drove her van in the rain. It was around eleven when I heard Sasha calling "Mommy!" from the alley behind the house. She was standing at the gate alone. I saw the back of Alex's red van as it ca-reened down the alley blowing iridescent plumes of rain off the back tires.

Sasha was pale. "She's going to beat up Sheri," she said. "We went to eat hamburgers after the movie and she thought Sheri was laughing at her. She started yelling. I mean, yelling really bad. The worst I've heard. We were in the backseat. Sheri whispered that she wanted to spend the night here. She's afraid of Alex. Alex wouldn't let her. She wouldn't even let her walk me in."

I pressed the heel of my hand to my forehead. "We have to do some-thing," I said. I tried to dial Alex's cell phone. She hung up when she heard my voice. I tried again. Again she hung up. I tried Simin's number but there was no answer.

Sasha was sniffling now, nibbling at the edges of her fingernails.

"We'll go there," I decided.

I remember the way the streetlights reflected on the wet asphalt, the WHOOSH of my car tires on rain-soaked streets.

"What's wrong?" Simin said. She stood at the open door of her apartment holding a glass teacup filled with amber liquid, a nervous half-smile on her face.

"Are they here?" My eyes shot in the direction of the bedroom Alex and Sheri shared.

"I just got here," Simin said, her voice low, conspiratory. "Come in. Don't stand outside."

"Sheri was asleep on the couch," Simin said. "And when I came in she got up and went to the bedroom."

Everything in the apartment looked the same: the tall upright piano made of dark wood, Persian carpets of blue and gray, gold and maroon. On the wall a framed photograph of a tribe of Persian women crossing a river. Thick trees turn the river water green and cool as the women wade through, bundles of clothing and household goods strapped to their backs. They wear colorful chadors and veils, the brightest of pinks, purple, yellow, as they silently look for the next home, the next resting place.

I told Simin what happened. None of us knew what to do. Sasha rocked from foot to foot, biting the skin around her fingernails.

Simin knocked lightly on the bedroom door. "Sheri," she said in a voice too cheerful for the occasion. "Someone's here to see you."

The door flew open and Alex stood there, her pale skin sallow, sickly-looking, her dark eyes wild and full of rage.

"We don't want to see you!" she shouted. "You are not going to tell me how to raise my daughter! Mind your own business. Leave us alone!"

"Fuck you, Alex." My own voice sounded weak and watery, and my words met Alex's back as she slammed her door so hard that the glass in the living room windows rattled.

Simin looked at me, resigned. "Don't fight with her. Can't you see she's crazy?" I listened to the rain outside, the palm fronds scraping cement. Sasha hadn't sat down. She was still rocking, biting. "Let's go, Mommy," she said. Sasha blamed me halfheartedly for what had happened. "Why did you have to say 'Fuck you' to her?"

The next morning Sasha received a furtive e-mail from Sheri. "We are moving on Monday," it said. "I cried all night. I begged my mother to let me see you before we go but she wouldn't even listen. You are my best friend. I am wearing the Sponge Bob necklace we got in San Francisco. I will never take it off."

With shaking hands I dialed the number of Child Protective Services. The woman who took my call was no monster, nothing like the huge presence that had loomed over me in my small house twenty years ago. She took down my story and said she would go to Sheri's school the next day to investigate.

On Tuesday Sasha and I waited for the locksmith with Simin. Outside the sky was gray, overcast. Sasha played "Für Elise" on the piano with her jacket hood pulled up. We drank tea from glass teacups.

Sasha pushed open the door of the bedroom that Sheri and Alex had shared. It was empty now except for an overflowing wastepaper basket under the window. The lonely room reminded me of the way I'd moved so many times as a single mom, of the low-rent stucco apartments emptied of our meager belongings, endless attempts to make a home. Sasha bent over the wastepaper basket, her hood still up, removing papers and flattening the creases out of them on her leg, searching for a clue as to Sheri's whereabouts or a small memento, some proof she had been there. She smoothed a crumpled piece of blue lined paper against her leg. "Look," she said, "this is from Sheri's school folder." Sheri had written her name ten or fifteen ways on the paper, practicing her signature, I suppose.

I watched Sasha hunched over the trash can. She was unprotected too; she had to live in the world just like I did. It didn't matter how much I loved her. I had dedicated the years since my diagnosis to building something for Sasha that I was never able to build for Jon and Sara. I tried to build it as best I could for Sheri too. But despite my efforts we were all still naked and exposed to the world.

The weekend after Alex and Sheri left, Simin invited us for dinner. The house was clean and lit with candles. The melancholic violins of Armenia floated from the stereo. We drank Persian tea. I found myself watching the slightly open bedroom door where Sheri and Alex had lived for these months.

All I saw was darkness inside.

Julia

Anna Fels

Anna Fels is a psychiatrist and the author of *Necessary Dreams: Ambition in Women's Changing Lives,* a book that should be required reading for every woman in America. Anna has also written for *The New York Times, Harvard Business Review, The Nation, Self,* and other publications. A faculty member of the Weill Medical College of Cornell University at New York Presbyterian Hospital, Anna lives with her husband and two children in New York City. We all have a Julia, a woman who serves as a touchstone for our career and family choices, reflecting how our life might have been if we'd made different decisions at the crossroads.

As I woke up, I felt the harsh tufts of the industrial carpet indenting my face. I was lying on my office floor, still in my house-staff whites after admitting psychiatric patients to the hospital throughout the previous day and night. I knew from the dull afternoon light coming through the window that I'd slept too long. The tongue depressors from my jacket pocket had cascaded into a small pool by my head; my stethoscope flopped next to them. I had meant only to take a short nap. I hadn't been able to face going home to my four-year-old daughter after being away for twenty-four hours and immediately collapsing into bed. I wanted to be able to sit down and play with her, to give her my full attention. In my exhausted state the decision had seemed to make sense: I would come home cheerful and awake. The good mother.

At the hospital entrance, waiting to grab a taxi, I noticed the maintenance men pulling up the chrysanthemums in a small garden by the driveway. They seemed to be replacing them with some sort of evergreen. What season was this, Christmas already? Three years into my psychiatric residency, I seemed to always be behind, still wearing my fall jacket as it began to snow, emerging into the soft spring air with my woolly hat and gloves. Trying to keep it all together—family, job, friends—I often found it hard just to keep my bearings.

As I waited at the curb, staring at the small piles of dirt and the fading flowers, I reflexively began to think of Julia.* Even in college, when we were close friends majoring in pre-med, the similarities of our backgrounds and interests had made it hard not to compare ourselves, questioning our choices when they differed. I wonder sometimes if everyone doesn't have a person like this in their life. As always, I pictured my college classmate on the porch of her suburban Victorian home surrounded by her four children. Was Julia sitting on a rocker enjoying the last

*Julia's name and certain details have been changed.

falling leaves with a baby or two in her lap? Was she in her spacious kitchen poring over a cookbook, planning a fragrant dinner to welcome her husband home from a business trip?

Julia—or rather, my fantasies about Julia's life—had become a permanent feature of my mental world. At any moment, this ever-cozy alternate universe, this idyll of domestic bliss, would spring to mind, leaving me confused about my life choices and envious of hers. I, too, had a husband, a child, and a home, albeit a city apartment that still needed furniture. But Julia had *time,* the most precious commodity I could imagine. I craved time with my family, time with friends, time to shop for furniture or stylish clothes, to read gossip magazines, to walk around the city, to cook, even to get my nails done.

It was only a small consolation that Julia seemed no less haunted by me than I by her. Whenever we saw each other, she oozed ambivalence: canceling dates or changing them at the last minute, insisting that she had to arrive late or leave early. It was always something. At our last attempt to meet for lunch she stood me up, then called with a feeble excuse. The friendship pretty much ended there. At a college reunion a few years later we had a brief, tense chat. She was aggressively cheerful as she stood encircled by the four children, like a battleship defended by a fleet of small gunboats. When I later attended a class fund-raiser Julia hosted, I heard that she was angry that I didn't give more money. Why did she take it so personally? A college with a billion-dollar endowment just isn't where I wanted to put my meager donations.

The collapse of the friendship seemed puzzling at first. But then, as my kids, now teenagers, would say, actually not. One of my psychiatric professors told me during my residency that the intensity of a person's hostility correlates directly with his or her own of sense of vulnerability. And Julia and I both felt intensely vulnerable in each other's presence; we each represented the road not taken. Each time we met, our choices in life were put into stark relief. She felt defensive about her lack of career, and I envied her soccer-mom life. We had both agonized over how to balance our needs with our children's. In the end, we had made radically different choices that left us both uneasy.

I tried to shake Julia out of my thoughts that day as my cab pulled up in front of our apartment building. At home, Molly was in her bedroom playing with a friend from next door. I gave her a hug and kiss, anxiously scanning her face for anger or coolness. She calmly gave me a hug and hello, caught up in her game, oblivious to my worries. I felt at once relieved and bewildered by her contented indifference. As usual, it was hard to sort my child's reality from my own demons regarding motherhood; preconceptions left over from *The Brady Bunch,* scolding pseudoscientific reports in popular magazines, and a lifetime of Betty Crocker TV advertisements featuring Mom happy in the kitchen.

I was certainly not alone in these concerns; all too many women with careers are preoccupied by the possibility that they are not good enough mothers, wives, and homemakers. It's hard for any young adult, male or female, to be a medical resident, but for a woman with children at home, it has a cruel, guilt-inducing, almost unbearable dimension that has no counterpart in men's lives. All too many men are not held responsible for their children's emotional well-being. Devotion to work is largely a win/win for them—a full career and a relatively guilt-free family life. No inevitable decisions and losses.

Women bear not only the chief responsibility for child care, they bear the entire moral burden of raising children. If, God forbid, anything goes wrong with the child of a working mom, she pays a steep price. I've often wondered how the media would have reacted if Chelsea Clinton, by all reports a lovely young woman, had been arrested multiple times for underage use of alcohol instead of the daffy Bush twins. I suspect that Hillary Clinton, lawyer and politician, would have been raked over the coals. Yet there has been nary a whisper about Laura Bush's mothering skills or failures. The ever-vigilant Motherhood Police have given her a pass.

Years after that December day when I awoke on my office floor, I heard through the grapevine that one of Julia's sons had a drug problem. After an inexcusable moment of schadenfreude, I experienced a sensation of terror that still intermittently haunts me. I could barely imagine the guilt and confusion I would feel about my career if my child developed a substance-abuse problem. And I could easily imagine the unspoken opprobrium of my family. In truth, I know Julia has always been a devoted mother. I am also, as a psychiatrist, keenly aware of the strong genetic component to addiction. And I have been humbled enough myself by motherhood to know the myriad, powerful influences that mold children.

So why do career women take the heat for all the maladies of our children? There seems to be a small army of self-appointed gumshoes always tracking working mothers and wringing their hands about the destruction of "the soul of childhood and the joy of family life" (*Newsweek*, 2001) as a result of working moms. I suspect these Motherhood Police are simply the current incarnation of the doomsayers who have been admonishing working women for the past 150 years. These academics, medical "experts," and journalists have ceaselessly predicted the dire consequences of women's increased access to education as well as political, medical, and legal rights. Barbara Ehrenreich and Deirdre English's book, *For Her Own Good: 150 Years of the Experts' Advice to Women,* gives a wonderful overview of these (mostly male) writers weighing in on the catastrophic results of women venturing outside the domestic sphere. In the early twentieth century, women who sought higher education were told that they risked losing "their mammary function" and becoming unfit to marry. G. Stanley Hall, perhaps the preeminent psychologist of that era, concluded that only "agamic or agenic [sterile] women" should attend college.

I have no doubt that these writers truly believed their own grim prognostications. Change is always alarming, particularly when it involves something as fundamental to the survival of the human race as male-female relationships. But it's hard not to notice the self-serving aspect of these arguments. Men have a great deal to lose when women become their social and economic equals. I recently experienced a rather vivid example of such a loss. At the twenty-fifth reunion of my Ivy League college (which had a relatively small number of women at the time I graduated), the dean announced helpfully to the assembled alumni that half of the men there would not be accepted into the freshman class if they were applying now; the spots would be taken by women. In a similar fashion, men currently have twice the competition for professional schools and for jobs, at least in fields that have become open to women. They are also at risk of being called upon to do more of the housework and child care—activities they have not exactly been lining up to do.

The historical concerns voiced early in the century about educating women now seem comically misguided. But perhaps we've just moved on to our next overblown threat: Women who work are bad mothers. This concern is particularly frightening because Americans, more than virtually any other people on earth, have an obsession with mothering. From the early twentieth century, Americans, having meritocratic ideals and a relatively fluid social system, have seen children as almost infinitely malleable, small protobeings who can be carefully shaped to maximize their social and economic advancement.

We have a near-religious belief that superattentive mothering produces super kids and anything less risks children who are unhappy, troubled, or underachieving. As with most religious beliefs, scientific evidence to the contrary has little impact. But massive amounts of research looking at the children of working mothers has failed to show that they differ significantly from the children of their nonworking peers. The one possible exception is infants placed in day-care centers during their first months of life.

Although these findings (or lack of findings) may at first seem counterintuitive, on reflection they fit well with much of our collective experience. It's surprisingly hard to put together a persuasive case for intensive, full-time mothering. Most cultures throughout the world have multiple caretakers for children: aunts, uncles, grandparents, siblings, neighbors, teachers, cousins. Certainly the British, our closest cultural ally, are not great believers in full-time mothering, with the upperclass sending many generations of future leaders off to boarding schools as eight-year-olds. If you take down nearly any biography of a distinguished person, you're overwhelmingly likely to read a hair-raising tale of childhood misery. Not exactly what Penelope Leach or T. Berry Brazelton would lead you to expect.

When I worried aloud to my mother about not being at home full-time with my children, she looked at me with puzzlement. She noted that my brother and I were the only generation of her family in memory that had not had full-time nannies. (Her own mother had been hospitalized for much of my mother's childhood.) But somehow, mysteriously, she, her relatives, and her ancestors had grown up to be productive adults. My father, motherless from early childhood and an orphan from his teens, went to boys' camp every summer and military academy the rest of the year. Yet he grew up to be a much-loved father and respected academic.

As a psychiatrist, I am acutely aware that disproportionate exposure of a child to one parent can be a mixed blessing. The limitations, deficits, and needs of a primary caretaker can leave a problematic, lifelong imprint. Furthermore, the valorization of motherhood has left us almost totally ignorant of the role fathers play in their children's development. The impact of poor or absent fathering has been largely ignored by both the scientific community and the popular press. We simply do not scrutinize the children of sixty-hour-a-week male professionals the way we scrutinize the children of working mothers. Nor is there a hue and cry about the rapidly increasing number of men of every class who have children out of wedlock and do not provide them with financial and emotional support. Sociologists who have noted this demographic trend away from fathering refer to it as "the feminization of kinship."

Presumably, if our society were truly concerned about a lack of parenting for children (as opposed to being queasy about increasing opportunities for women), it would implement government and corporate initiatives to support quality child care. You might expect the creation of nursery schools of the type run by the French government, or extended maternity leaves for mothers, as most European countries offer; you might even predict paternity leave for fathers, as in Sweden. Yet the United States has virtually the worst record of provision for child welfare of any Western country.

The difficult truth is that, despite endless developmental theories, we have surprisingly little evidence about the combination of adult caretakers, temperament, and even adversity that creates productive and happy adults. We just don't know when or how much individualized attention is required for children, particularly after infancy. My opinion is that children need different amounts and kinds of responses from adults at various stages of their lives. The more adults in children's lives to whom they can attach, at different ages and for different reasons, the better. These adults may be parents, camp counselors, grandparents, teachers, housekeepers, or friends' parents. For my father, the man who ran his summer camp became, during his adolescence, a role model and father figure. I hear about these diverse, powerful, life-altering figures from friends as well as patients.

What we *do* know about child care can be easily summarized: Children need responsive adults available to care for them. Parents per se don't need to be constantly on call, nor do they need to be perfectly "at-tuned" to their children, to use the psychiatric lingo. But children do need caring adults to tend to their needs.

And it is here that we get to the real problem facing women today, both the stay-at-home Julias of the world and career women like myself. Except in unusual circumstances, the workplace currently makes no provision for adults caring for children, despite the fact that by 1995, over two thirds of married women in the United States worked for a wage, including 64 percent of married women with preschool children.

The irony is that for most of the twentieth century, these same employers subsidized the most expensive, full-time, individualized child care that exists—namely, the stay-at-home wives of their male employees. Now the same companies employ vast numbers of women in pink-collar and lower-management positions while making no accommodation for child care. At the same time, real wages were lowered so that two earners are now required to maintain the middle-class standard of living that required only one income in the 1970s. In effect, employers passed the full cost of child care on to individual families *and* significantly increased the hours of labor per family. Businesses, for the most part, still act as if there's a full-time housewife at home taking care of the kids. The reality is that currently only 3 to 7 percent of households in the United States have the family configuration of the nonworking wife, working husband, and children at home. It's simply too expensive.

The lack of any reasonable adjustment of the workplace to the needs of parents and children means that choices available to women are inadequate. We can choose a full-on career designed for men with wives at home, full-time motherhood, or part-time work with little chance of a substantial career at any point in our lives. Certainly, there are women who want nothing more than to be full-time moms. There are others who just want careers. But the vast majority of women would like a life between these extremes.

An early study on this issue published in the late 1970s highlighted the dilemmas that women still face. Judith Birnbaum investigated the consequences of life choices made by a group of women honors graduates from the University of Michigan; she published the results in a paper titled "Life Patterns and Self-Esteem in Gifted, Family-Oriented and

Career-Committed Women." Birnbaum compared findings from a prior investigation of women during their twenties with her own study of the same cohort in its late thirties and forties. The earlier research had found that women who pursued careers were "far more troubled with self-doubts and [had] low self-esteem during their twenties and early thirties" than the women who were housewives. In other words, right at the age when women are typically starting families, the career women were painfully struggling with pressures and questions about their life choices. By the time the same women arrived in their mid-thirties, however, the relative gains and losses had shifted dramatically, Birnbaum found. Career women were doing much better than homemakers. Fifteen to twenty-five years after college graduation, the homemakers had "the lowest self-esteem and the lowest sense of personal competence, even including childcare and social skills." The study found that the self-esteem, mental health, and even marital happiness of the career women were all higher by midlife than that of the homemakers.

Both of the options studied by Birnbaum exact a steep price. A full career plus having a family—the life I chose—is extremely stressful early on. I completely understand why Julia rejected it after a few pre-med courses. On the other hand, by their thirties and forties, the women who abandoned their ambitions to be full-time mothers often feel socially adrift and regret not having meaningful work. In truth, at this point in my life, with one child in college and another soon to follow, I can't imagine not having my profession. Many mornings as I walk across the park to my office, I reflect on the privilege of listening to the intimate, compelling, and unpredictable life stories that my patients bring me. I enjoy thinking about how the mind works and discussing it with my colleagues. And I don't think I would have been a great full-time mom; it's just not who I am.

Women, like men, have an array of talents, temperaments, energy levels, and aspirations. So why are women's options so limited? Why do our choices so often require the sacrifice of important aspects of our lives? The answer is that the massive transformation of American women's lives that has occurred over the last two centuries is still incomplete. In the United States, women's life spans have nearly doubled; the number of children born to each woman has decreased with practically every generation (in the early nineteenth century women had, on average, *seven* live births); birth control has become available; legal rights, including divorce, voting, and political rights, have been won.

During this time, women slowly gained access to training previously reserved for men. Their new opportunities advanced from childhood. First came access to grammar school, then high school, then came equal access to college, graduate school, and finally professional schools. During the last generation, women in unprecedented numbers won the opportunity to get entry-level jobs in the professions of medicine, law, and business.

That is where we are now. The new barrier that women face is the lack of realistic career paths beyond the entry level. Right now women can advance in their careers only if they conform to the life cycle of men with wives who don't work full-time, if at all. Women, well over half the population and nearly half the workforce, are too often asked to minimize, hide, or deny the realities of pregnancy, childbirth, and child care—in other words, their own life cycle.

Our next frontier is reconfiguring the workplace so that women—and men—can have rewarding careers *and* raise their children. My generation thought, as we began entering the professions in large numbers during the early 1980s, that we were at the end point in the struggle for women's equality. Most of us now see that we were much further from that goal than we ever imagined.

Many young women today are rejecting careers—the current crop of Julias. I sympathize. A full-on career plus motherhood can be brutal. But multiple studies document that full-time motherhood is at least as debilitating. There have got to be other choices. It is the losses built into women's current options that generate the defensive hostility of the "mommy wars." With no accepted cultural norms for women's lives and no societal provisions for adequate parenting, women struggle individually to construct and then justify their lives. Understandably, this lonely struggle leaves us worried and threatened by women who have taken a different path.

Julia pretty much disappeared from my life after the fund-raising debacle, although I'd hear about her from time to time from mutual friends. Then, recently, I ran into her on the street near my office. It was one of the last shopping days before Christmas, a miserable, rainy, windy day that left us both off balance, trying to hold on to our umbrellas while cradling purses and arms full of sopping bundles. It had been years since we'd laid eyes on each other. In truth, we both looked a bit the worse for wear, older of course. As we exchanged greetings and bits of news, I struggled to meld my old image of Julia with the face that was before me, and I could see her making the same complex adjustments as she scanned mine. We were the same but not the same. Getting to this moment, with our children nearly grown, had been hard for both of us, and our faces showed it. Promising to call each other, we tried awkwardly and unsuccessfully to embrace amid our bags and umbrellas. But it didn't matter. We were happy to see each other.

On Balance

Jane Juska

Jane Juska is the author of two books, *A Round-Heeled Woman: My Late-Life Adventures in Sex and Romance* and *Unaccompanied Women: Late-LIfe Adventures in Love, Sex, and Real Estate,* and a contributor to the anthology *Single Woman, Of a Certain Age.* For more than forty years she has taught English to high school, college, and prison students. Many of her articles on teaching and students have appeared in professional journals, and she received the Best Article on Teaching from the Education Writers of America in 1986. Born in Ann Arbor, Michigan, in 1933, Jane grew up in Archbold, Ohio. In 1955 she moved to California, where she has lived, with brief intermissions, ever since. She has one adult son and a granddaughter.

Life can only be understood backwards,
but it must be lived forwards.
—Søren Kierkegaard

I f abortion had been legal when you were pregnant with me," my son, then in his mid-thirties, asked, "would you have gotten one?"

He was born in 1965, six years before *Roe* v. *Wade,* when I was thirty-two. Remembering the look on his face when I answered, I wish now I had lied. I wish I had said, "No, of course I wouldn't have gotten an abortion." Instead, I told the truth. I explained the facts of life as they were for me in 1964 when, as an unmarried woman, I learned I was pregnant. "I would have lost my job; I wouldn't have been able to support you."

Unwed mothers were not allowed to be classroom teachers in 1965. Maternity leave did not exist even for wedded mothers, and certainly not for women who had made the mistake of becoming pregnant outside of marriage and thus, according to the moralists of the day, were ipso facto unfit to teach the children in our schools. I could not afford to spend eight months of unpaid leave in a Florence Crittenden Home for Unwed Mothers, the exact locations of which I was unsure. I could not afford to get fired. I could not afford to have this baby who became my son. My mother had told me, when I was a senior in high school, "If a girl gets pregnant outside of marriage, she has only herself to blame. Men have desires and cannot be held accountable." So slinking home to my parents in Ohio was out of the question. And always, in the back of my mind, were two friends who had had illegal abortions, each in a different foreign country, who had almost died and who later recounted the grisly details to me. Given all that, I did the only thing I could think of: I threw myself on the mercy of the man who fathered my baby, a man I did not love. A good Catholic boy, he offered marriage and I accepted.

In 1965 the rule was that a pregnant teacher could work through the first six weeks of her pregnancy. Then, because she would Begin to Show, she would have to take a leave of absence—unpaid, for after all, it wasn't the school's fault she got pregnant. My husband was in graduate school; I could not afford eight months without pay. So I lied to the school district, and, amid tears that threatened to flood the examining room, begged the doctor, a young man sympathetic to my plight, to lie too. He moved my due date from the real one, February, to the necessary one, April. My son, who was born in February, was "premature." Six weeks later, in accordance with the school district's rule, I returned to work.

When I told my son all this, he was amazed. He has turned out to be a splendid young man—smart, independent, funny, kind. Maybe he's even forgiven me for the lousy job I did finding proper day care. At that time, in the town where we lived, day-care facilities did not exist, not even bad ones. Young parents relied on older family members. My family lived almost three thousand miles away and, in any case, had no intention of being relied on by their daughter whose baby's early arrival had all their friends and neighbors counting on their fingers. I had to depend on my friends who lived nearby, and my infant son did not like my friends. He screamed when I dropped him off in the morning, screamed for hours, so I was told, and hiccupped tears when I picked him up at the end of the day. My good friend, whose husband's income had allowed her to stay home to care for her daughter, gave up on my son after less than a month. She handed him back to me and said, "This child needs his mother."

It was not the last time I would suffer the angst of motherhood. Another friend offered to try her hand at soothing my baby along with her own son; this time, things were better, at least good enough so that I could give most of my thinking over to my teaching. Most, not all, for now I was a mother and would never be free to devote my time and concentration to the work I loved. With me or absent from me, my son tugged and pulled, and I knew my friend was right: "This child needs his mother."

But I could not be his mother. Not the kind my mother had been, always there, Mrs. Cleaver before Mrs. Cleaver had been born. When I was sick and couldn't go to school, my mother made me orangeade from real oranges squeezed into a syrup she cooked on the stove and cooled over crushed ice. She carried the drink to me in my bed where I lay propped up on pillows (goose-down) with pillowcases (ironed) beneath clean white sheets (also ironed). My throat would feel better just looking at the orangeade and my mother who had made it. When my own little boy was sick, I sent him to school anyway until the day the teacher pinned a note to his jacket that said, "Do not send this child back to school until he is well." In the early days after my son's birth I was a wreck and my milk dried up. I could not even feed my child properly. In the later days I did what I had to do—sent my sick child to school—and it was wrong.

Looking back, I cannot blame my misfortunes on the times that dictated sex after marriage, not before. The choice I made—to enter into a sexual relationship with little or no thought of consequences—was mine alone, and it took a long time on the couch under the aegis of Dr. Freud before I could understand why I made that choice and then to forgive myself for having made it. But I do blame the times, then and now, for the paucity of affordable child care. How is it possible, when we have come so far in our thinking about the worthiness of women and their work, that we do such a slapdash job of caring for our children?

Beginning with *Roe* v. *Wade,* I became pro-choice and remain so not only when it comes to carrying a pregnancy to full term but also when it comes to choosing whether or not to return to work. Before the sixties, like an angry child, blew the roof off the house of convention, any self-respecting mother who could stay home did stay home. She needed and got, no questions asked, the financial support of her husband, whose job it was to make money so the mother of his children could do the right thing—take care of the kids. Indeed, a man was suspect if his wife worked; clearly, he was not doing his job, was not a real man. My college friends, all of whom had done things in the right order—marriage first, then babies—never questioned whether or not they should go back to teaching or nursing, to women's work. Women's work was short-term, a time-filler, not as important as men's work, something women did only until they married and took on the role for which they were destined: child rearing. Eventually, they hired poor women who couldn't afford to stay home with their kids to clean their houses and sometimes to take care of their children. Poor women had jobs; very few women had careers, and those who did, most of them, remained childless. By choice. Interestingly, though choice was available to my contemporaries somewhere out in the ether, nobody in what my twelve-year-old niece calls the Olden Days sought it out; they followed tradition, they fit their roles, and they reared great kids who have turned out to be terrific adults and good parents themselves. Maybe having a choice isn't all it's cracked up to be.

Did I envy my friends? Not really. Taking care of children full-time is overtime without pay. Children are little vampires. Nothing is enough; neither is everything. They turn their adorable faces up to us, and we hardly mind that we haven't had a full night's sleep since they were born. They are adorable, of course, for reasons of evolution: If they were ugly, they wouldn't live beyond age one. My son wondered some years ago in response to my complaints about sleep deprivation, "How long have you had problems sleeping?" I answered, "Well, let's see, you're thirty-two, so . . ." He did not laugh. He also didn't laugh when, foolishly, I applauded myself on the smoking of Camels and the drinking of martinis that helped me through my pregnancy, when I spoke with scorn of the prohibitions dominating today's pregnancies. "You turned out all right," I said. "Yeah," he said, "maybe that's why I'm short." Whoops. So I never told him how much I loved my job, my career, my teaching, and how, torn as I was to leave him every morning, I could not deny the rush of freedom I felt when I drove off, watching his diaper bag dangle from my friend's arm in my rearview mirror.

Given the choice, would I have quit teaching and stayed home to care for my baby? Yes, I would have, for I was a woman of my times, though there was another reason, one I could not bring myself to think about when my son was young and I had no choice about whether to work. My son was not a child who was ready for a mother's friend or a nursery-school teacher to care for him, and I knew it. He was not ready to leave home at the age of six weeks; he was not ready at three to spend eight or nine hours in the basement of the Lutheran church. He was not ready at five to begin kindergarten. Some kids are. Some kids take early separation from their mothers in stride and adapt, more or less quickly, to strange houses and strange cribs and strange ladies asking them if they want to go potty. But some aren't. And as mothers we know which of our kids is which. So yes, I would have stayed home, and I have come to believe that my not staying home with this particular little boy accounts in some ways for his problems in school and in his life beyond: A year as a drunk, a pill popper, and a runaway on the streets of Berkeley had its roots in his early childhood and his need, at seventeen and at any cost, to get out of my life and into his own. This may sound overly dramatic, but I knew then as I know now: This child needed his mother.

Today, the times do not dictate a mode of mothering, unless you consider "Whatever" a dictate. Things are all mixed up except for one constant: money. Without sufficient money, women have no choice; they live with the obligation to make the money and care for the children, and they depend on the kindness of friends, family, and strangers. Life is tough. On the other hand, for those women who can afford to stay home, life and the choices it provides can be its own kind of hell.

On the sidewalks of the college town in which I live, young mothers push strollers around, up the ramp to the library, to the park, the grocery store, the pet shop, and woe betide the pedestrian who fails to get out of their way. "Excuse me!" they call. "Stroller on your right!" They come barreling along, eyes straight ahead, determined to get to the crosswalk before the light changes. These mothers do not seem to be having fun. Indeed, there is a frightening grimness to many of them and, though I am guessing here, a resentment. They have elected to stay home but as a compromise have brought their seriousness and their professional skills with them: the aggressiveness of business, the argumentativeness of the law, the omniscience of medicine. By God, if they're going to give up their degrees and all that training in order to be mothers, they're going to be good ones. Out of the way! Granted, the world is a much scarier place now than it was in 1965. Dangers abound: mercury in food, asbestos in walls, sugar everywhere, sunlight all over the place. A mother of young children is faced with entire days of saying no, of rationalizing that, well, maybe a little bit won't hurt, it's just butter. Butter! Oh God, I gave my child butter! Salt is a bad word; so is fat. Soy is good, as is broccoli (organic). Hopping on a tricycle without a helmet is unthinkable. The decisions to be made are endless; no wonder mothers are exhausted.

But a stay-at-home mother is no less exhausted than the mother who has chosen to go back to work. There she is in the boardroom or the courtroom or the laboratory trying to concentrate fully on the task at hand. And she does—for about ten minutes—and then, in her inner ear, she hears Maria or Elsa or Kharzid talking to her child and, in a blinding flash, knows that her child will never learn English. Then, of course, there is the husband and the father of the child: Is he doing his part? Is he helping to provide the balance that must be present in the home of the child who is to grow up damn near perfect?

There has been lots of talk lately about balancing home and work: part-time work, working at home, that sort of thing. Balance would ensure that the mother's intellect won't rot and that her natural love for her child will show itself in ways the child will understand—that is, she would be around, not gone all the time. Articles and books detail the conflict mothers face and suggest ways to find balance in lives that, with the advent of children, are out of whack.

Let me save you some money: In a life with children, balance does not exist. Once you're a parent, you can figure you'll be out of whack for the rest of your life. So spend your time and energy on something productive like writing letters to Cheerios thanking them for providing the mainstay of your kids' diet. Children are not born to provide balance. Children are made to stir us up, to teach us how angry we can get, how scared we can be, how utterly happy, happier than we'd ever imagined was possible, how deeply we can love. Children turn us upside down and inside out; they send us to the depths and heights of ourselves; but they do not balance us. We can't balance them either, and a good thing, too. They're finding out how to live in this world, and the most we can do is make them as safe as possible and have a good time with them.

I am in favor of choosing, consciously, to have a good time with kids. You can do this whether you work full-time, part-time, or overtime. Peekaboo, in all its infinite variations, will see you through three good years at least, and with "I'm-gonna-get you" as backup, everybody can have fun. It was a choice I must have made way back in the Olden Days, albeit unconsciously, because my son tells me he remembers a happy childhood. (Could he be telling the truth?)

When he was eight years old, a child of divorce and a quick study in Standing Up for Himself, we squared off yet again. At the end of this unusually noisy argument, something about who was the boss ("You're not the boss of me!" "Oh, yes I am!"), a shouting match that deteriorated quickly (into "Am!" "Not!"), my son asked me another question: "Do you think we should get a divorce?"

For a fleeting moment, I considered the pleasures of a trial separation but chose instead to tell the truth: "Never ever; I am your mom and you are my son forever."

On balance, some choices are easy.

My Baby's Feet Are Size 13

Iris Krasnow

The author of *I Am My Mother's Daughter: Making Peace with Mom Before It's Too Late,* journalism professor Iris Krasnow has been credited with kicking off the stay-at-home trend in 1997 with the bestseller *Surrendering to Motherhood,* which describes the happiness she discovered at home with her four young sons after leaving her career in daily journalism. Iris found herself in the eye of the catfight between office moms and homebodies, receiving hundreds of testimonials from fast-track women who told her they quit their jobs because of her book, as well as endless barbs from staunch feminists who accused Krasnow of setting the women's movement back by glorifying home life over professional life. The controversy put her in the center of vein-popping discussions on *The Oprah Winfrey Show,* the *Today* show, and *Good Morning America,* and led to the books *Surrendering to Marriage* and *Surrendering to Yourself.* Krasnow maintains that the definition of true liberation for women is "doing whatever makes you feel like your strongest, best self. And if it's staying home with kids, follow your gut, not political ideology or the judgments of your peers."

My six-feet-three son, Theo, is celebrating his fifteenth birthday today, and I'm trying to kiss him and he's standing stiffly. Perched on my toes, I finally manage to brush my lips against his forehead. He pushes me away and grumbles, "Okay, Mom, enough."

It is never enough.

How can we get enough of our children, those creatures we are bound to by tears and blood and genes? His voice is as deep as his father's, and he's wearing a red T-shirt picturing Che Guevara. The subzero night he was born in Washington, D.C., December 22, 1989, seems like a week ago. I close my eyes and see my baby boy, watching the world for the first time with wide-set blue eyes, my eyes. I touch my shoulder and I can still feel him slumped there, coming home from the hospital on a Christmas Day long ago, seven and a half pounds stuffed into a red flannel stocking.

Today he wears size 13 black Converses, belts his jeans halfway down his butt, and has three younger brothers, ages thirteen and eleven (twins), who also stiffen when I try to kiss them. They are pulling at my reins; soon the worn leather straps will snap and they will be free. I was home a lot when they were small, needy, and adoring, and I'm grateful I didn't miss much of that fleeting magic of young motherhood.

Because now it's over.

As the author of *Surrendering to Motherhood,* the 1997 book on the joys of ditching the office to stay home with young children, I helped start the ongoing battle between professional women who buy Twix for school parties and stay-at-home mothers who bring butterscotch bars, wearing thermal mitts to handle the still-hot pans.

Yes, I am guilty of fanning the early embers of the mommy wars, by suggesting to women that if they choose to have children, they have a fundamental commitment to spend a lot of time with them. The book's detractors called me "antifeminist," for writing snippets like these:

Despite all these long debates among ambitious women on ways to balance our lives, the task is insurmountable—with young children there can be no balance. When you surrender to that fact then real balance comes, of having your soul and mind and heart in sync.

Mothers around me who work 60 and 70 hours a week outside the home talk of being stretched so taut they feel as if they might snap. They feel guilty at the office because they are not at home with their children, and guilty at home over what's not getting done at the office.

You can't win this tug of war until you let go of one side of the rope. No one can do it all, all at once. That is not living; it's suffering.

Finding a job that gives you more time with your children is the most important task you can spend energy on. It may mean whittling down, even walking away from, your hard-earned profession. But it also means assuring that your children are protected and loved by the human being who can protect and love them better than anyone else.

If that didn't shove the guilt on working mothers, nothing did. I'm sorry if you were someone I made sad or mad. I was hormonal and blissful, mesmerized by mundane tasks like washing baby bottles with long-handled brushes, layering quiche, and reading *Cosmo,* all while listening to vintage Fleetwood Mac. My kids had captured me, and I was surrendering, with gratitude, to no longer wearing pantyhose and racewalking through my life. I could not imagine that every woman with a new baby did not feel like I did.

If I were revising the book today, I would soften some of the language. But I wouldn't change any of the choices I made. I'm happy I left a job in daily journalism at United Press International to hang out with Theo, Isaac, Jack, and Zane, who at the time I conceived the book were ages three and under. But I'm also happy that I kept a finger in the artery of my old life, launching a freelance writing career and becoming a journalism professor. Because now that the all-consuming phase of motherhood is history, I still have an identity to fall back on beyond the "Mommy Mommy" self.

No one calls me Mommy anymore; in fact, thirteen-year-old Isaac sometimes calls me babe.

I have grown into the woman I was addressing in my book, the one who needs to be reminded that the dawn of motherhood is over in a finger snap, so savor every second when you have children around. I am the woman who now knows it is true that you can always go back to your big career but you can never go back to this incandescent moment when kids cling to you like monkeys. I still believe that mothers of young children should surrender, and be with them, as much as possible.

Because soon, too soon, they are teenagers with stubble, hooked up to headphones and wiping off your kisses with indignant huffs.

The comment has been made to me "It's easy to surrender to motherhood if you can afford to." Yet, after hearing hundreds of stories from a diverse cast of women, rich and poor, I find it's often the people with the most money who have the toughest time surrendering, which I define as "yielding to the higher power of children." And it's the mothers with the least money and no help at home who embrace the notion of surrender. They have watched the surrender of their own mothers and grandmothers to raise a family right.

I was greatly moved when I was a guest on *The Oprah Winfrey Show* in the summer of 1997 to discuss the book. Single mothers shared stories of how they work night shifts so they could be there for children in the day; others told of husbands who work two and three jobs so they can stay home. Oprah Winfrey is one of the least-conflicted women I've ever met when it comes to the issue of work and family. At the beginning of the show, she told of her own clear choice not to have kids because she pours all of her time into a job she loves and is not the type of woman who would want to turn child rearing over to a nanny.

Nor would I—it's been too much fun. Newly fifty, with lots of gray hair, I'm glad I took my own advice. As I write this sentence, I am sniffling at the kitchen table where I once fed four boys with rubber-coated spoons, their pink mouths opening like tiny birds. Jack and Zane are now eleven and play poker at night. I am overcome with images of nuzzling my firstborn, squirmy Theo with honey-red curls who nursed until he was two and wore a polyester Superman costume the whole year he was three, over his coat by day, over his pj's to bed. He is now more connected to his iPod than he is to me.

As a gift for his birthday, I bought him a round-trip train ticket to visit camp friends in New York City. It was his first train ride alone. I walked him to the track, and he boarded the train without a backward glance. I imagined this moment a thousand times when the boys were in preschool. Those were the days they would turn around as they walked away from my Suburban, often running back to me to clutch my knees and get one last sniff of Mommy. I grimaced then at the thought of this day to come when my children would walk away from me without looking over their shoulders.

And there I was. Sending off a son, ecstatic to be leaving his mother, to Penn Station in New York on a day when thousands of other travelers were bound there as well to the adjacent Madison Square Garden to watch the ball drop on New Year's Eve. Suddenly, I was gripped by catastrophic fantasies: He will get seduced, kidnapped, a bomb is on the train! I grabbed a man in an Amtrak uniform who was shooing in the last of the passengers and told him there was a tall, skinny young man on board with wild curls and headphones who was taking a train for the first time by himself. "Please take care of him," I pleaded.

The man promised me he would keep an eye on Theo. "I do this for mothers all the time," he said.

Watching the train leave the station in Baltimore, I realized the person who needed to be taken care of then was not my son but me. I flashed forward to the day when it will be just me and my husband, Chuck, eating supper in silence at a table where milk would routinely spill and boys would be imitating teachers and teasing one another about girls. The day is rapidly coming when it will be just me, mothering me, in a house of yowling memories but no whooping laughter.

I am thankful that I still have an evolving self beyond the Mommy Self, that I have a passion of the soul beyond my children—to publish, to teach, to travel. I am relieved that I never stopped writing because that love will never leave me. My children will.

When revisiting some of the women I originally interviewed in *Surrendering to Motherhood,* I learned that the ones who are the most content are those who also kept a finger, or a hand, in their pre-mommy professions, the lawyer who retained a couple of clients, the catering executive who started a home-based bakery. We are thrilled we got to have our cake and eat it too, appeasing both our primal hungers—to keep growing as individuals while we mother our brood.

I am proud to say my kids have turned out well. They are confident, kind, and respectful of grown-ups; they make friends easily. I cannot say that they would have turned out any differently had I spent more time in an office than I did at home. What I can say is that *I* would not have turned out all right. Surrendering to my children, you see, was a very selfish act. I needed to be home.

When Theo was a baby I interviewed Zelda Fichandler, a mother of two grown sons who worked her entire adult life to build Arena Stage theater in Washington, D.C. I asked the sixty-five-year-old Fichandler if she had any regrets in a remarkable career that birthed the first regional theater in the United States. "If I had a perfect life to live over again, I would spend the first five years of my children's lives at home," she started out, her black eyes piercing. "But at the time, I never felt guilty about leaving the kids. I kept feeling 'This is worth it.' Now I give advice to young women embarked on missions to be very careful whether it's worth it. I'm not absolutely positive now that it's been worth it. Because of life not lived, books not read, art not seen, vacations not taken, conversations not held, flowers not smelled."

Fichandler stopped, then added: "Yeah, there is an upside and a downside. I never had enough of my kids. I do feel like I was always there when they needed me. But I don't think I was always there when I needed them."

We all know women who did not skip a beat in their full-time professions once babies were born, except for taking a few weeks off to nurse, do sit-ups, and find great nannies. And most of their kids turned out all right. But some of those mothers tell wrenching stories of how *they* aren't turning out all right, tales of crying the whole way home from driving children to college, asking themselves, How could this have happened? How could my baby be eighteen? Where was I?

I invite those women with consuming office jobs to think hard about whether it's worth it, before they turn into a sixty-five-year-old success story like Zelda Fichandler, with a huge career and a hole in the heart that can never be filled. There I go again, throwing another log onto the smoldering fires of the mommy wars. But I'm telling you the truth. Your kindergartener is going to be fifteen tomorrow, and you cannot go back to the sweet, golden era when he eagerly leapt into your arms.

Soon after being struck by Zelda Fichandler's words, I had what I call my "scrambled-egg epiphany," which moved me from the newsroom to the playroom, as recorded in *Surrendering to Motherhood:*

> Amid the noise of the boys and my swinging emotions, I suddenly got very still inside. Wrapped in the bathrobe four babies had nestled against while they nursed, my brain started clanging this jubilant message: There are no shackles in this house, this is no jail. These kids are your ticket to freedom like nothing you have ever tasted, the kind that is not hinged on TV appearances or being a size 6 again. It's the liberation that comes from the sheer act of living itself. When you stop to be where you are, then your life can really begin.
>
> On that gray carpet, with egg under my nails and egg in my hair, I realized that for the first time in my life I was exactly where I was supposed to be.

When the boys started school, I became a journalism professor at American University, a three-day-a-week position that usually gets me home in time to pick them up. Again, this is my need, not theirs—I love to hear their first rush of stories from the day. *They* love it when our male babysitter, Devin, a high school senior, takes them home. He drives them through McDonald's, listens to Eminem, and doesn't grill them for stories about "what you did today." When I car-pool, I give them individual bags of raw almonds for snacks and make them hear my old Aretha Franklin tapes. Who would you rather ride with if you were eleven, thirteen, and fifteen?

In the spring of 1998 I spoke about my own work-family choices to the Lawyers at Home Forum of the Women's Bar Association; the event was called "Beyond the Mommy Wars." Feminist pioneer Betty Friedan was sitting next to me on the panel. With a vein throbbing in her neck, she accused me of setting the women's movement back, by glamorizing home life over professional life. I'd offer the same response today that I gave then: There is nothing more powerful, more liberating, for women than choosing to surrender to motherhood, and to align our careers with the vision in our hearts, not political correctness.

A year later, in New York City, I was on a panel for a national women's convention that addressed balancing kids with career. At that event, another famous feminist scolded me, her neck vein popping too. She railed that I just *did not understand* that there are many women who quit jobs to stay home and raise children only to end up feeling like they, and I quote her, "wanted to kill their kids."

To this, I was speechless.

As a college student in the middle-1970s, I wanted never to suffer from what Friedan, in her book *The Feminine Mystique,* called "the trapped housewife syndrome." Yet, I ended up being exhilarated by the wife-mother role I once believed to be the death of dreams. Choosing to spend lots of time with our children is actually the convergence of the feminist ideals our era of women embraced—power, freedom, self-expression, and independence. Nothing ever felt so powerful, so free, so right, as becoming a militant mother who fights for her children on every front.

What I know a decade after *Surrendering to Motherhood* was published, and after speaking to hundreds of women on work-family balance, is that there are plenty of mothers who love their kids as much as I love mine who simply can't stand to be in the house all day. They don't want to kill their kids, they are just itching for stimulation beyond Milton Bradley. I know now there are lots of mothers who, like me, are following the compass in their hearts, only their arrows point to offices. Just like I need my home to feel whole and fulfilled, they need colleagues and desks miles away from their kitchens.

I am not better. These women are not wrong.

Three years ago, I wrote an article for the "Style" section of *The Washington Post,* titled "The Mommy Wars Are Over," in which I spoke of signs that feminism and motherhood were finally converging. Ha! That's what I thought. The mudslinging persists. Perhaps, sadly, there is no end to the fight. Our mother-lion instincts make us fiercely self-righteous and defensive about how we raise our own kids. There may always be harumphs from homebodies when law-firm partners come rushing from court into class parties, toting plastic 7-Eleven bags filled with Oreos. Some female executives may never stop rolling their eyes and ripping into moms who are home full-time, saying that they need to "get a life."

At least the crossfire is a bit more friendly than it was when the term came into our vocabulary. The first writer to label the tension between baby boom mothers "mommy wars" was Jan Jarboe Russell, in a 1989 *Texas Monthly* article that drew the battle lines this way: "Working moms think stay-at-home moms are idle and self-indulgent. Stay-at-home moms think working moms are neglectful and egotistical."

Russell described a scene in a supermarket where she felt "penetrated by another mother's stare." Waiting in the checkout line, Russell, in office-appropriate red wool suit and navy pumps, began talking to a blonde in her mid-thirties wearing a pale pink sweatshirt and matching sweatpants. Russell asked innocently: "What do you do?"

Red-faced with rage, the other mother hurled a head of lettuce at her and hissed: "I stay home with my children, which is what you should do."

What should you do? Heed your gut instincts, do what you need to do, and you'll be making the right choice. The mother who is living her truth, whether it be mostly at the office or mostly at home, is the best role model for children.

My own mommy war is internal, waged as a battle against the swift passage of time. My soft toddlers are now sinewy and hard. They steal my Victoria's Secret catalogs and get instant messages that make me more certain than ever that the definition of a good mother is "a woman who spends enough time with her children to know what the hell they are doing."

I hope this is a definition we can all agree on.

My mother was always home, raising three children close in age. And today, at the age of eighty-five, she says that the happiest she has *ever* been was when we were young and "I had you all to myself," seated around her kitchen table.

When she was dating my dad, she sold perfume at Saks Fifth Avenue, on Michigan Avenue in Chicago. She quit her job when they married and had three children quickly, becoming a 1960s housewife, buried in laundry. When we walked from school through the kitchen doorway at 3:15

P.M., she was sitting at the kitchen table, a dish towel over her shoulder, smoking a Kent and doing crossword puzzles. Her deviation from this routine was to grocery shop, attend PTA meetings, or walk down the street to play Scrabble with Shirley.

I cannot recall one afternoon that Helene Krasnow was not there waiting for us. When her kids were in college, she hung up her plastic apron, put on a black suit, twirled a silk scarf around her neck, and got a full-time job selling men's clothes at Lord & Taylor on Michigan Avenue, a block away from Saks.

My evolution into domesticity was nothing like my mom's. I had an adrenaline-charged career before bearing children, roaming the world for UPI, immersed in exotic countries and enthralling characters. I've interviewed rock stars and presidents, kings and queens, even Mr. Rogers. Yet, despite glamorous past lives and a packed Rolodex, when I'm eighty-five and asked to list my best times, I, too, will put mothering young children at the top. I, too, will whimper when recalling how full I felt with four squirmy sons in one embrace.

I will revel in these dwindling, glory days when my Suburban still smells like rancid Go-Gurt, squirted on the car seats en route to basketball, karate, bowling parties. I was right when I finger-wagged in *Surrendering to Motherhood:* "Be there, moms. Because it's over in an eye blink." As I speak, there is a guide to colleges next to Theo's computer, and he's talking about going to school in Los Angeles because he likes the "atmosphere in California," like his mother did when she bolted out of the Midwest to Stanford twenty-five years ago.

Ignited by the Bay Area, and by guest lecturers like Angela Davis with her huge Afro and huge voice against female oppression, I was angry over my mother's choice to stay home instead of becoming a real *somebody*. Today I know my mother was hugely accomplished, that she was the biggest somebody she could ever have been: a person who structured the lives of three children and gave them stability. I am not home all the time like she was, but I'm home enough to know I didn't miss out on much.

But I do miss my babies, and I'm curious about how they will remember me. Theo is sprawled on his bed, Converse tennies on and his huge feet hanging over the end, buried in a book on filmmaking, which he wants to study when he gets to L.A. I heard him mumbling into his cell phone to his best friend, Ben, that he's also interested in New York University, a prospect this mama prefers (I can visit by train *every* weekend) but wouldn't dare tell him because then he'll start researching colleges in Alaska.

I sit next to him and stroke his cheek, and he doesn't look up. I want to shake him and remind him how much he loves me and needs me.

"Was I around enough?" I ask him.

Long silence, still no eye contact.

"Mom," he tells me, "you were around too much."

This answer will soothe and amuse me when I'm alone in a still house at 5 P.M., drinking Cabernet, waiting for the boys to call from their dorm rooms. There will be many mornings when I'm staring out my kitchen window at the pink of dawn on the Severn River, expecting them to come down for breakfast. But they'll be sitting with girlfriends at Starbucks.

Who will I be when they're gone? What am I supposed to do with 126 Beanie Babies, including the Princess Diana bear we paid fifty bucks for and waited in line three hours to buy? My later book *Surrendering to Yourself* explores the importance of developing ourselves beyond our families. Children do leave. Parents die. Jobs change. We can count only on ourselves.

This hard and lonely destiny we all face is a great incentive to discover a self beyond Mommy while kids are still at home so we don't fall apart when they are gone.

I pick up a photograph shot a few years back on our trip to Disney World. The children are wearing Flap Happy sun hats and goofy grins that show lots of missing teeth. Oh God, this is tough, letting go. When Chelsea Clinton was at Stanford, President Clinton wore two watches; one with East Coast time, the other displaying West Coast time. He needed to feel connected to his daughter, who no longer needed to be near him. We give our children roots and love, and they can grow and thrive anywhere. My friend's son moved to a village outside Tokyo after college and just announced he was staying because of a young Japanese woman he described as "the one."

My own pack of puppies could scatter too. The idea of wearing two watches or three, or embarking on a fourteen-hour flight to see a grand-child, takes my breath away. I pull my smallest son, Jack, onto my lap, where he will fit for only another year or so. In a hypnotic chant, I whisper in his ear, "I will live in Maryland, I will live in Maryland, I will live in Maryland." My face is buried in his silky head, and I am thankful he is still too young to put gel in his hair like his brother Theo.

Ending the Mommy Wars

I tuck my three children into their own beds, in their own rooms, every night. A few hours later Max, Morgan, or Tallie usually shows up on my side of the mattress, solemnly poking me to announce his or her arrival. The last thing I need is to have my sleep interrupted by kicks and squirms. But to be so close to my children, at the one time of day when they are too bleary to fight with one another, is priceless to me.

My husband is always on the far side of the bed, lying still as a corpse, hoping the children will not notice he's there.

In the dark of night (and many times during the day) it makes no difference whether I'm a working or stay-at-home mom. Like all mothers, I have undergone a spiritual metamorphosis as powerful as adolescence and menopause. *The Velveteen Rabbit* gets me every time with that paragraph about becoming Real. "Here she goes!" my son laughs as I start to tear up.

> "Real isn't how you are made," said the Skin Horse. "It's a thing that happens to you. It takes a long, long time. That's why it doesn't often happen to toys that break easily, or who have sharp edges, or have to be carefully kept. When a child REALLY loves you, then you become Real."

This is the beautiful side of motherhood, whether one works or not.

Unfortunately, motherhood is not always so pretty.

Talking with hundreds of women during the three years I worked on this book taught me quite a lot about myself and the struggles between working and stay-at-home mothers today.

First and most undeniable: The mommy wars are not really between different cliques of women over what kind of motherhood is superior. The real battles rage inside each mother's head as she struggles to make peace with her choices.

Second: Whether you work or not has no bearing on whether you are a good mom.

Period.

Is Dawn Drzal, author of "Guilty," a better mom than her New York City neighbor Ann Misiaszek Sarnoff, COO of the WNBA, because Dawn gave up her career as an editor while Ann kept on working? Does Terri Minsky's string of hit TV shows make her a better (or worse) mother than Inda Schaenen, the radical feminist stay-at-home mom? Each woman has high standards, impossible standards, for what kind of mother she strives to be. Our fanatical, soul-changing love for our children makes us all want to be the best mothers we can be. We have this much in common.

Third, I found that some women don't experience tension between working and stay-at-home moms—or at least nothing they'd call a war. But even these moms agree that we all struggle to feel good about our unique brand of motherhood. An innocent desire, but one that makes us vulnerable. Politicians and the media exploit stereotyped images of "soccer moms" and "welfare moms," because they know women want to be classified as "good" and "bad" on some level. Worst of all, this need to feel good makes us very, very critical of one another and ourselves.

Positive messages for mothers in twenty-first-century American society are harder to find than swim diapers at Target in August. When was the last time you told another woman "You're a good mom"? How about the last newspaper or magazine article that said: "Relax, you're not perfect, but since you love your kid deeply, it's all going to turn out okay in the long run"? Even if you don't breast-feed for at least six months, don't devote twenty-four hours a day to developing your kid's IQ, and occasionally down a glass of wine before 6 P.M. because the kids are driving you crazy.

Love for our children, and the immense task of caring for them, burns up large portions of our pre-mom selves. Think of Leslie Lehr, Monica Buckley Price, and Catherine Clifford, who gave up work they cherished to stay home with their children. Some of us pay dearly with our careers, our bodies, our marriages, our friendships, our relationships with our parents and siblings, our very selves. Then, after years spent diapering babies and fixing school lunches, we look up and find little to no sincere affirmation from our friends, our families, or greater society that we've done an admirable job rearing our children. The only moms who do feel genuinely proud are women with rock-solid self-esteem in this area. All two of them. So how, then, can the rest of us feel like good moms?

When you want to feel good about yourself, and cannot despite repeated attempts, the next best thing is to feel better than others. Ask any seventh-grade girl. Starting when I was eleven or twelve, the goddesses in my life—older girls—trained me in the ancient art of comparing and ranking females endlessly on the traits that mattered then: weight, hair color, breast size, butt shape, nose prominence, stomach size, appeal to the opposite sex, and so on. Most of this indoctrination took place in locker rooms, girls' bathrooms, classrooms, and hallways emptied of boys and teachers.

I've never been happy plying this trade. The competitiveness of the female tribe led me to a teenage bout with anorexia, endless hours wasted trying to get a 360-degree view of my butt in the mirror, and four years at Harvard proving that I was smart even if I'd failed in my quest to be physically perfect. It's not the kind of interior monologue that makes one feel particularly fine about the fairer sex. But I've never been able to rid myself of this need to judge women, including—perhaps most of all—myself.

When I became a mother, this ability to classify myself vis-à-vis other women slammed me headfirst into a stone-and-mortar wall. Who ranks as best mom? How can I win the potty-training round? The talking-first round? The I'd-do-anything-for-my-kids round? On my most insecure days, I'd trade my diamond earrings to know on an absolute and indisputable scale who is a better or worse mother than I am, to line up every mom in the world from best to worst, myself somewhere in the front to middle.

I want to know. I need to know. I will never know.

There's no divining who's best when it comes to motherhood. We are all completely unprepared for the job; our mothers lived in such a different world that they seem as baffled by motherhood today as we are. We do the best we can with our decisions on work and family. As Beth Brophy wrote, we are all trying to convince ourselves we are good enough.

Whether to work or not after having kids is a profound choice; it splits women into two groups with publicly distinct theories about motherhood. Our internal monologue about whether we are good mothers morphs into an external catfight in which we disparage other mothers. We're talking age-old us-versus-them rivalries: the Capulets versus the Montagues, *Lord of the Flies, Animal Farm* . . . working versus stay-at-home moms.

Not coincidentally, all of these rivalries end badly.

When I lived in New York after college, I interviewed a female Freudian psychiatrist for an article on eating disorders. I asked her why people came to see her. She paused to gather her thoughts before answering, "They come to change the past."

Long after the article was published, I remembered her words.

It's no coincidence that so many women in this book wrote about their mothers and their childhoods. As mothers, we all, to various extents, carry the baggage of our pasts; we all try to re-create the good facets of our childhoods and to compensate for the painful ones. The memory of what we did and did not receive as children shapes—some would say warps—our approach to motherhood. We try to give our children (and by proxy ourselves) what we lacked as children. For some, it's financial security, a nice house, an unending supply of beautiful clothes and toys. Others give guidance and boundaries, a focus on goals and achievement. Still others want to give laxity, freedom, and unconditional love.

What I most want to give my children is the one thing I didn't have in a childhood filled with pets, books, barefoot summers in New Hampshire, and a pony when I turned thirteen. I want to—I need to—give my children a happy mom. And for me, being happy means working.

Before tackling this book, I had no idea why some moms stayed home. I had no clue what they were doing there. I didn't know if they were faking happiness or were truly content without work and a paycheck in their lives. And I had no inkling why I raged against them so bitterly at times. I know these women now—and I see that their decisions differ only slightly from my own.

I never hated other mothers. My anger came from years of competitiveness with other women, and my own internal agony of seeing, in stay-at-home moms, what I was missing at home when I was at work, and in ambitious working moms the career sacrifices I was making by working part-time. It's clear to me now that comparing myself to other moms is pointless. It's also clear that other moms' choices suit them and my choices are (mostly) right for me and my kids, which is not the same as perfect. But I'm not out to be perfect. I'm out to be better than perfect, as Anne Marie Feld writes. I'm out to be happy. And that's a personal quest no one but I can judge, fulfill, imitate, or envy.

We all need other moms regardless of our personal decisions about working or staying home. That's why I needed this book. The stories on these pages made me laugh, and cry, and regret a few things, and analyze—yet again—my decisions about how much of my life to devote to my work and my children and myself.

There are no easy answers. But I no longer feel alone in my struggle to balance work and family. There are millions of women in America keeping me company as I fight my internal mommy war, and very good company you are.

Leslie Morgan Steiner

Acknowledgments

Thanks to Cathi Hanauer for letting the bitch out of the house.

Thanks to the women in this collection who shared their hearts and minds and words.

Thanks to my agent, Alice Fried Martell, and my editor at Random House, Susanna Porter, good mothers themselves.

Thanks to Don Graham, Bo Jones, Steve Hills, Susan O'Leary, Katharine Weymouth, Peggy Schiff, Linda Baquet, Julie Gunderson, Doug Dykstra, and my other friends and colleagues at *The Washington Post,* for giving me the time to write this book. Thank you to Willie Joyner for visual inspiration.

Thanks to Leslie McGuirk of McGuirk's Quirks for creative inspiration. Thanks to Ann McDaniel, Elsa Walsh, and Tom Shroder for reading early drafts and urging me to explore the inner catfight. And thanks to David Steinberg and everyone at SwapDrive Backup for providing twenty-four-hour peace of mind.

Thanks to all the moms in my life, especially Elin Cohen, Michele Dreyfuss, Jennifer Brown Greenberger, and Jodi Peterson.

Thanks to Stephanie Modder, our blue-haired friend from Wisconsin, whose soul rings out in her voice.

Thanks to Perry, who still owes me a list of the reasons he married me.

Most of all, thanks to Max, Morgan, and Tallie, for being themselves.

About the Author

LESLIE MORGAN STEINER is an executive at *The Washington Post*. She started her career at *Seventeen* magazine before getting her M.B.A. at the Wharton School of Business and working in marketing and public relations for Johnson & Johnson. In addition to writing for the *Post* she has contributed regularly to such national publications as *Money, Mademoiselle,* and *New England Monthly.* She lives in Washington, D.C., with her husband and three children.

About the Type

This book was set in Sabon, a typeface designed by the well-known German typographer Jan Tschichold (1902–74). Sabon's design is based upon the original letter forms of Claude Garamond and was created specifically to be used for three sources: foundry type for hand composition, Linotype, and Monotype. Tschichold named his typeface for the famous Frankfurt typefounder Jacques Sabon, who died in 1580.

6e789